T0319795

Integrating Europe's Infrastructure Networks

Integrating Europe's Infrastructure Networks

The Political Economy of the European Infrastructure System

Colin Turner

Institute for Infrastructure, Heriot-Watt University, UK

Edward Elgar
PUBLISHING

Cheltenham, UK • Northampton, MA, USA

Published by
Edward Elgar Publishing Limited
The Lypiatts
15 Lansdown Road
Cheltenham
Glos GL50 2JA
UK

Edward Elgar Publishing, Inc.
William Pratt House
9 Dewey Court
Northampton
Massachusetts 01060
USA

A catalogue record for this book
is available from the British Library

Library of Congress Control Number: 2021946154

This book is available electronically in the **Elgar**online
Political Science and Public Policy subject collection
http://dx.doi.org/10.4337/9781839105487

ISBN 978 1 83910 547 0 (cased)
ISBN 978 1 83910 548 7 (eBook)
Printed and bound by CPI Group (UK) Ltd, Croydon, CR0 4YY

Contents

Preface

This is third time I have found myself writing about the European infrastructure. These previous works (co-written with a now retired colleague) were very much set within the context of the Trans-European Networks (TENs) policy initiative. Throughout the late 1990s and early 2000s, TENs seemed to be the 'big idea' emanating from the European Commission. Initially this was a complement to the Single Market and – more latterly – as a catalyst for the EU's comparatively lethargic economic growth. In between, the ambitions of the programme expanded along with the expansion of the EU to include the former Soviet satellite states of Central and Eastern Europe. However reflecting upon TENs after more than 20 years it is evident that the hype heavily outstripped the reality of the process, with its efficacy (as a supranational initiative) directly curtailed by the inability/unwillingness of states to fund the TENs projects, and also of the lack of available finance available from other sources. This trend has been especially evident in transport (see Chapter 2). In other sectors, whilst more diverse and commercial sources of finance have been available, these have not always resulted in TENs being developed as envisaged (see Chapters 3 and 4). Nonetheless TENs – as a policy programme – remains very relevant to the pattern of infrastructure development across the EU. As such, TENs (and various supporting and flanking initiatives) will form a focal point of analysis within this book. However – as will also be evident throughout this book – there are (in practice) a multitude of processes promoting the interconnection of national systems.

Within the context of the expansive literature on regionalism, this work continues the theme of previous works in viewing the development of European infrastructural integration as essentially intergovernmental in nature. This reflects a prevailing perspective that infrastructuring is a territorial strategy deployed by states to assert and reinforce their territoriality. In this context, the core building block of the regional systems is interconnection between what are (normally) mature national systems with supranational bodies operating as forums for co-operation and co-ordination between states. It is through such mechanisms that national systems adapt to the tension placed upon them by the process of regionalism. It is also evident that this regionalism within infrastructure systems is also fuelled by a desire to use co-operation and co-ordination to address issues of common concern. These processes – as highlighted throughout the work – reflect an emergent overlap between territorial and geo-strategies. However despite such tensions national systems still overwhelmingly evolve to meet national needs due not just to the nature of traffic that flows among/between them but also due to the political economy of how such systems are financed.

The sectoral focus within this work is upon those infrastructures identified within the initial TENs strategy (i.e. transport, energy and telecommunications/information infrastructures). However the degree of policy activism within each of these now varies markedly. In transport and energy, there is sustained activism by the EU (though often through operator-driven programmes). In telecommunications/information, any degree of activism in hard infrastructure has been replaced by the indirect measures associated with the reform of what has become termed 'soft infrastructure'. The emergence of soft infrastructure as a theme within infrastructure systems reflects not merely a market-driven process in their development but also a need to take holistic views of the development of such systems. Indeed such holism has led to a claim that regionalism needed to extend beyond these 'classic' economic infrastructures into water and/or social infrastructure systems. However in both, regionalism seems to be very limited.

The book was written against the background of the UK's formal departure from the EU. This often meant that statistics included data from the EU that included the UK. I have tried throughout the book to exclude the UK the data sets used. However it was important throughout to look at non-EU Western European states and to include them in the offered analysis wherever possible. Across each of the sectors examined the degree of interconnection between EU and non-EU states in the infrastructural integration process does vary quite markedly. Nonetheless the interconnection across Europe is not simply an EU process, and it is important to include this in the offered analysis. Overall the importance of infrastructural integration in the geographic region of Europe is an important area of study, and one that has direct relevance to other regions. Europe is a region where economic integration has progressed the furthest, and its experience in integrating national systems offers an important exemplar for other regions. Europe's experience underscores the importance of both formal and informal integration in shaping the interconnection of national systems. However, arguably of more importance is that Europe's experience underlines just how difficult that process can be as states seek to balance their territorial needs with the desire to adapt to a broader shifting geostrategic context.

Colin Turner
Edinburgh

Abbreviations

ACER	Agency for the Co-operation of Energy Regulators
BEMIP	Baltic Energy Market Interconnection Plan
BRI	Belt and Road Initiative
CCNR	Central Commission for the Navigation of the Rhine
CEE	Central and Eastern Europe
CEF	Connecting Europe Facility
CENELEC	Comité Européen de Normalisation Électrotechnique (European Committee for Electrotechnical Standardization)
CEN	Comité Européen de Normalisation (European Committee for Standardization)
CEPT	European Conference of Postal and Telecommunications Administrations
CER	Community of European Railway
CIA	Central Intelligence Agency
CTP	Common Transport Policy
DAE	Digital Agenda for Europe
DSM	Digital Single Market
EaP	Eastern Partnership Agreements
EC	European Commission
ECA	European Court of Auditors
EEA	European Economic Area
EES	European Energy System
EFSI	European Fund for Strategic Investment
EIB	European Investment Bank
EII	European Information Infrastructure

EIS	European Infrastructure System
ENISA	European Network and Information Security Agency
ENTSO-E	European Network of Transmission System Operators for Electricity
ENTSO-G	European Network of Transmission System Operators for Gas
EP	European Parliament
ERMTS	European Railway Traffic Management System
ETNO	European Telecommunications Network Operators
ETS	European Transportation System
EU	European Union
EU+4	The 27 EU states plus Switzerland, Norway, Iceland and the UK
EU27	The 27 member states of the EU
GDP	Gross Domestic Product
GDPR	General Data Protection Regulation
IEA	International Energy Agency
IEM	Internal Energy Market
IGU	International Gas Union
ITF	International Transport Forum
ITU	International Telecommunications Union
IWW	Inland Waterways
KM	Kilometre
LNG	Liquefied Natural Gas
Mbps	Megabits per second
MoS	Motorways of the Sea
MoU	Memorandum of Understanding
NES	National Energy System
NGA	Next Generation Advanced Broadband Infrastructure
NII	National Information Infrastructure

NIS	National Infrastructure System
NSI	North South Energy Interconnectors
NSOG	North Sea Operating Grid
NTS	National Transportation Systems
OECD	Organisation for Economic Co-operation and Development
OSJD	Organization for Cooperation of Railways
PCI	Projects of Common Interest
RIS	Regional Infrastructure Systems
SEM	Single European Market
SGC	Southern Gas Corridor
TEM	Trans-European Motorway
TENs	Trans-European Networks
TEN-E	Trans-European Energy Networks
TEN-T	Trans-European Transportation Networks
TEN-Telecom	Trans-European Telecommunication Networks
TER	Trans-European Railways
TINA	Transport Infrastructure Needs Assessment
UIC	Union Internationale des Chemins de Fer (International Union of Railways
UNECE	United Nations Economic Commission for Europe
UNESCAP	United Nations Economic and Social Commission for Asia and the Pacific
WEF	World Economic Forum

1. Territoriality and the European infrastructure system

INTRODUCTION

The territorial state is at the core of the international system, with each state seeking to assert its territoriality (through a set of enabling strategies) over the portion of the earth's surface that is recognised by all other states as being under its jurisdiction (Taylor 1994, 1995). Central to these territorial strategies is the provision of territorially extensive economic infrastructures (see below for formal definition) with sufficient capacity and development to enable the intense and prompt flow of both state and non-state tangible and non-tangible resources to enable the state to control, integrate, secure and develop that territory under its jurisdiction (Turner 2018, 2020). This underlines that the state needs to offer universal access to the infrastructure system as a means of enabling its territoriality. These territorial strategies have been subject to the adaptive tensions formed by economic, social and technological change. One such adaptive tension was and is the trend towards regionalism within the international system, where regionalism is defined as the formal and informal processes of economic, social and political interaction, interdependence and even integration across and between contiguous and semi-contiguous territorial states (Dehousse et al. 1990, Söderbaum 2012).[1]

This chapter explores the form and nature of the adaptive tension of regionalism on the territorial state largely within the context of the pressures this places on national infrastructure systems (NIS). In particular, the chapter will focus on the exemplar of this trend provided by the ongoing processes of European integration and how this is creating adaptive tensions promoting the re-infrastructuring of NIS as a response to these forces of change. In so doing, the focus is upon contemporary events and processes, not upon the history of regionalism and regional infrastructuring across Europe.[2] Initially the chapter explores the form and nature of regionalism within the context of state strategy, arguing that it represents a strategy of co-operative territoriality between states. Building on this conceptual development, the chapter moves on to examine the interface between territoriality and regionalism in NIS across Europe. In so doing, the notional adaptive tensions upon NIS created by the process of regionalism through both formal and informal processes of economic integration will be examined.

THE NATURE OF STATE STRATEGY

The state here is defined as a territorially bounded entity that seeks to secure and preserve its territoriality through a series of mutually support-ing policy actions formed exclusively and implemented by a centralised institutional system across a demarcated and (normally) contiguous space (Krasner 1978, Auster and Silver 1979, Skocpol and Theda 1979, Nordlinger et al. 1988, Kofman 2007). These sets of actions to establish, preserve and enhance state territoriality lie at the core of state strategy. State strategy is treated as the exclusive area of the state, reflecting notions of sovereignty where such a strategy is formed and undertaken in a discretionary manner autonomous of socio-economic pressures (Skocpol 1985, Mitchell 1991, Jackson and James, 1993). Expressed in functional terms, state strategy can be synthesised into two overlapping elements (see for example Cerny 2010). The first are those actions by the state that have the demarcated territory over which the state exercises sovereignty as their objective: so-called 'territorial strategy'. The second aspect of state strategy is how the state (given emergent inter-state inter-dependencies) seeks to position itself in an international system of states to secure its core territorial and extra-territorial objectives: defined here as 'geostrategy'.

In terms of territorial strategy (see Sack 1983, 1986), the objective of the state is to assert legitimate control across a territory. This rests upon the notion that not only does the state have the legitimate right – by both the population of a territory and other states (Taylor 1995) – to assert control over the territory, but also that it has the capability to undertake the measures to assert its territoriality (Vollaard 2009). This reflects that state strategy does not solely depend upon the state possessing the monopoly of physical violence to enable its rule-making authority (Weber 1968); it also depends upon the ability of the state to provide the public goods that legitimise its right to assert its territoriality within the demarcated space (Holsti 1996, Fukayama 2004, Lemay-Hébert 2009).

As such, the core objective to such strategy is to ensure that the state meets its own and its population's desire for internal order, external security, socio-economic cohesion and the promotion of economic growth (see for example Painter and Jeffrey 2009). Conventionally, this treats the state as a 'bordered power container' (Giddens 1985) with limited or no overlap between respective state territorial jurisdictions (Scholte 2005).

The second dimension of state strategy is geostrategy, which reflects the need for states to position themselves to support their territorial objectives within the system of states (Skocpol 1985, Moisio 2019). Geostrategy – as defined here – concerns those actions (both formal and informal) by the state that seek to manage the evolution and consequences of extra-territorial events and processes that impact the capability of the state to meets its territorial objectives (Walters 2004, Browning and Joenniemi 2008). These formal geostrategic actions involve a mix or sole use of geopolitical and geo-economic techniques to influence the behaviour of other states (as well as non-state agents) so that they work for (or at the very least not against) the interests of the state and its territorial objectives (see for example Katzenstein 1978, Taylor 1994, Cerny 1995, Keohane 2002). Alongside these methods are those actions to manage the everyday interactions between states across contiguous and semi-contiguous space where there is evident spillover/territorial overlap between states. These result in the actions of a state in one territory impacting on another. These actions are often unintentional but reflect longstanding socio-economic and political links (Arrighi 1994).

The interface between territorial and geo-strategies underlines that there is no neat divide between domestic and international systems (Agnew 1994), and that not all events that happen in a national territory are national events (Brenner 1999, Sassen 2013). Thus, according to Agnew (2005), the state and territory are no longer synonymous as territoriality can impact on and be impacted by political and socio-economic processes beyond the borders of the state. This stresses that strategy is no longer focused purely on activity within defined borders (see also Painter 2010, Carpenter 2019). Furthermore this process underscores that the conventional notion that discretionary territorial strategy is curtailed by globalisation is too simple a perspective (see for example Weiss 2005). The tensions acting upon discretionary state strategy are formed by a mix of contemporary issues (such as the trend towards globalism) and longstanding factors by territorially overlapping social, political and economic processes (see for example Taylor 1994, Sassen 2013).

Such complexity reflects that territoriality is not simply the outcome of a single state's actions but of an assortment of behaviours by a range of actors. Furthermore some components of territorial strategy are not strictly national as they operate in a larger operational space that can involve the debordering of activities beyond established state boundaries. Thus the conventional territorial function of sovereignty can also be configured within imperial (where one state asserts and contests rights over others), integrationist (pooling of sovereignty) and globalist (networks that are defined by geography) configurations (Carpenter 2019). Nonetheless given this context, the state will develop strategies to reflect its own interests and to also manage the needs of its territory even if it cannot directly control all the forces acting upon it (Harvey 2010). The legacy of these processes is that the public good elements of the state in terms of security, control, cohesion and growth are to some extent externally influenced (Agnew 2000). In some cases, states may be pro-active in this adaption through – for example – applying the logic of the competition state where the state seeks to increase both the permeability of borders and penetration of territory by international forces as a partial enabler of territorial strategy (Cerny 1995, Weiss 2005). The efficacy of state strategy to adapt in a discretionary manner to these tensions will reflect the relative power of the state. The larger regional and even global hegemonic states have more capability to shape the system to their advantage than smaller or less economically powerful states. This renders smaller states into a position of vulnerability (Katzenstein 2003). This can – amongst states – stimulate the development of alternative less independent/more interdependent state strategy as a means of securing their territorial objectives (Palan et al. 2001). It is within such contexts that a clear strategic rationale for regionalism can emerge (see below).

REGIONALISM AS CO-OPERATIVE TERRITORIALITY

The commonality underpinning the rationalisation of regionalism as state strategy rests upon the extent to which the flows between two or more territorial states and the mutual penetration of space that results create common territorial problems (Hass 1958, Keohane 2002, Gritsch 2005).[3] These can emerge through common security issues, cross-border cohesion, the mutual desire for growth and competitiveness, the push for sustainable economic systems and the desire to sustain territorial control in the face of more open territorial systems. These common interests form the foundation for inter-state co-operation/co-ordination to solve these common problems for mutual benefit. Such commonality is formed against a context where freer mobility, the erosion of flow filtering and discrimination between the states works for mutual advantage. This is based upon the existence of mutual confidence by each state that another's actions do not compromise any other state's territoriality. Thus, regionalism results from the actions of self-interested rational states in a global system of states that seek to preserve their own (aligned) interests (most notably their survival) through collective action. Such strategies limit state discretion through the pooling of specific activities where this is a more effective means of attaining territorial objectives through co-operation and co-ordination (Axline 1994, Payne and Gamble 1996, Rosamond 2000, Schimmelfennig 2010, Börzel 2016). This process is underpinned and legitimised by the notion that these states leak power across each other's borders. Consequently inter-state co-operation seeks to ensure that such processes are managed so as to mutually support each other's territoriality (Jackson and James 1993, Taylor 1994, Mann 1997). Indeed Vaubel and Willett (1991) argue that states have an incentive to engage in regionalism where cross-border externalities result in the under-production of public goods, where international co-operation occurs in the production of public goods and where non-co-operative behaviour produces sub-optimal outcomes (Axelrod 1984). The efficacy of regional processes to support state territoriality relies upon trust and commitment between partners to ensure the mutual legitimacy of flows. Such legitimacy is based on a commonality of risk and the alignment of the objectives of co-operating states.

Despite this trend toward regionalism, there is little evidence of any sense of an independent supranational strategy being developed in any regional grouping either at the territorial or the geo-strategic level (Vollaard 2009). For most regional groupings, bar the EU (see below), there are limited erosions of internal borders, and no real intention for the group to develop any real common geostrategic positions beyond trade. Consequently – in most regional agreements – territorial and geo-strategy remain the sole preserve of the state. Wissel (2014) argues that regional bodies, even where they are most developed (such as in the case of the EU), lack infrastructural power with there being no direct link to civil society, with regionalism being an elite-driven process devoid of popular consensus. Thus regionalism does not erode the salience of the state in its territory or its position as a building block of the global system. Regionalism does though create an adaptive tension upon states to which they need to respond (Brenner 1999). As suggested, any adaptations occur without fundamentally altering the nature of the territorial state as the challenges of regionalism are often at the periphery of the main objectives of territoriality (Mann 1984, Hurrell 1995, Weiss 1998). Regionalism does not tend to penetrate deep into the state's socio-economic and political structures, with co-operation being limited in scope and impact upon a state's territorial functions (see for example the work of O'Tuathail et al. 1998, Weiss 2005).

This strategic adaption to the tension created by regionalism results in strategies that can best be characterised as co-operative territoriality. This is a discretionary strategy followed by states to adapt to tensions created by the rising complexity, intensity, extensity and velocity of cross-border flows and their legacy for state territoriality. Co-operative territoriality represents a strategy of proactive engagement between states to enhance the efficacy of their own strategies, often (though not always) via co-ordinating supranational/international structures (Held et al. 2000). The strategy is based on the notion of inter-governmental co-ordination as advanced by Hettne and Söderbaum (1998). This stresses strategies of co-operative action by states for mutual benefit based on rising inter-connections between economies with minimal loss of sovereignty (Cini 2010). This process can reflect a mutualisation of risks (both internal and external to the states) where state territory is penetrated by both formal and informal interactions that can be both legitimate and illegitimate (see below). As such, territoriality cannot neatly be delimited by borders (see for example Agnew 1994). Thus, as Brenner (1999) stresses, co-operative territoriality as a strategy is rationalised through the recognition that the state is not a self-enclosed block of space but forms strategy on the recognition that it operates on a series of overlapping domains. This does not change the territory of the state, but it does require a re-scaling so as to enable it to create and manage socio-economic political relations that impact upon its territoriality.

Conceptualising regionalism as co-operative territoriality embeds the analysis in this research within intergovernmental approaches to the study of regional integration, with the process ultimately shaped by domestic political economy (Moravcsik 1993, Cini 2003, 2010). This eschews any sense that any pooling of sovereignty generates an embedded dynamic process of ever closer integration (Keohane and Nye 1975, Rosamond 2000).[4] These approaches reflect realist methodologies to the study of the subject matter, where the territorial state seeks only compromises (based on inter-state bargaining) regarding its sovereignty when it is in its own interests (based on its domestic agenda) (Schmitter 2007). The emergence of centralised decision making and the pooling of sovereignty emerges as a rational act by states as they seek to strengthen the credibility of inter-state commitments and also aid dispute resolution (Börzel 2013).

One evident rationale for co-operative territoriality is for the state (especially smaller, less powerful ones) to utilise regional forces to support/enhance state geostrategy. Axline (1994) notes that regionalism is an adjunct to state strategy where it is used as a means to supplement, support and enhance state power. In this context, regionalism is about the state – through the regional system – acquiring a competency to adapt to globalism; it is through the region that the state can better adapt to global interdependencies (Hettne and Söderbaum 1998, 2000). This can possibly reflect security concerns and a feeling of vulnerability in the presence of global/regional hegemons (Buzan and Waever 2003, Börzel 2013). The logic of regionalism as a commercial strategy for state competition has been more widely accepted (Palan et al. 2001). In this context, smaller states see the benefit of regionalism, with economic integration offering the capability to scale up markets to increase power in a geostrategic sense.

These themes were also evident within the shift towards 'new regionalism'. With this trend, regionalism began to take on a more geostrategic slant as it became less about the region looking inwards and more about utilising regionalism as a tool for participating states to attain influence in the global system (Hettne 2005). In short, the regionalism process became more about the economic interests of the state – though some blocs have evolved to have a strong security focus. However, what is increasingly common is that states are choosing to selectively (in many cases) promote the erosion of national borders to promote territorial seamlessness (Söderbaum 2012).

Much of the literature on regionalism focuses on the formal processes, where power is proactively ceded to supranational/international organisations based on multi-state co-operation. Alongside these formal processes are informal mechanisms between states (Hurrell 1995). In this context, informal integration can reflect everyday cross-border non-state actor interactions that stand outside any formal agreement (such as business networks especially where there are diasporas) (see Kurian 2004). Such informality can also reflect bilateral and multilateral agreements that stand apart from any formal integration process and where the process is explicitly co-operative, with no intent to transfer any powers to a supranational entity (Börzel 2016). It is the intensity of these informal cross-border interactions that is seen as one of the more powerful drivers towards the legitimisation of formal integration as states seek to embrace rather than restrict such interactions. These processes underscore the complexity of regionalism where parallel formal and informal process can coexist, especially where common problems are 'localised' or bilateral and not relevant to third states. This informality of integration can reflect a more pragmatic localised solution to common problems on an issue-by-issue basis. The complexity of regionalism is underlined by the fact that some regional agreements have established supranational bodies that are designed to be informal to allow consensus, flexibility and non-confrontation (Heeg and Ossenbrügge 2002, Acharya and Johnston 2007). Wissel (2014) argues that regionalism does not cause inter-state differentials to vanish, and nor does rivalry cease: states still have divergent interests. As such, regional blocs are still very fragmented – something that can only increase as they expand their membership and as their degree of heterogeneity expands as a consequence. Such emergent divergences can limit areas of mutual beneficial co-operation and constrain the efficacy of state strategies that have embedded co-operative territoriality.

THE TERRITORIAL STATE AND ITS INFRASTRUCTURE SYSTEM

As Bridge et al. (2018) identify, infrastructures are 'the open and closed veins of territory' (p. 3). The infrastructuring process represents a means of enabling state strategy though the creation and maintenance of territory-wide physical networked systems that facilitate the transmission, storage, processing and distribution of tangibles and intangibles within and between territories to support their functioning (Finger et al. 2005, Larkin 2013). Through the generation and management of intra-territorial flows, the state is able to penetrate space to secure its territoriality (Mann 1984, Van der Vleuten 2004). In practical terms, this requires that infrastructure is embedded (to the point of invisibility at the point of usage) into socio-economic systems and that it enables 'valuable' relationships between users creating communities of practice (Star and Ruhleder 1996). The notion of value in infrastructure systems also highlights that they are only effective as a tool of state strategy insofar as a user intends to use that infrastructure (Edwards 2003). Thus universal provision does not mean it is useful to every citizen within a territorial state. In systemic terms, the value of any single component of an infrastructure system operates as part of a larger system where a failure of any single component can create cascade effects elsewhere within the territorial system. Such vulnerabilities have focused states on issues of criticality where such cascade effects could challenge state territoriality (Rinaldi et al. 2001). The link between infrastructure and state territoriality does offer an evident rationalisation for the position of authors such as Larkin (2013) who argue that the notion of an embedded NIS can make little sense when the state can use it as an expression of power and legitimacy and offer a means of discourse within its population (see Turner 2020). As a means of reinforcing its territoriality, the state has an incentive to pursue what Larkin terms 'suprastructures'. These are those components of the NIS that are intentionally not embedded within systems but whose existence is made explicit to users.

The NIS represents the totality of the networked infrastructures located within the territorial state. The systemic nature of the NIS underscores that it is more than just the sum of infrastructure located within the borders of a state. For simplicity, the NIS is sub-divided into differing types of infrastructure (Turner 2020): economic infrastructures (that is those that facilitate the flow of economic products/processes within a territory); and enabling infrastructures (those social and institutional structures and systems that enable the effective operation of economic infrastructure) (Howe et al. 2016). Whilst much of the focus within the NIS has been upon the physical economic infrastructures (as indeed reflected within the structure of this book), there has been – over time – an increased focus upon soft infrastructure systems (Niskanen 1991). These soft infrastructure components represent a core enabler of economic infrastructure through the provision of institutional systems for the establishment, usage and evolution of the NIS (Turner 2020). The salience of soft infrastructure has increased within its spatial and operational complexity as well as in diversity of ownership. As the NIS becomes more polycentric – both in terms of ownership of its components and sources and destination of flows – so there has been an increased policy focus upon ensuring that such complexity does not come at the price of system functionality, especially with regard to critical infrastructures (see below). Indeed, as noted below, the need to harmonise soft infrastructure between states is arguably the most salient impact of the development of regional systems. These emergent rules – arising from more complex NIS – are complemented by longstanding soft issues in infrastructure systems formed by the need to ensure that user behaviour is compliant with the territorial needs of the system (Turner 2020).

According to Mann's notion of state power, states depend on extensive infrastructure systems that allow them to universally penetrate, secure and bind territory as well as create the conditions for economic growth and development (Mann 1984). The interface between state strategy and the NIS is reflected within the infrastructural mandate and underlines the multiple functions of infrastructure in enabling state territoriality (Turner and Johnson 2017, Turner 2018). Briefly these are:

- *Control*: an extensively developed infrastructure system allows the state to penetrate civil society through its ability to generate and move resources (both tangible and intangible) around a territory. Through such penetration the state is able to exercise ideological, economic, military and political control (Mann 1997).
- *Security*: as the guarantor of security, one of the main functions of the state is guarding the NIS against external disruption and in utilising infrastructural gateways to exclude illegal/illicit flows (Gilpin 2011). This underlines that the state has the right to vet the de- and re-territorialisation of flows.
- *Integration*: there is an expectation that the services offered by the NIS are reliable, affordable and of high quality, and that these characteristics are universal across both physically remote or peripheral regions and those areas (both urban and rural) where there is social, political and economic exclusion.This notion of infrastructure as a tool of territorial integration has found a high-profile expression within the 'modern infrastructural ideal' (Marvin and Graham 2001).
- *Development/growth*: the state of the NIS is important in influencing growth through promoting the efficient circulation of resources (see for example Canning and Pedroni 2004). This should enhance productivity and aid the spread of knowledge within an economy (Martin and Rogers 1995, Estache 2010). Alongside this NIS are also configured to support international interaction between states.
- *Sustainability*: the development and utilisation of the NIS should be 'efficient' in its use of natural resources (World Bank 2012). There is an expectation that infrastructure systems should be structured and operate in a manner that does not harm the social, economic and ecological processes necessary to facilitate and sustain human equity, diversity and the functionality of natural systems (Dasgupta and Tam 2005). This seeks to decouple (at least in relative terms) infrastructure development and usage from environmental degradation (see Hickel and Callis 2019).

These drivers of infrastructuring within states were formed against a backdrop of what Schipper and Van der Vleuten (2008) term 'infrastructure nationalism'. This was a period throughout most of the 20th century where there was a pattern of national preference (if not outright discrimination) within NIS. Often this meant that core (critical) economic infrastructures came under state (frequently monopoly) ownership based on a desire to ensure that these developed in a manner that supported and enabled state territorial strategy. This pushed themes of universal access, state control and cohesion to the fore, with states often financing NIS development through a mix of user charges and taxation. This was supported by national preference in procurement and standardisation. Inevitably, this strategy of infrastructure nationalism promoted systemic fragmentation, though not outright isolation as it did not preclude NIS interconnection; it was just not a priority. Whilst states would not want to promote spillover between systems (where one state could benefit from another's infrastructure investment) there was an acceptance of the need to facilitate interconnections between NIS due to economic and social flows between these systems. However such flows would face the bottlenecks created by the existence and probable underdevelopment of border infrastructure where state infrastructuring exists to undertake the simultaneous (and seemingly contradictory) acts of facilitating, monitoring and filtering the de- and re-territorialisation of flows.

REGIONAL INFRASTRUCTURING AND CO-OPERATIVE TERRITORIALITY

As a strategy of co-operative territoriality, regional infrastructure systems (RIS) are rationalised on the basis of states seeking to integrate national systems so as to increase the velocity, efficiency and penetration of flows from partner states so as to reinforce (or, at the very least, not compromise) the infrastructural mandate (see Table 1.1). In this context, RIS are based on the fixed national infrastructures that are produced, reconfigured, re-differentiated and transformed to enable accelerated and expanded movement that accompanies regionalism (Brenner 1999). Such regional processes impact (both directly and indirectly) upon each of the identifiable properties of infrastructure (see Table 1.2). These impacts reflect that RIS emerge out of retrofitting the respective NIS to its shifting context to create a network of national networks where flows are rendered seamless by expanding capacity and/or removing frontier/ border infrastructure (where necessary) and co-ordinating/harmonising soft infrastructure (Howe et al. 2016). Inevitably, balancing a desire for the largely economic benefits from the increased velocitisation of cross-border flows has to be reconciled with the need for bordering and filtering to ensure state security and control (Harvey 1985). This means discriminatory filtering by states between partners and non-partner states at the region's borders, creating pressure to establish a network of hard and mutually supporting soft infrastructure systems between states (Van der Vleuten 2004, Turner 2018). Border infrastructure tends to defy the convention that infrastructure should disappear into the background and be transparent in usage (Star 1999). Border infrastructure is an expression of state power and is designed to be a visible expression of that power (Larkin 2013). This reflects what Turner (2020) terms the process of suprastructuring so as to support territoriality.

Table 1.1   Regionalism and infrastructure mandate

Component of Infrastructural Mandate	Example of Regional Dimension
Control	This can be shaped by cross-border flows of people and ideas, especially where ethnic groups straddle border areas. There is a need for states to monitor flows to the extent that external borders are policed so as not trade off economic interaction without comprising control of any single state within the group. This may also require police co-ordination and cooperation.
Security	The erosion of internal borders will need to be replaced by external borders at the region's edge. The common concern is based on consensus between states as to the nature of any external threat.
Cohesion	To promote social and economic cohesion so that any flows between states do not destabilise any single state or region within any state. The process must also militate against any threat to social cohesion of any group within the region.
Growth	The state seeks the growth of easier trade and investment between states within the region in the expectation that it will benefit economic growth and/or development.
Sustainability	Integration of economic systems renders resource efficiency in the use of infrastructures (or a component of) an issue of collective concern.

Regional infrastructuring as a form of cooperative territoriality has to reflect that co-operation between states can militate against conflicts and inconsistencies between the respective members of the regional grouping as well as operating (as mentioned) as a platform for the solution of common problems. As such, at the core of the development has to be that the respective NIS are at similar stages of development, and that soft infrastructure components can be approximated. Beyond this, states must see a mutual benefit from the integration of NIS, possibly from the perception that cross-border economic interactions are either stymied or under-developed from the absence of interconnection. In some cases, it could be that landlocked states require regional systems to aid fuller integration into regional systems as a precursor to fuller integration into the global system. Importantly these efforts must also be supported by uniformity over the commonality of state strategy with regard to notions of security, economic development with further approximation of the control objectives that allow co-operation between respective civil units. This also reinforces the aforementioned point that co-operative territoriality has to be supported by trust between partners, especially with regard to the mutual legitimisation of flows.

Whilst regionalism as co-operative territoriality is seen as a pragmatic strategy to reinforce state territorial strategy in a complex international system, there are aspects (especially with regard to the territorial role of NIS) where the process can operate as a constraint upon its effectiveness as a tool of territorial strategy (especially with regard to state security). The immediate impact of regionalism in infrastructural terms is the erosion of the importance of aforementioned border infrastructure and lowering their ability to operate as filters and points of control to ensure state security. As mentioned, the logic of regionalism is to remove (or at least reduce) such impediments and increase capacity either side of the border to capture the benefits of lower transaction costs associated with freer flows between these territories (Sohn 2014). This views the removal of border infrastructure through a neo-liberal lens of trade liberalisation – though broader economic, social and political processes can be at work in this process. In some cases the border is an artificial barrier that inhibits longstanding socio-economic interactions.

There are cases where extra-territorial infrastructure can represent a potential territorial challenge when it becomes a 'choke point' within the international system and where any disruption to this 'hub' has cascade effects on a number of NIS. Where such choke points are regional in nature or are a common concern for a group of states, co-operation is a rational strategy. Such decisions are also rationalised where – in an international system of flows – agents other than the state can penetrate and gain legitimacy within its civil society. This is especially salient where infrastructure relations cannot be demarcated to the borders of the state (Glassman 1999, Painter 2010). Where such relations are part of international value chains (or other such pan-national configurations) then infrastructures lose their sense of 'pure' nationality as they operate as part of a larger socio-economic space (Sassen 2013).

Table 1.2　　Infrastructure properties and the tensions of regionalism

Infrastructural Property	Impact of Regionalism in Infrastructure System
Embeddedness	The process implies that national systems become in operational terms indistinguishable from one another and that such differences as there are become invisible.
Transparency	When a user moves from one NIS to another there is no adaptation to be made by users in terms of behaviour and terms and form of use.
Reach or scope	A single piece of territorial infrastructure has the potential to have extra-territorial effects should its operation be either enhanced or disrupted.
Learned as part of membership	The norms and processes of moving between systems creates learning processes as users develop common understandings of cross-border mobility and of utilising seamless but differentiated NIS.
Links with conventions of practice	Movement between national systems requires an understanding of mutually agreed conventions with regard to usage. Whilst conventions of usage can reflect a system's history and pattern of evolution, such differences do not inhibit seamless/relative ease of movement within and between systems.
Embodiment of standards	To ensure mutual recognition of conventions, embeddedness and transparency, systems agree common (mutually agreed) standards allowing each NIS to interoperate without the need for regular policing/ regulation of non-domestic sourced flows.
Built on an installed base	The regional system builds upon the processes and physical systems of pre-existing national and international systems.
Becomes visible upon breakdown	In operational terms, the national system (or a part thereof) only becomes visible once it either fails or begins to act as an impediment to seamless international flows. Such visibility can be driven by human, technical or natural factors.
Is fixed in modular increments, not all at once or globally	Whilst any component of any national system has some degree of regionalism, its maintenance and development are undertaken on a piecemeal basis such that the system improves/develops incrementally, potentially creating uneven patterns of infrastructure evolution across the regional system.

This means that states need to adapt to the process of regionalism through the production, re-configuration, re-differentiation and transformation of NIS across contiguous and semi-contiguous space (Brenner 1999). The result is that RIS emerge as a complex amalgam of NIS based upon inter-state co-operation to reflect the respective interests of the component parts. Despite such adaptive tensions created by the shift in infrastructural relations, the larger system is still state-based as a source, destination or transit of flows through the regional system (Keating 2013). This reflects the absence of regional territoriality due to states being unwilling to cede many of their competences to supranational bodies (Murphy 2013). Thus the regional system emerges out of state needs, with supranationality (at best) being limited to stimulating inter-state co-ordination to militate inconsistences and gaps between NIS rather than directly facilitating a de facto regional system (Turner 2018). Co-operation between states reflects commonality of interest and the intentional absence of a higher regional body.

As such, regional infrastructuring will reflect co-operative territoriality on two processes. The first is the promotion of a virtual regional system via the interworking, interoperation and interconnection of separate national systems. This will focus on aligning soft infrastructure systems, increasing capacity at key pinch points and on building missing links within the system which (both directly and indirectly) hinder physical flows within the region. The second is co-operation to create single regional infrastructures that operate across multiple contiguous territories. The co-operation is rationalised as these territories are the source, destination and/or place of transit for transnational flows. Despite their inherent transnationality, these systems are still state-dependent as they rely upon state sanction either for transit or the de/re-territorialisation of flows (Table 1.3 reflects a fuller list of the types of re-infrastructuring evidenced). This reflects that – as an adaptive tension – regionalism is placing pressure on NIS to adapt, and is doing so through one or more of the following (Turner 2018):

- Formal regional agreements between states that stimulate increased cross-borders flows;
- Bilateral agreements between states to recognise longstanding interdependence through the interconnection of NIS;
- Global/regional hegemonic pressure may also seek to stimulate closer NIS integration as a means of promoting systemic stability as a reflection of their own political and economic interests;

- Multi-lateral agreements to build multi-state regional infrastructures.

Whilst this list is not definitive, it is important in that it underlines that regionalism within infrastructure systems is not synonymous with the formal integration process. Indeed (as noted below), in the case of Europe, inter-state (informal) processes of integration have a long and continuing presence in the ongoing regionalisation of NIS across the continent. Thus co-operative territoriality as a state strategy need not be expressed solely within formal integration agreements as states may be unwilling to cede power to supranational bodies even in the presence of common problems, and existing bilateral links may be the more effective method of NIS interconnection. The forms of regional infrastructuring evidenced in Europe are highlighted in Table 1.4.

The salience of co-operative territoriality within and between NIS depends upon the impact of the flows between states. This, in turn, is driven by the type of flow (formal/informal) and the extent to which the erosion of internal regional borders are legitimised, and state confidence in the ability of external regional borders to replace internal filters. Across different regional groupings there are variances as regards the intensity of co-operative territoriality due to variations in the erosion/eradication of internal borders and of the consequent degree of integration of NIS. The erosion of internal borders reflects a belief that bottlenecks are seen as bad for the efficiency of the system without clearly recognising their strategic value to territoriality, especially at borders where the slowing of traffic is necessary as part of the security process.

Underpinning the notion of co-operative territoriality is that the formal integration of infrastructure systems allows states to – at least partially – mutualise infrastructure risk. This infrastructure risk has been reflected in themes on criticality. Criticality is defined here as concerning those parts of the NIS whose failure would pose a direct challenge to state ter- ritoriality (Turner 2018). Interconnection between NIS means that a local failure within a national system can be – at least in part – mitigated by connectivity with other NIS that allows flows to be sustained into a state, thus minimising disruption. Inevitably this focusses the state upon key pinch points in the system and seeking to develop alternatives to such bottlenecks to erode such vulnerabilities. Through such processes the regional system creates a process of mutual support under scenarios of rising infrastructure risk. The degree of interconnection can also create its own risk where outright integration creates regional infrastructure dependencies that can create a contagion of failure throughout the system based on localised issues. As such, co-operative territoriality has to involve managing these spatial interdependencies. The fuller interface between the core requirements of the NIS and the enablement offered by RIS is outlined in Table 1.3.

Table 1.3   *The interface between national and regional infrastructure systems*

NIS Facet	Role of Regional System
Universality	The promotion of regional systems has the potential to increase access to infrastructure services in frontier regions which are often characterised by infrastructural under-development due to their frequent peripherality to main centres of state activity and population.
Connectivity	The growth of regional connectivity can aid trade across the region as well as enabling flows between component NIS.
Globality	States (especially if landlocked) could use regional systems to access global logistical channels. These regional links can also be used to generate security of supply by enabling access to diverse globally sourced energy.
Criticality	The risks across respective NIS can be mutualised through the connection of NIS to allow sustained flows in the presence of local failure.
Quality	The promotion of interconnectivity between NIS of differing quality can force a state with lower-quality systems to upgrade systems to ensure full interoperability.
Quantity	The interconnection between systems can stimulate states to increase NIS capacity at key potential pinch points within regional systems.

REGIONALISM AND THE EUROPEAN INFRASTRUCTURE SYSTEM

Underpinning processes of regionalism within European NIS has been an emergent sense of co-operative territoriality within the European region (Wallace 1999) where aspects of the aforementioned infrastructural mandate (notably growth, cohesion and security (see below)) can be enabled, supported or enhanced by action at the supranational level of governance (see also Table 1.2). This reflects that there is no sense of coherent separate territorial or geo-strategy being developed at the EU level. At best, any notion of EU territoriality is a reflection of inter-state co-operation and co-ordination (Mamadouh 2001, Bialasiewicz et al. 2005, Pullano 2011) with the EU Europeanising state strategy to offer advantages of scale (Perkmann 2007, Vollaard 2009).

Thus, where there are elements of territorial strategy they are at best shared competences, with supranational action being secondary to state strategy (Walters 2004, Vitale 2011, Faludi 2013). Thus, regionalism as a territorial system is an amalgam of state territoriality, the willingness of states to allow penetration by intra-group flows and the trust by states that the external boundaries of the region can be adequately policed. Consequently the notion of a separate EU-wide regional territoriality above the state is largely illusory as states limit co-operation in terms of scope and scale (Scott 2009). This is also evident in the absence of independent EU geostrategy; though, as the European Infrastructure System (EIS) is embedded within a global network of infrastructures, it has an evident geostrategic dimension (Newman and Paasi, 1998). This geostrategic dimension reflects not just notions of the security and reliability of externally sourced flows (in the absence of internal borders) (Scott and Van Houtum 2009) but also how aspects of the EIS depend upon external infrastructures (and the sustenance of flows through them) for their effectiveness (Carr 2016). To promote this security of flows, EU states co-operate to use their economic power to influence the behaviour of states within its neighbourhood and beyond (Pace 2007, Browning and Joenniemi 2008, Browning 2018). These patterns reflect that the EIS is not a closed infrastructure system, and that part of the logic of integration is to enable all states to interconnect securely with global transmission systems by connecting into those states which have pre-existing access (Schipper and Schot 2011).

Bialasiewicz et al. (2005) suggest that the EU eschews the notion of hard territoriality associated with infrastructuring in favour of an 'aspirational territoriality' that seeks to promote territorial cohesion by creating a space of common values and solidarity. EU narratives surrounding notions of territorial cohesion reflect this approach as this is more about a shared political vision than a 'hard' sense of creating a uniform space (Faludi 2009). This reflects that the notion of 'cohesion' as a common territorial goal has to coexist with the hard territoriality of states (Faludi 2014). This aspirational territoriality has to be agreed and co-ordinated between states to be attained. The EU – the authors argue – is riddled with territorial ambiguities where the EU's ideals run up against an absence of territorialising competences at the supranational level of governance (Bialasiewicz et al. 2005).

These notions of Europe and its aspirational territoriality shape the infrastructuring process within the EU. This is a region of pre-existing systems that have evolved to serve national needs, but where there are (or have been) links between these national systems. However across these states the quality, quantity and maturity of NIS can differ markedly. This is also compounded by NIS not always responding to the adaptive tensions placed upon them by regionalism as well as other forces. The aspirational territoriality of the EU has an ideal EIS in mind that enables Europe to operate and function as a cohesive group supporting competitiveness and sustainability whilst not compromising state concerns of security and control. Table 1.4 indicates the numerous forms of infrastructuring that are evident throughout the European system of NIS that lies at the core of the EIS.

Table 1.4   *Forms of infrastructuring in the European regional system*

Infrastructural Process	Description
Interconnection	This process is based on the physical interconnection of pre-existing systems by the establishment and maintenance of physical links between NIS to support the reliability, resilience, security, consistency and/or predictability of flows between states.
Interoperability	This process seeks to ensure that flows between NIS are rendered seamless through the adoption of common standards and protocols so as to allow national systems to interwork.
Transit	Parts of the regional system are needed to ensure flows between non-contiguous states. These systems are required not merely for the benefit of the state in which the transit infrastructure is located but because without it flows across the wider region could face bottlenecks or long diversionary routes.
Regional by Design Systems	These are dedicated systems that cross multiple territories. They are designed to promote pan-regional flows where there is a regional dislocation between flow source and destination and where existing national systems are inadequate or not for the nature of the flow.
De-infrastructuring	The ease of flows across borders requires the removal of those border infrastructures that seek to operate as checks and bottlenecks within the regional system.
Re-infrastructuring	These are parts of the system that need to be re-purposed as a result of regionalism. They are infrastructures built to serve national needs but which now operate as key hubs/links within the regional system. This may mean an increase in capacity or adaptation to new standards/protocols.

Contextualising regional infrastructuring as a largely state-driven phenomenon shaped by an ongoing process of both formal and informal integration underscores the variety of measures that promote infrastructural integration across Europe (Opitz and Tellmann 2015). The EIS is defined here as the totality of interacting and mutually dependent networked national and transnational infrastructure within the geographic space of Europe (Turner 2018). This conceptualisation of the EIS (as suggested above) sees it as a regional network of networks built from the state-based system (Van der Vleuten and Kaijser 2005). Indeed Misa and Schot (2005) see the process as long term, referring to hidden integration of European infrastructural integration as inter-state agreement, and disagreement has led to a successive linking and delinking of infrastructures. Such state-based processes became subsumed within supranational initiatives – notably the Trans-European Networks (TENs) programme (see below), which has contextualised bi- and multilateral initiatives within the context of a broader supranational strategy (Dülffer 2009). Overall, the development of the EIS involves multiple levels of governance.

Inter-State Processes

As will be mentioned throughout, the development of the EIS is largely a state-based process formed around a series of bilateral and multilateral interconnections. In a continent with a high degree of state-based territorial fragmentation, inter-state collaboration is normal across both soft and hard aspects of NIS (Van der Vleuten and Kaijser 2005, Badenoch and Fickers 2010). Such actions reflect a long history of infrastructural integration, much of which pre-dates (by about a century) both the current territorial configuration and the push towards supranationality within the system (Johnson and Turner 1997, 2007, Van der Vleuten and Kaijser 2006). The integration of both hard and soft systems form the basis of the European-wide system – a process driven by the rational actions of states as they seek to manage the overlap between territorial and geo-strategies (Darian-Smith 1999). Transnational infrastructures were – and are – the norm across Europe by strategic intent, with the international dimension of the NIS being an inevitable component in system development and design (Badenoch and Fickers 2010). Such strategies did not inhibit states pursuing their own interests in the development of their respective NIS. Sometimes this was in isolation, with the result of emerging incompatibilities between systems which have only been rendered interoperable retrospectively. The most evident legacy of this long-term trend is that discretionary supranational action is largely unnecessary as states can develop the EIS in a piecemeal fashion operating in their own interests (Schipper and van den Vleuten 2008, Högselius et al. 2013).

Alongside these multiple bilateral interconnections are multilateral infrastructures based upon the interconnection and/or traversing of three or more states. Such infrastructures reflect the need for security of flows by either a single state (where, for example, it is landlocked and requires such systems to access global logistical systems) or where such systems are necessary to transport flows across and to multiple states driven by spatial disparities in the availability of resources (Walters 2004). In the former, this is a process of interconnecting, multiple national systems to create pan-European mobility by lowering the transaction costs associated with fragmented and/or isolated NIS. In the latter, there is dedicated pan-European infrastructure to securely transport flows across and between multiple states (Kandiyoti 2012).

Whilst infrastructure nationalism (Schipper and Van der Vleuten 2008) was the predominant model of infrastructure development throughout Europe in the 20th century this did not remove tensions to seek to interconnect or even integrate these national systems. Throughout this period, there were a number of initiatives, not necessarily to counter infrastructural nationalism but to ensure that this process did not 'Balkanise' the European system. Thus there was US pressure to integrate systems as part of post-war reconstruction and, alongside, these assorted Europe-wide co-operative forums emerged to promote continent-wide inter-NIS interoperability (see below).

International Initiatives

Before the EU gained competences for the creation of single markets for the various network services provided over the EIS, there were and remain longstanding international agreements and organisations between states to ensure interoperability between national systems. Some of these reflect the fact that certain networks pre-dated the current territorial configuration of Europe and that there needed to be agreement on interworking of national systems. The International Union of Railways/Union internationale des chemins de fer (UIC) was established in 1922 to standardise practices and to limit any fragmentation of the European rail system. Its remit included a revenue-sharing agreement between respective national systems based on a 'UIC code' that defines rules and best practice. These rules now operate globally, though much of the EU-based standards work is now done by the European Rail Agency. Similar inter-state agencies exist in telecommunications, where the European Conference of Postal and Telecommunications Administrations (CEPT) – established in 1959 – exists to develop agreed standards in telecommunications across technical, operational, regulatory and commercial issues as does the International Telecommunications Union (ITU). There are also standard-isation organisations in the energy sector, with the European Committee for Electrotechnical Standardization/Comité Européen de Normalisation Électrotechnique (CENELEC) covering the evolving European electric-ity system and gas through the European Committee for Standardization/ Comité Européen de Normalisation (CEN). These have more latterly been supported by operator-driven initiatives through the European Network of Transmission System Operators for Gas (ENTSO-G) and the European Network of Transmission System Operators (ENTSO-E), both of which have a standardisation and network integration mandate (see Chapter 3).

In practice, there are a range of co-operative agreements between states and national and international operators, as well as other stake-holders, to develop national networks in a manner that renders them both interconnectable and interoperable. These inter-state/interopera-tor co-operative arrangements reflect both longstanding and emergent interdependencies that pre-dated the formal integration process and/or have emerged as a response to it. In some cases, the process was driven not only by a desire to sustain interconnectivity against a fragmenting territorial system but also to facilitate integrated systems for emergent infrastructures in a post-war environment. The creation and sustenance of such co-operative frameworks underpins the arguments of Van der Vleuten and Kaijser (2005) that – in many cases – co-ordinated suprana-tional action is rendered unnecessary.

Supranational Initiatives

Whilst there have been a number of sectoral policies at the supra-national level on the respective economic infrastructure sectors, the Trans-European Networks (TENs) programme was the first attempt to give the EIS a more systemic treatment (Johnson and Turner 2007). Launched in 1990 and contextualised by the emergence of the Single European Market (SEM), which exposed the inadequacies of the prevail-ing infrastructure system, TENs formalised many bilateral and multilat-eral programmes within a single strategy for European infrastructuring

(Johnson and Turner 1997). This single strategy sought to reinforce and add impetus to pre-existing processes as well as stimulating new structures to promote more widely developed systemic interconnection, interoperability and access through the framework of open and competitive markets. This process represented an attempt to undertake a geostrategic infrastructuring of the EIS as a means of using the scaling up of infrastructure systems to EU-wide level as a platform for exercising its geo-economic and geopolitical power. However, these processes were still largely state-led, with the EU limited to a largely marginal role in facilitating trans-European mobility by promoting border infrastructure capacity, better infrastructure services and socio-economic cohesion (Johnson and Turner 1997).

For states, TENs as a policy strategy was legitimised by a desire to co-operate to promote secure supplies of essential products, facilitating trade and lowering investment costs. Consequently, the importance of TENs lies more in its role as a catalyst for state-led development, high-lighting systemic deficiencies, missing links, uneven maturity of systems and soft infrastructure requirements of the EIS (Johnson and Turner 1997). In this context, TENs emerges as an attempt to reconcile state overlap between territorial and geo-strategies to co-ordinate infrastructural integration. That infrastructuring remains a state-based competence reflects the aforementioned absence of a sense of European territoriality, and that the erosion of internal borders requires states to address gaps within and between their respective NIS (Mamadouh 2001, Bartolini 2005). Thus TENs as a policy strategy operates within the context of state-based infrastructuring strategies with the EU having very little discretion.

For the EU, TENs are justified on the basis that the failure of an overarching body to act would lead to the under-provision of cross-border infrastructure, with the EIS tending towards fragmentation and sub-optimal operation conditions due to this absence of co-operation and scale (Vaubel and Willet 1991). For the EU, only a supranational body can do this; though, as suggested above, states have tended to be more pragmatic than strategic in establishing cross-border links. For the EU, as a forum for co-ordination, it is the most appropriate body to realise network effects throughout the EIS. Connectivity to attain network effects is the prime strategic objective of the integrative elements behind TENs. This means not just the existence of a link to all parts of Europe, but that the link has sufficient capacity in that it promotes intra-regional economic convergence.

Whilst the plan laid the basis for a common infrastructure policy, it was in retrospect a policy of very limited efficacy. This was largely due to the large funding gaps within many of the projects (especially transport and energy), driven by the programme's reliance on state finance for its realisation (see Chapters 2 and 3). Throughout its evolution as a policy programme there were numerous attempts by the European Commission to establish less state dependency in project finance (see Johnson and Turner 1997, 2007). However this was always resisted by states and it was only in information infrastructures that significant sources of non-state finance were available (see Chapter 4). The main source of EU finance for TENs projects is currently (2021) through the Connecting Europe Facility (CEF), which only provides very limited financial support for the development of priority projects. The European Investment Bank (EIB) can also offer support, though this is less through direct grants and more through seeking to arrange the desired levels of funding from the financial markets.

However, as noted above, the EU is not the only option for the development of an EIS. In some areas, states preferred to co-operate outside of supranational frameworks that some considered too restrictive. The development of TENs as a distinct public policy area built upon existing co-operative frameworks, often bypassing or replacing longer-standing international bodies involved in establishing transnational interoperability and interconnection. The result has been a rather muddled framework of co-operative bodies shaping the evolving EIS.

Arguably a greater impact of the EU (alongside pre-existing inter-governmental bodies on issues such as standards) has been in the area of soft infrastructure. These will be examined in more detail in the respective chapters; but – both in a generic and a sectoral sense – the EU has (through its impact on soft infrastructure) proved a proactive body in facilitating the integration of NIS. The development of the SEM programme, with its elimination of internal borders, necessitated the creation of institutional frameworks to ensure that this did not compromise state control or security (see Chapter 2). This builds on longstanding common policies in the economic infrastructure sectors, notably transport and energy, which also focused on soft infrastructure in promoting interoperability and liberalisation of national systems. These policies did little more than seek to co-ordinate national policies to promote sectoral rather than infrastructural integration.

The EU has also started to become more proactive with regard to the co-ordination of member states' critical infrastructure with its focus on those national infrastructures whose failure would impact upon two or more states (Pursiainen 2009). This reflects a desire to mitigate cascade effects within the EIS via co-operation between states and in setting agreed standards of resilience (Burgess 2007). This strategy seeks to ensure that common threats (even if the impacts are local) do not fragment the system (Hämmerli and Renda 2010). However, power remains with the states that have shown they are willing to suspend regional flows if their territoriality is threatened. Many states are resorting to inter-state agreement rather than using supranational systems which tend to merely offer an awareness of the opportunities of collaboration and the spreading of best practice. Van der Vleuten et al. (2013) argue that longstanding collaboration between states negates the need for any supranationality, especially as a decentralised system tends to work well (see also Van der Vleuten and Lagendijk 2010). This reflects a longstanding process of 'hidden' integration that lies outside of the EU's institutional structure.

CONCLUSION

Whilst the development of the EIS involves a multiplicity of actions at multiple levels, it is the states that ultimately drive its development. This is based on a rational act by states that want to secure and enhance their territoriality. The evident overlap between a state's territorial and geo-strategies reflects an adaptive tension to which states are responding. This they do via a strategy of cooperative territoriality. Regionalism as an adaptive tension places pressure on states to adapt NIS to ensure that territorial strategy and geo-strategies are aligned to support state territoriality. In Europe, such interconnections reflect longstanding links between states. These links have been increasingly integrated into the formal integration process through the EU's Trans-European Networks initiative.

NOTES

1　Formal integration refers to those measures to promote integration that are encapsulated within state-led, policy-driven programmes. Informal integration involves those 'everyday' flows (both official and unofficial) of capital, products and people between states by non-state actors that are of an intensity that generates some degree of interdependence.
2　Readers interested in his aspect of the process of European infrastructuring should consult the volume edited by Van der Vleuten and Kaijser (2006).
3　The region here is viewed through the lens of IPE, and as such is treated as a supranational subsystem of the international system based upon a number

of clustered states drawn together by interdependence across a usually contiguous or semi-contiguous space (Hettne and Söderbaum 2000, Hettne 2005).

4   Smith (1992) stresses that regionalism varies between groups according to its scope (the array of policy issues included in agreement), depth (the degree of uniformity of policy actions), institutionalisation (the degree of formal building of common institutional systems) and centralisation (the extent to which centralisation of authority is pursued).

REFERENCES

Acharya, A., and Johnston, A. I. (eds) (2007). *Crafting cooperation: Regional international institutions in comparative perspective.* Cambridge: Cambridge University Press.

Agnew, J. (1994). The territorial trap: The geographical assumptions of international relations theory. *Review of International Political Economy*, Vol. 1, No. 1, pp. 53–80.

Agnew, J. (2000), Global political geography beyond geopolitics, *International Studies Review*, Vol. 2, No. 1, pp. 91–99.

Agnew, J. (2005). Sovereignty regimes: Territoriality and state authority in contemporary world politics. *Annals of the Association of American Geographers*, Vol. 95, No. 2, pp. 437–461.

Arrighi, G. (1994). *The long twentieth century: Money, power, and the origins of our times.* London: Verso.

Auster, R., and Silver, M. (1979). *The state as a firm: Economic forces in political development.* Boston, MA: Martinus Nijhoff.

Axelrod, R. (1984). *The evolution of cooperation.* New York: Basic Books.

Axline, A. W. (ed.) (1994). *The political economy of regional cooperation: Comparative case studies.* London: Pinter.

Badenoch, A., and Fickers, A. (eds) (2010). *Materializing Europe: Transnational infrastructures and the project of Europe.* Basingstoke: Palgrave Macmillan.

Bartolini, S. (2005). *Restructuring Europe: Centre formation, system building, and political structuring between the nation state and the European Union.* Oxford: Oxford University Press.

Bialasiewicz, L., Elden, S., and Painter, J. (2005). The constitution of EU territory. *Comparative European Politics*, Vol. 3, pp. 333–363.

Börzel, T. A. (2013). Comparative regionalism: European integration and beyond. In Carlsnaes, W., Risse, T., and Simmons, B. A. (eds), *Handbook of international relations*. London: Sage, pp. 503–530.

Börzel, T. A. (2016). Theorizing regionalism. In Börzel, T. and Risse, T. (eds), *The Oxford handbook of comparative regionalism*. Oxford: Oxford University Press, pp. 41–63.

Brenner, N. (1999). Beyond state-centrism? Space, territoriality, and geographical scale in globalization studies. *Theory and Society*, Vol. 28, No. 1, pp. 39–78.

Bridge, G., Özkaynak, B., and Turhan, E. (2018). Energy infrastructure and the fate of the nation: Introduction to special issue. *Energy Research and Social Science*, Vol. 41, pp. 1–11.

Browning, C. S. (2018). Geostrategies, geopolitics and ontological security in the Eastern neighbourhood: The European Union and the 'new cold war'. *Political Geography*, Vol. 62, pp. 106–115.

Browning, C. S., and Joenniemi, P. (2008). Geostrategies of the European neighbourhood policy. *European Journal of International Relations*, Vol. 14, No. 3, pp. 519–551.

Burgess, J.-P. (2007). Social values and material threat: The European programme for critical infrastructure protection. *International Journal of Critical Infrastructures*, Vol. 3, No. 3–4, pp. 471–88.

Buzan, B., and Waever, O. (2003). *Regions and powers: The structure of international security*. Cambridge: Cambridge University Press.

Canning, D., and Pedroni, P. (2004). The effect of infrastructure on long run economic growth. Harvard University Working Paper, Vol. 99, No. 9, pp. 1–30.

Carpenter, M. J. (2019). Understanding aterritorial borders through a BIG reading of Agnew's *Globalization and Sovereignty*. *Borders in Globalization Review*, Vol. 1, No. 1, pp. 123–126.

Carr, M. (2016). *Fortress Europe: Dispatches from a gated continent*. London: New Press,

Cerny, P. G (1995). Globalisation and the changing logic of collective action. *International Organization*, Vol. 49, No. 4, pp. 595–625.

Cerny, P. G. (2010). The competition state today: From raison d'état to raison du monde. *Policy Studies*, Vol. 31, No. 1, pp. 5–21.

Cini, M. (ed.) (2003). *European Union politics*. Oxford: Oxford University Press.

Cini, M. (2010). Intergovernmentalism. In Cini, M. and Borragán, N. P.-S. (eds), *European Union politics* (3rd edn). Oxford: Oxford University Press, pp. 86–104.

Darian-Smith, E. (1999). *Bridging divides: The Channel Tunnel and English legal identity in the new Europe*. Oakland: University of California Press.

Dasgupta, S., and Tam, E. K. (2005). Indicators and framework for assessing sustainable infrastructure. *Canadian Journal of Civil Engineering*, Vol. 32, No. 1, pp. 30–44.

Dehousse, R., Weiler, J. H. H., and Wallace, W. (1990). *The dynamics of European integration*. London: Pinter.

Dülffer, J. (2009). The history of European integration: From integration history to the history of integrated Europe. In Loth, W. (ed.), *Experiencing Europe*. Baden-Baden: Nomos, pp. 17–32.

Edwards, P. N. (2003). Infrastructure and modernity: Force, time, and social organization in the history of sociotechnical systems. In Misa, T. J., Brey, P., and Feenberg, A. (eds), *Modernity and technology*. Cambridge, MA: MIT Press, pp. 185–226.

Estache, A. (2010). Infrastructure finance in developing countries: An overview. *EIB Papers*, Vol. 15, No. 2, pp. 60–88.

Faludi, A. (2009). Territorial cohesion under the looking glass: Synthesis paper about the history of the concept and policy background to territorial cohesion.

European Commission, Regional Policy, Inforegio. Available at http://ec
.europa.eu/regional_policy/consultation/terco; date accessed 25/11/2020.

Faludi, A. (2013). Territorial cohesion, territorialism, territoriality, and soft planning: A critical review. *Environment and Planning A: Economy and Space*,
Vol. 45, No. 6, pp. 1302–1317.

Faludi, A. (2014). Territorial cohesion beyond state territoriality. In *CIST2014:
Fronts et frontières des sciences du territoire/Frontiers and boundaries of
territorial sciences*. Proceedings du 2e colloque international, 27–28 March
2014. Paris: Collège international des sciences du territoire, pp. 179–183.

Finger, M., Groenewegen, J., and Künneke, R. (2005). The quest for coherence
between institutions and technologies in infrastructures. *Competition and
Regulation in Network Industries*, Vol. 6, No. 4, pp. 227–259.

Fukuyama, F. (2004). *Statebuilding: Governance and world order in the 21st
century*. New York: Cornell University Press.

Giddens, A. (1985). *The nation-state and violence*. Los Angeles: University of
California Press.

Gilpin, R. (2011). *Global political economy: Understanding the international
economic order*. Princeton, NJ: Princeton University Press.

Glassman, J. (1999). State power beyond the 'territorial trap': The internationalization of the state. *Political Geography*, Vol. 18, No. 6, pp. 669–696.

Gritsch, M. (2005). The nation-state and economic globalization: Soft geo-politics
and increased state autonomy? *Review of International Political Economy*,
Vol. 12, No. 1, pp. 1–25.

Hämmerli, B., and Renda, A. (2010). Protecting critical infrastructure in the EU.
Brussels: Centre for European Policy Studies.

Harvey, D. (1985). The geopolitics of capitalism. In Gregory, D. and Urry,
J. (eds), *Social relations and spatial structures*. Basingstoke: Macmillan,
pp. 128–163.

Harvey, D. (2010). *The enigma of capital: And the crises of capitalism*. New
York: Oxford University Press.

Hass, E. B. (1958). *The uniting of Europe: Political, social, and economical
forces, 1950–1957*. Notre Dame, IN: University of Notre Dame Press.

Heeg, S., and Ossenbrügge, J. (2002). State formation and territoriality in the
European Union. *Geopolitics*, Vol. 7, No. 3, pp. 75–88.

Held, D., McGrew, A., Goldblatt, D., and Perraton, J. (2000). *Global transformations: Politics, economics and culture*. London: Palgrave Macmillan.

Hettne, B. (2005). Beyond the 'new' regionalism. *New Political Economy*, Vol.
10, No. 4, pp. 543–571.

Hettne, B., and Söderbaum, F. (1998). The new regionalism approach. *Politeia*,
Vol. 17, No. 3, pp. 6–21.

Hettne, B., and Söderbaum, F. (2000). Theorising the rise of regionness. *New
Political Economy*, Vol. 5, No. 3, pp. 457–474.

Hickel, J., and Kallis, G. (2019). Is green growth possible? *New Political
Economy*, Vol. 25, No. 4, pp. 1–18.

Högselius, P., Åberg, A., and Kaijser, A. (2013). Natural gas in cold war Europe:
The making of a critical infrastructure. In Högselius, P., Hommels, A., Kaijser,
A., and Van der Vleuten, E. (eds), *The making of Europe's critical infrastruc-*

ture: Common connections and shared vulnerabilities. Basingstoke: Palgrave Macmillan, pp. 27–61.

Holsti, K. (1996). *The state, war, and the state of war.* Cambridge: Cambridge University Press.

Howe, C., Lockrem, J., Appel, H., Hackett, E., Boyer, D., Hall, R., ... and Ballestero, A. (2016). Paradoxical infrastructures: Ruins, retrofit, and risk. *Science, Technology, and Human Values*, Vol. 41, No. 3, pp. 547–565.

Hurrell, A. (1995). Explaining the resurgence of regionalism in world politics. *Review of International Studies*, Vol. 21, No. 4, pp. 331–358.

Jackson, R. H., and James, A. (1993). The character of independent statehood. In Jackson, R. H. and James, A. (eds), *States in a changing world.* Oxford: Clarendon, pp. 3–25.

Johnson, D., and Turner, C. (1997). *Trans-European networks: The political economy of integrating Europe's infrastructure.* Basingstoke: Macmillan.

Johnson, D., and Turner, C. (2007). *Strategy and policy for trans-European networks.* Basingstoke: Palgrave Macmillan.

Kandiyoti, R. (2012). *Pipelines: flowing oil and crude politics.* London: IB Tauris.

Katzenstein, P. J. (ed.) (1978). *Between power and plenty: Foreign economic policies of advanced industrial states.* Madison: University of Wisconsin Press.

Katzenstein, P. J. (2003). Small states and small states revisited. *New Political Economy*, Vol. 8, No. 1, pp. 9–30.

Keating, M. (2013). *Rescaling the European state: The making of territory and the rise of the meso.* Oxford: Oxford University Press.

Keohane, R. O. (2002). *Power and governance in a partially globalized world.* London: Routledge.

Keohane, R. O., and Nye, J. S. (1975). International interdependence and integration. In Greenstein, F. I. and Polsby, N. W. (eds), *Handbook of political science* (Vol. 8). Reading, MA: Addison-Wesley, pp. 363–414.

Kofman, D. (2007). The normative limits to the dispersal of territorial sovereignty. *The Monist*, Vol. 90, No. 1, pp. 65–85.

Krasner, S. D. (1978). *Defending the national interest: Raw materials investments and US foreign policy.* Princeton, NJ: Princeton University Press.

Kurian, N. (2004). Fungible borders and informal regionalism: Rethinking China's international relations. *East Asia*, Vol. 21, No. 1, pp. 7–17.

Larkin, B. (2013). The politics and poetics of infrastructure. *Annual Review of Anthropology*, Vol. 42, pp. 327–343.

Lemay-Hébert, N. (2009). Statebuilding without nation-building? Legitimacy, state failure and the limits of the institutionalist approach, *Journal of Intervention and Statebuilding*, Vol. 3, No. 1, pp. 21–45.

Mamadouh, V. (2001). The territoriality of European integration and the territorial features of the European Union: The first 50 years. *Tijdschrift voor economische en sociale geografie*, Vol. 92, No. 4, pp. 420–436.

Mann, M. (1984). The autonomous power of the state: Its origins, mechanisms and results. *European Journal of Sociology*, Vol. 25, No. 2, pp. 185–213.

Mann, M. (1997). Has globalization ended the rise and rise of the nation-state? *Review of International Political Economy*, Vol. 4, No. 3, pp. 472–496.

Marvin, S., and Graham, S. (2001). *Splintering Urbanism: Networked infrastructures, technological mobilities and the urban condition.* London: Taylor & Francis.

Martin, P., and Rogers, C. A. (1995). Industrial location and public infrastructure. *Journal of International Economics*, Vol. 39, No. 3–4, pp. 335–351.

Misa, T. J., and Schot, J. (2005). Introduction: Inventing Europe: Technology and the hidden integration of Europe. *History and Technology*, Vol. 21, No. 1, pp. 1–19.

Mitchell, T. (1991). The limits of the state: Beyond statist approaches and their critics. *American Political Science Review*, Vol. 85, No. 1, pp. 77–96.

Moravcsik, A. (1993). Preferences and power in the European Community: a liberal intergovernmentalist approach. *JCMS: Journal of Common Market Studies*, Vol. 31, No. 4, pp. 473–524.

Moisio, S. (2019). Re-thinking geoeconomics: Towards a political geography of economic geographies. *Geography Compass*, Vol. 13, No. 10, e12466.

Murphy, A. B. (2013). Trapped in the logic of the modern state system? European integration in the wake of the financial crisis. *Geopolitics*, Vol. 18, No. 3, pp. 705–723.

Newman, D., and Paasi, A. (1998). Fences and neighbours in the postmodern world: Boundary narratives in political geography. *Progress in Human Geography*, Vol. 22, No. 2, pp. 186–207.

Niskanen, W. A. (1991). The soft infrastructure of a market economy. *Cato Journal*, Vol. 11, No. 2, pp. 233–238.

Nordlinger, E. A., Lowi, T. J., and Fabbrini, S. (1988). The return to the state: Critiques. *American Political Science Review*, Vol. 82, No. 3, pp. 875–901.

O'Tuathail, G., Herod, A., and Roberts, S.M. (1998). Negotiating unruly problematics. In Herod, A., O'Tuathail, G., and Roberts, S. M. (eds), *An unruly world? Globalization, governance and geography.* London: Routledge, pp. 1–24.

Opitz, S., and Tellmann, U. (2015). Europe as infrastructure: Networking the operative community. *South Atlantic Quarterly*, Vol. 114, No. 1, pp. 171–190.

Pace, M. (2007). The construction of EU normative power. *JCMS: Journal of Common Market Studies*, Vol. 45, No. 5, pp. 1041–1064.

Painter, J. (2010). Rethinking territory. *Antipode*, Vol. 42, No. 5, pp. 1090–1118.

Painter, J., and Jeffrey, A. (2009). *Political geography.* London: Sage.

Palan, R., and Abbott, J. with Phil Deans (2001). *State strategies in the global political economy.* London: Pinter.

Payne, A., and Gamble A. (1996). Introduction: The political economy of regionalism and world order. In Gamble, A. and Payne, A. (eds), *Regionalism and world order.* Basingstoke; Macmillan, pp. 1–20.

Perkmann, M. (2007). Construction of new territorial scales: A framework and case study of the EUREGIO cross-border region. *Regional Studies*, Vol. 41, pp. 253–266.

Pullano, T. (2011). *The evolving category of territory: From the modern state to the European Union.* Warwick: University of Warwick, Centre for the Study of Globalisation and Regionalisation.

Pursiainen, C. (2009). The challenges for European critical infrastructure protection. *European Integration*, Vol. 31, No. 6, pp. 721–39.

Rinaldi, S. M., Peerenboom, J. P., and Kelly, T. K. (2001). Identifying, understanding, and analysing critical infrastructure interdependencies. *IEEE Control Systems*, Vol. 21, No. 6, pp. 11–25.

Rosamond, B. (2000). *Theories of European integration*. Basingstoke: Palgrave Macmillan.

Sack, R. D. (1983). Human territoriality: A theory. *Annals of the Association of American Geographers*, Vol. 73, No. 1, pp. 55–74.

Sack, R. (1986). *Human territoriality: Its theory and history*. Cambridge: Cambridge University Press.

Sassen, S. (2013). When territory deborders territoriality. *Territory, Politics, Governance*, Vol. 1, No. 1, pp. 21–45.

Schimmelfennig, F. (2010). Integration theory. In Egan, M., Nugent, N., and Paterson, W. (eds), *Research agendas in EU studies*. Basingstoke: Palgrave Macmillan, pp. 37–59.

Schipper, F., and Schot, J. (2011). Infrastructural Europeanism, or the project of building Europe on infrastructures: An introduction. *History and Technology*, Vol. 27, No. 3, pp. 245–264.

Schipper, F., and Van der Vleuten, E. (2008). Trans-European network development and governance in historical perspective. *Network Industries Quarterly*, Vol. 10, No. 3, pp. 5–7.

Schmitter, P. (2007). Regional cooperation and region integration: Concepts, measurements and a bit of theory. Unpublished manuscript. European University Institute, Fiosele, Italy.

Scholte, J. A. (2005). *Globalization: A critical introduction*. Basingstoke: Macmillan.

Scott, J. W. (2009). Bordering and ordering the European neighbourhood: a critical perspective on EU territoriality and geopolitics. *Trames*, Vol. 13, No. 3, pp. 232–247.

Scott, J. W., and Van Houtum, H. (2009). Reflections on EU territoriality and the 'bordering' of Europe. *Political Geography*, Vol. 28, No. 5, pp. 271–273.

Skocpol, T. (1985). Strategies of analysis in current research. In Rueschemeyer, D., Evans, P. B., and Skocpol, T. (eds), *Bringing the state back in*. Cambridge: Cambridge University Press, pp. 3–43.

Skocpol, T., and Theda, S. (1979). *States and social revolutions: A comparative analysis of France, Russia and China*. Cambridge: Cambridge University Press.

Smith, P. H. (1992). Introduction: The politics of integration: Concepts and themes. In Smith, P. H. (ed.), *The challenge of integration: Europe and the Americas*. New Brunswick, NJ: Transaction, pp. 5–39.

Söderbaum, F. (2012). Formal and informal regionalism. In Shaw, T. M., Grant, J. A., and Cornelissen, S. (eds), *The Ashgate research companion to regionalisms*. Aldershot: Ashgate, pp. 51–67.

Sohn, C. (2014). Modelling cross-border integration: The role of borders as a resource. *Geopolitics*, Vol. 19, No. 3, pp. 587–608.

Star, S. L. (1999). The ethnography of infrastructure. *American Behavioral Scientist*, Vol. 43, No. 3, pp. 377–391.

Star, S. L., and Ruhleder, K. (1996). Steps toward an ecology of infrastructure: Design and access for large information spaces. *Information Systems Research*, Vol. 7, No. 1, pp. 111–134.

Taylor, P. J. (1994). The state as container: Territoriality in the modern world-system. *Progress in Human Geography*, Vol. 18, No. 2, pp. 151–162.

Taylor, P. J. (1995). Beyond containers: Internationality, interstateness, interterritoriality. *Progress in Human Geography*, Vol. 19, No. 1, pp. 1–15.

Turner, C. (2018). *Regional infrastructure systems: The political economy of regional infrastructure*. Cheltenham, UK and Northampton, MA, USA: Edward Elgar Publishing.

Turner, C. (2020). *The infrastructured state*. Cheltenham, UK and Northampton, MA, USA: Edward Elgar Publishing.

Turner, C., and Johnson, D. (2017). *Global infrastructure networks: The trans-national strategy and policy interface*. Cheltenham, UK and Northampton, MA, USA: Edward Elgar Publishing.

Van der Vleuten, E. (2004). Infrastructures and societal change: A view from the large technical systems field. *Technology Analysis and Strategic Management*, Vol. 16, No. 3, pp. 395–414.

Van der Vleuten, E. and Kaijser, A. (2005). Networking Europe. *History and Technology*, Vol. 21, No. 1, pp. 21–48.

Van der Vleuten, E., and Kaijser, A. (eds) (2006). *Networking Europe: Transnational infrastructures and the shaping of Europe, 1850–2000*. Sagamore Beach, MA: Science History Publications.

Van der Vleuten, E., and Lagendijk, V. (2010). Interpreting transnational infrastructure vulnerability: European blackout and the historical dynamics of transnational electricity governance. *Energy Policy*, Vol. 38, No. 4, pp. 2053–2062.

Van der Vleuten, E., Högselius, P., Hommels, A., and Kaijser. A. (2013). Europe's critical infrastructures and its vulnerabilities: Promises, problems, paradoxes. In Högselius, P., Hommels, A., Kaijser, A., and Van der Vleuten, E. (eds), *The making of Europe's critical infrastructure: Common connections and shared vulnerabilities*. Basingstoke: Palgrave Macmillan, pp. 3–19.

Vaubel, R., and Willett, T. D. (eds) (1991). *The political economy of international organizations: A public choice approach*. Boulder, CO: Westview.

Vitale, A. (2011). The contemporary EU's notion of territoriality and external borders. *European Spatial Research and Policy*, Vol. 18, No. 2, pp. 17–27.

Vollaard, H. (2009). The logic of political territoriality. *Geopolitics*, Vol. 14, No. 4, pp. 687–706.

Wallace, W. (1999). The sharing of sovereignty: The European paradox. *Political Studies*, Vol. 47, No. 3, pp. 503–521.

Walters, W. (2004). The frontiers of the European Union: A geostrategic perspective. *Geopolitics*, Vol. 9, No. 3), pp. 674–698.

Weber, M. (1968). *Economy and society*. New York: Bedminster.

Weiss, L. (1998). *The myth of the powerless state*. Cambridge: Polity Press.

Weiss, L. (2005). The state-augmenting effects of globalisation. *New Political Economy*, Vol. 10, No. 3, pp. 345–353.

Wissel, J. (2014). The structure of the 'EU'ropean ensemble of state apparatuses and its geopolitical ambitions. *Geopolitics*, Vol. 19, No. 3, pp. 490–513.

World Bank (2012). *Inclusive green growth: The pathway to sustainable development*. Washington, DC: World Bank.

2. The European transport infrastructure system

INTRODUCTION

The integration of the European Transport System (ETS) has a long precedent, with the process dating back as far as the 1830s with many states seeking to establish strong international dimensions to national systems early in their development (Van der Vleuten and Kaijser 2005).[1] Whilst such systems could suffer from inter-state co-ordination problems, many states saw the virtue of such connections. In the aftermath of 20th-century European conflict, pan-European connectivity stalled or was even reversed as infrastructure nationalism came to the fore (Nijkamp 1993). State control (often via state monopolies) over national transportation systems (NTS) remains the core model of the development of transportation systems in Europe, though inter-governmental co-operation to maintain pre-existing and build new links has become a higher-profile policy priority (ERT 1990). These trends reflect how transport infrastructure integration has ebbed and flowed across Europe, and that such integration has been uneven between states due to both state preference and to variances in the maturity of transportation systems. Nonetheless, interconnection and flows between states remain the norm (Badenoch and Fickers 2010). Van Exel et al. (2002) see three components to European systems, namely: those national projects with benefits to neighbouring states; cross-border projects (i.e. those that have a direct connection between two states across an agreed border); and multinational transport corridors (see below).

Whilst acknowledging the importance of the above precedent in the development of the ETS, the themes addressed in this chapter are largely shaped by contemporary policy strategy. Due to the high degree of policy proactivism and maturity of interconnection, the focus will be on EU states and the creation of a common transport area, but the analysis will be extended (where relevant) to other non-EU Western and Eastern

European states. Initially, the chapter will focus on an examination of the main trends in the ETS. Thereafter it will examine the main contextual drivers shaping transport infrastructure integration across Europe – notably the Trans-European Network initiative, the enabling soft infrastructure system and the push towards pan-European interconnection. Before conclusions are reached, the chapter seeks to contextualise the evolution of the ETS within the broader context of developments in neighbouring and global transportation systems, notably the European dimension of China's Belt and Road Initiative.

Table 2.1   Share of intra-EU traffic flows by mode (2020)

Mode	Percentage Freight (tkm)[a]	Percentage Passengers (pkm)
Road	51	81.5
Rail	12.6	8.4 (1.5 for trams and metro)
Aviation	0.1	9.6
Maritime, including inland waterways (IWW)	29.2 (of which 4 IWW)	0.4

Note: [a] The remainder comprises oil pipelines (addressed in Chapter 3).
Source: EC (2020)

TRENDS IN THE EUROPEAN TRANSPORT SYSTEM

Whilst the focus of this chapter is on those processes shaping the creation of an integrated ETS, the evolution of this system is built upon national systems and the trends in terms of flows within and between these states. The following section seeks to explore the prevailing configuration of the ETS with regard to the relative salience across passenger and freight traffic of the respective modes and their development across Europe. Before moving on to examine the respective modes in more detail, Table 2.1 offers a broad overview (as of 2020) of the share of EU passenger and freight traffic across the respective modes of transport. Of the two main types of flow in 2018, intra-EU freight movement was almost 3.5 billion tonne-kilometres (tkm),[2] with total passenger movements within the EU27 of almost 6 billion passenger-kilometres (pkm).[3]

Road

Europe's road networks are both intensively and extensively developed. The density of the road network for all European OECD states is 140 km of road per km^2 (OECD 2019). This varies between as much as nearly 900 km per km^2 in Malta to around 15 km per km^2 in Portugal. Road investment dominates state spending on inland transport infrastructure. According to the International Transport Forum, Its share has been consistently around 70 per cent of the total between 1990 and 2017. However between 2000 and 2017, road investment as a share of GDP was broadly static at around 0.7 per cent of GDP, with road infrastructure spend per capita also largely dormant at around $150 per head (ITF 2019).

For the EU27 (in 2018) road remains the dominant form for both freight and passenger transport (see Table 2.1). For freight transport, road comprised just over half of total intra-EU flows as measured by tonne per kilometre. This dominance is even stronger for intra-EU passenger traffic, where over 80 per cent of passenger kilometres is by road (Eurostat 2019). However this pattern is not repeated for longer distances, where only about 16 per cent (by value) and 3 per cent (by weight) of extra-EU trade occurs through road traffic. This is also reflected in the fact that (at most) 10 per cent of trans-EU freight traffic (by weight) goes through the road system (Eurostat 2019). In terms of quality of road infrastructure, a crude indicator is the ratio of paved to unpaved roads. Here there is a broad East–West split, with Western European states having a broad ubiquity of paved roads whilst some Eastern European states (notably Romania) have relatively high levels of unpaved road infrastructure. Across the EU27 there are nearly 5000 km of paved roads for every 1000 km^2. Some Nordic and Baltic states have a high share of unpaved roads – Sweden has 75 per cent unpaved roads and Estonia and Latvia have 62 per cent and 78 per cent respectively (CIA 2019). However, these are all states where urban roads represent a relatively low share of the total road network. Overall (in 2016) the share of the urban road network in Europe as a portion of the total network varied from nearly 75 per cent in Austria to just over 8 per cent in Lithuania (ITF 2019).

This comparatively high quality of road infrastructure has to be sustained through constant maintenance. Evidence from the European Parliament indicates that this has fallen since 2009 where road maintenance spending has been cut across many states as public sector budgets (still overwhelmingly the main financiers of European road infrastructure) have become tighter (EP 2014). As a share of total road infrastructure spending by states, maintenance has fallen since 2000 (when it was 35 per cent of total spend) to less than 30 per cent in 2016 (ITF 2019). Poor maintenance impacts not only the quality and reliability of the infrastructure but also its safety.

The scale of the EU's motorway network is also a barometer of the comparative quality of the European road system. In 2019, the EU27 had 73.8 km of motorway for every 1000 km of road network. This is below both the average for both the US and China but above Japan and Russia. Across all states of the EU27, the motorway network is a small fraction of the total road network. For most states, motorways – as a share of total road networks (in 2017) – comprise on average 2.6 per cent (up from 1.2 per cent in 1990). The only outlier in this is Portugal, where motorways comprise over 20 per cent of the road network (Eurostat 2019).

Motorways – as a metric of road infrastructure quality – remain unevenly developed across Europe. According to the United Nations Economic Commission for Europe (UNECE 2018), motorway density is highest in the small Western European states; for example, the Netherlands has over 60 km of motorway per 1000 km². Most Western European states have 20–30 km of motorway per 1000 km², whereas many Eastern European states have less than 10 km. These Eastern European states (as suggested above) have been those states where there have been the fastest increases in motorway density, with Romania seeing over 220 per cent growth between 2006 and 2016. Between 1990 and 2017, the EU27's motorway network grew by over 80 per cent. This growth has not only been evident in Eastern Europe: other 'lagging' states have also seen growth. Ireland – for example – has seen the highest growth, almost over 3000 per cent, over the period. Meanwhile the mature industrialised economies of the EU have seen a broadly static share of motorway infrastructure over this period.

In the absence of physical impediments, roads across Europe have demonstrated a high degree of connectivity throughout their development (Schipper 2008). The legacy of history and state formation have sought to ensure that national road systems had a European dimension built into their design, in part to ensure the effective navigation of trans-European flows but also to recognise historical interdependencies. State security concerns did not match the desire for interconnection, with ease of flows constricted across borders either via divergent system capacities or through physical impediments, compressions on flows and/or divergent soft infrastructure. Thus the issue is not so much that a physical interconnection exists between states, but that the movement can be seamless via the absence of physical barriers/restrictions and that mobility is directly facilitated. The pan-European nature of the road system has been promoted since the late 1940s through UNECE's E-road initiative (see below) which sought the virtual integration of the system via a bottom-up process of state-based upgrades to national road systems (Schot 2010). This bottom-up process remains the core building block of the European road system, and highlights the importance of national systems to the process of pan-European road infrastructure.

Rail

Many European states place great strategic emphasis on rail systems (both local and long-distance). In part this is driven by themes of modernity and, more especially, the role of high-speed rail infrastructure as state suprastructure (Larkin 2013). Like road, there is a long precedent within Europe for the integration of national rail systems (van der Vleuten and Kaijser 2005). For a long period of time, states have sought to remove any barriers, initially on a piecemeal basis but more latterly through the creation of the Single European Railway Area (see below) (EC 2010). However by 2018, just over 1 per cent of total rail journeys (as measured by passenger numbers) in the EU27 were international (EC 2020).

As with its road system, the European rail system has a comparatively high intensity of development. Though, of the 39 European states covered by OECD data, rail density has remained static at 4.8 km per 100 km^2 for the past decade (OECD 2019). The network may be extensively developed but it is of variably quality, with Western European systems tending to be of a better standard (WEF 2019). In terms of the density of rail infrastructure systems across the EU (km of railways per 1000 km^2 in 2016), those states with the highest density are Switzerland, Germany, the Czech Republic (Czechia) and Luxembourg. The Swiss and the Czech systems have over 120 km of rail per 1000 km^2, while the other states have between 100 and 120 km per 1000 km^2 (UNECE 2018a). In the decade to 2016 some states (such as Spain) saw a growth in rail density. However others (notably Denmark, Poland and Latvia) witnessed a decline as infrequently used lines were closed. Between 1990 and 2017, rail's share of inland transport investment has fallen from around a third to less than a quarter, with average per capita spend falling by 25 per cent over this period and such investment comprising around 0.2 per cent of the combined European OECD states' GDP (OECD 2019). This has corresponded with a decline in the extent of European rail systems, with coverage falling back by over 20,000 km to just over 217,000 km between 1996 and 2017. Of the remaining lines, 54 per cent are electrified (as of 2017), though this varies markedly between states, with Luxembourg having 95 per cent electrification and Ireland less than 6 per cent. Outside of the EU27, Switzerland stands alone in having a universal electrified rail system. According to OECD data (2019), in Western Europe as a whole some 52 per cent of the rail system is electrified, a rise of 5 per cent since 2000.[4]

High-speed rail is less extensively developed, with only a patchwork system in operation.[5] Across the EU27, less than 4 per cent of the network is high speed, with much of this being within Western European states and 60 per cent of the network being in two states alone (Spain and France). Beyond these states, high-speed networks are only being slowly expanded (Eurostat 2019).[6] The OECD (2019) indicated that of those states that had high-speed rail its share of the total network had risen from 3.2 per cent in 2000 to 12 per cent in 2017, with the most significant extensions (as share of total network) being in Denmark and Spain; in China – by comparison – around a third of the network is high speed. Full interoperability of the rail system is also being limited by divergences in gauge between states on non-high-speed lines. Whilst much of Western Europe uses the standard gauge, there are still large sections of the system that continue to diverge, notably in Northern and Eastern Europe (CER 2015).

Aviation

The European aviation system is defined by the interface between the physicality of the hubs and the soft system of airspace management. This interface has been encapsulated within policy narratives on the creation of the Single European Sky (Pellegrini and Rodriguez 2013). In this section, the focus will be upon the hard elements of the aviation system. The hard elements of an airport include not just runways but also the system's capability to physically queue arrivals and departures, as well as terminals and docking facilities. All of these are subject to physical limits in their capacities and are expected to be the main sources of congestion within the European system (Eurocontrol 2017). The strong interrelationships between hard and soft infrastructure systems in European aviation reflects the interdependencies created by a hub and spoke system across the continent where national systems are intertwined around a series of regional hub airports.

Whilst comprising less than 10 per cent of EU27 passenger traffic, aviation saw the biggest increase in passenger growth between 1995 and 2017 – by 123 per cent. In 2018, 46 per cent of this traffic was intra-EU, 16 per cent national and 37 per cent extra-EU (Eurostat 2019). Across the EU27 (plus the UK), there were 325 major airports, with 44 that handled in excess of 10 million passengers annually. Across Europe, there are over 850 airports that have international connectivity. These are supported by many domestic only facilities (frequently unpaved). The CIA (2019) estimates that there are over 3700 airports across Europe in total (included paved and unpaved), with the population density of airports being 1.9 per million inhabitants across European OECD states, though this figure can rise to as near as 40 per million inhabitants in the case of Iceland. In terms of the spatial density of provision, Europe has almost 30 airports per 100,000 km^2.[7] The main airports in the EU (i.e. those handling more than 10 million passengers) are highly concentrated in the larger states, namely Germany, France and Spain (with London Heathrow remaining a key non-EU hub). The driver of these traffic flows is airport connectivity, both direct and indirect, as measured by the number of facilitating flights.[8] Those airports with the highest direct connectivity also tend to be those with the highest indirect connectivity. Thus airports such as Frankfurt, Paris Charles de Gaulle and Amsterdam, which exhibit both strong direct and indirect connectivity, are prominent in the European aviation system (ACI 2019). Indeed, Europe dominates the global hub system, with nine of its airports in the top 20 for connectivity (ACI 2019). Europe itself has a hierarchy of hubs, with the core global hubs being complemented by secondary and niche hubs that differ in terms of traffic form and flows as well as degree of connectivity. The niche hubs tend to have limited indirect connectivity focusing on one or two regions, and are often in the peripheral states. The secondary hubs are more widely focused but lack the scale of the global hubs.

Maritime

The European maritime infrastructure system is a multi-faceted system comprising networks of ports (both inland and littoral), inland waterways (IWW) and short sea shipping routes that enable the intra- and extra-European movement of passengers and freight (EP 2015).[9] In terms of extra-European movement of freight, maritime systems are the dominant points of entry to the European system (EC 2020). The maritime system covers over 50 per cent of the EU's external trade by value and more than 75 per cent by weight. Maritime transport also has a strong traditional role in the intra-European freight systems, comprising nearly 40 per cent of internal trade by volume (Eurostat 2019). EU27 maritime flows (both internally and externally sourced and destined) grew by around a quarter between 1990 and 2017 and now comprise some 45 per cent of total freight flows (billion tonnes per km) (Eurostat 2019). In 2015, nearly two-thirds of port traffic was extra-EU, a quarter was intra-EU and less than 10 per cent was between ports within the same state (Eurostat 2019). In terms of passenger traffic, maritime channels are only of real significance in those states where a significant proportion of the population is island based – such as Greece, Italy and Denmark (Eurostat 2019). For intra-EU freight, 39 per cent of all flows through EU ports are intra-EU. This rises to as high as 78 per cent for Sweden (Eurostat 2019).

The importance of maritime transport for intra-EU flows (as well as sustainability themes) has been highlighted within the prioritisation of short sea shipping through the EU's TEN-T 'Motorways of the Sea' (MoS) project (see below). Short sea shipping represents about 60 per cent of traffic for EU ports. Whilst European port traffic is relatively fragmented, it is evident that those ports that are on the main East–West logistics route (mainly based around the North Sea) have the highest volumes of freight (as measured in tonnes). Indeed, in 2017 Rotterdam (the Netherlands) received more than twice as much as the next nearest port, Antwerp (Belgium), with only three ports receiving in excess of 100 million tonnes of freight (Eurostat 2019). Overall Rotterdam handles 20 per cent of total freight by volume received by the EU27 top 40 freight ports. These flows are highly concentrated, with the top three EU27 container ports combined comprising a third of the bloc's freight traffic by volume. Of course, the efficacy of ports depends upon hinterland infrastructure where a mix of road, rail and inland waterway are used.

In 2018, the EU27 had over 400,000 km of inland navigable water-ways (more than the US but less than either Russia or China). These do not have universal reach but are important for states with limited direct reach to global maritime logistical channels. Finland has around 20 per cent of the EU's inland waterways, Germany 18 per cent and the Netherlands 15 per cent. These inland systems are especially important for those states through which Europe's major river systems flow (such as Bulgaria, Romania and the Benelux states). Thus, whilst inland waterways account for only around 6 per cent of total intra-EU freight movements (as measured by billion tkm), for those states on Europe's major river systems they can reach as much as a quarter of flows by weight. However, of the 147 billion tkm transported across the European inland waterway system in 2017, 70 per cent flowed through two states – Germany and the Netherlands, where these systems are used extensively to ferry freight to the main North Sea European ports, Rotterdam and Antwerp (EP 2015). Across the broader European continent, as measured by tonne-kilometres, freight by inland waterways almost halved between 1975 and 2017 (OECD 2019). Regarding passenger traffic, inland waterways are marginal.

Inland waterways are a primary means of moving goods from seaports to the hinterland. For North Sea ports, some 54 per cent of freight moves through this channel (Eurostat 2019). Integral to this process are Europe's inland ports that are used to link inland areas with inland waterways to allow penetration of maritime systems into less accessible locations (Wiegmans et al. 2015). These ports allow for containerisation, offering links to high-capacity hub ports and thereby aiding the rapid dispersal of freight across Europe (Rodrigue et al. 2010). According to the Central Commission for the Navigation of the Rhine, of Europe's inland ports, Duisburg (Germany) is by far the biggest, handling nearly three times more traffic (by weight) than the next biggest (CCNR 2018). Indeed, German inland ports dominate the Rhine-based inland waterway system where the transport of dry bulk (linked to the steel industry) is a major source of traffic. The Rhine-based ports dwarf the Danube-based ports, with the former delivering five times more traffic than the latter. The port of Paris is currently the EU's second biggest inland port, though this is driven by localised factors – namely the movement of materials associated with the extension of the Paris metro.

THE TRANS-EUROPEAN TRANSPORT NETWORK (TEN-T) PROGRAMME

Whilst most European states have well-developed infrastructure systems, the European Commission felt that these systems were not adapting to the pressures placed upon them by the processes and consequences of regional integration (Maggi et al. 1992, EC 2003). Whilst NTS have frequent points of interconnection, such connections often do not possess the capacity to support the free-and-easy circulation of freight and passenger traffic between EU states envisaged by the Single Market programme (ERT 1990, EC 2001). In particular, it is estimated that the ETS would not be able cope with rising transport demand where, by 2050, it is estimated freight traffic will increase by 80 per cent and passenger traffic by 50 per cent (EC 2011). This adaptive tension raises the prospect that territorial and geostrategies will become misaligned due to a purely national focus on the design and development of NTS (van Exel et al. 2002, Gutiérrez et al. 2011).

To seek to address these problems, the European Commission launched the TEN-T programme (EC 1998). TEN-T sought to promote missing interconnecting transport links in prioritised trade corridors, easier flows in pre-existing connections (by removing bottlenecks via adjustments to both hard and soft infrastructure) and system-wide interoperability (EC 1994, 2002, 2002a). The focus was on scaling up national systems to address systemic needs, most notably with regard to the development of national and international high-speed transport systems (Maggi et al. 1992). Thus, the theme for TEN-T was not connectivity between systems per se but interconnectivity that was seamless and expeditious (Johnson and Turner 1997, 2007, Mulley and Nelson 1999). This seamlessness extends beyond simple technical issues to include the interoperability of corporate (willingness of firms to offer interoperable services), judicial (i.e. that legal systems allow free flows) and cultural (such as attitudes to travel) themes. Full interoperability is only attained when all are aligned across NTS.

Whilst TEN-T has stressed other themes during its lifespan, it is as a flanking policy to longer-standing transport policy themes (notably the attainment of a Single European Transport Area) that TEN-T is currently framed (Maggi et al. 1992, HLG–TEN-T, 2003, EC 2010a). This prioritises the programmes in promoting a sustainable inter-modal transport system along designated inter-state 'core corridors' to channel both freight and passenger traffic to major economic, political and logistical hubs within the EU (see below) (EC 2011). This priority has to function alongside other tensions working on the programme, namely: the expansion of the EU (which exposed disparities in inter-state NTS), public sector austerity (the states remain the main financiers of transport infrastructure); a shifting technology base for NTS (largely based on the convergence of transport systems with information systems as well as evolving pre-existing links with energy systems); and by emergent themes of sustainability and energy transition.

Despite TEN-T's systemic ambitions, early actions (between 1990 and 1994) tended to be project-led. This resulted in TEN-T having a strong national focus in terms of impact assessment, with cross-border effects being ignored (van Exel et al. 2002). This should have been unsurprising as states – the primary financiers – were reluctant to fund projects where the beneficiaries might be non-national users. Thus states would focus upon those parts of TEN-T where the effects could be 'nationalised'. Indeed, states quickly took over the design of the programme to reinforce this process, merely using TEN-T as an extra source of finance to develop NTS (Turró 1999). As a result, member states' priorities diverged, with TEN-T emerging as a patchwork of national projects and transnationality becoming sidelined (Aparicio 2017). This was not helped by available funding being way below expectations and the vastly overstated ambitions of the TEN-T (Button 1998). Moreover, the plurality of transport systems was not developed, with co-modality under-deployed; for example, the importance of core nodes (such as seaports) remained under-developed as multi-modal hubs (TEN-T Expert Group 2010, EC 2010b). As such, TEN-T – as initially conceived – was in practice little more than a set of maps underpinned by an over-ambitious narrative. Indeed Aparicio (2017) argues that TEN-T was designed as a coalition (of both supranational and commercial forces) to place pressure on governments to increase infrastructure spending where such expenditure had been falling for decades; though it had stabilised at 1 per cent of GDP by the mid-1990s (Johnson and Turner 1997, ITF 2013).

This began to shift in 1994 with the adoption of a more systemic approach whereby any project selected by the European Commission for support was nominated – as guided by the Christopherson Report (see Johnson and Turner 2007) – for its ability to enhance pan-European mobility rather than for its own specific virtues. Despite this more systemic approach, the process reflected a scaling back of the ambitions of TEN-T: the number of priority projects was reduced to the 14 that were most attainable so as to add political impetus to the programme and make some degree of progress more achievable as the EU's limited funding would be more effective if was concentrated on fewer projects.[10] However, the programme retained its focus on national projects that were often developed on a standalone basis rather than for their systemic impact.[11] Whilst they were in part 'dedicated axes' these projects were, in fact, again a series of largely disconnected national projects, each designed to support a new emphasis within TEN-T on cohesion. This emphasis was driven largely by the EU's enlargement into Central and Eastern Europe (CEE) to ensure that those states did not merely upgrade their existing systems but did not fall further behind in NTS development and maturity (Aparicio 2017).

This focus on cohesion saw (in 2001) an expansion in the number of priority projects to 30, chosen according to their contribution to notional pan-European transportation corridors (Johnson and Turner 2007). Nevertheless, TEN-T (due to its market-driven strategy) still retained an apparent bias towards more developed states as the in-built conflict between cohesion and competitiveness within the programme was largely resolved in favour of the latter (Spiekermanfl and Wegener 1996). This was evident in the prioritisation of high-speed rail systems (both in terms of TEN-T funding and number of projects) within the 30 prioritised schemes, and the fact that such capital-intensive projects were better able to be funded in the more developed states where the state contributed nearly 80 per cent of the finance to TEN-T infrastructure; EU funding is incidental to the process at around 4 per cent. The result of this funding profile was states still not wanting to pay for cross-border projects with strong spillovers. This resulted in a poor completion rate (10 per cent) for TEN-T projects (Proost et al. 2011); and, where they were completed, the main driver was national needs rather than those of the wider European system (EC 2009). States were keen to push national projects and over-emphasised their European-ness so as to get EU funding, with the result that TEN-T became an extension of national planning processes. Indeed, as Table 2.2 indicates, there were clear alignments between the needs of territorial states from their own NTS and the TEN-T programme.

It was evident from a 2009 European Commission review that TEN-T – as a policy strategy – was of limited success. There was a tendency for states to view it as a means of reinforcing territoriality rather than as a device to align its territorial and geostrategic interests. The absence of any willingness by states to commit to policy in a meaningful sense meant that, by 2009, only 39 per cent of the priority projects had been attained (EC 2009). The review advanced a new policy framework which, although further scaling back on the ambitions of TEN-T, moved states away from the voluntarism of the old policy and towards compulsory adherence to the principles of TEN-T (notably with regard to adherence to EU standards), with the European Commission given more power of implementation. This meant formally treating national systems as sub-systems of TEN-T by refocusing the policy around two sets of corridors – those that are part of the core network and those integral to the more broadly defined comprehensive networks (Van Weenen et al. 2016). A large percentage of these prioritised corridors had already been built at the national level with the new compulsion on states to align (where relevant) NTS to these pan-EU corridors, especially with regard to systemic bottlenecks, missing links and the applications of technologies and soft infrastructure that support interoperability (see below). The focus on the corridors within TEN-T was also used to more effectively convey the purpose of the scheme (notably with regard to transport efficiency and the promotion of corridor multi-modality) as well as providing an effective framework for co-operation and collaboration, and to provide a means of conveying and realising the European value added within the EIS (EC 2018a). This will be created by dedicated institutional systems to support this process to ensure the core and comprehensive networks are completed within their respective time frames. However, this did not lead to the new policy becoming exempt from the politics of corridor determination, especially with the creation of a new funding system – the Connecting Europe Facility (CEF) – designed to channel money into the targeted core corridors.[12]

Table 2.2   Aligning TEN-T to the infrastructural mandate

Infrastructural Mandate Theme	TEN-T Objective
Control	Indirect improvement in state infrastructural power
Cohesion	Improve mobility by enhancing access
	Promote strategic economic development
	Pronto social development and inclusion
Security	Transport safety to promote substance and security of flows
	New technologies to increase reliability of flows
	Promote links to neighbouring states
Growth/Development	Transport efficiency
	Promote strategic mobility by addressing systemic inadequacies
	Promote single market
	Enable interactions with non-EU states
Sustainability	Promote environmental improvement at local, national and international levels
	Promote new technologies
	Promote new energy-efficient modes

Source: Based on Johnson and Turner (1997)

The nine corridors within the core network – to be established by 2030 (see Table 2.3) – involved identifying the core nodes (such as member state capitals and gateway ports), and then seeking to link them via appropriate hard and soft infrastructure (Schade et al. 2015).

Table 2.3   *Core corridors and non-corridor themes within TEN-T*

Core Corridor	State Connectivity	Number of Projects Identified (estimated cost)
North Sea–Baltic Sea	Joins Baltic Sea Region (BSR) to North Sea Region via Helsinki; Baltic States, Poland and Germany	520: 130 road; 127 rail; 76 maritime; 75 airport; 36 IWW; 18 MoS; 16 ERTMS (€98.7 billion)
Rhine–Alpine	Connects North Sea ports of Belgium and Netherlands with Mediterranean port of Genoa via France, Luxembourg, Germany and Switzerland	318: 110 rail; 41 IWW, with 37 in Switzerland
Baltic–Adriatic	Connects Polish ports with Italian and Slovenian Adriatic ports; route crosses southern Poland, Czech Republic and Slovakia and interconnects Vienna and Bratislava, the Eastern Alpine region and Northern Italy	535: 170 rail and ERTMS; 99 road; 115 maritime, IWW and MoS (€100 billion)
Mediterranean	A multimodal east–west link to connect Western Mediterranean ports to the centre of the EU via the southern member states	217: 124 rail and ERTMS; 28 IWW (€104 billion)
Orient–East-Med	This multi-modal corridor connects Central Europe with the North, Baltic, Black and Mediterranean seas using (where possible) rivers and channels in Germany and the Czech Republic	415: 177 rail and ERTMS; 24 IWW (€68 billion)
Atlantic	Connects Europe's South-Western regions (notably the Iberian Atlantic coastline)	217: 112 rail and ERTMS; 40 MoS (€44 billion)
North Sea–Mediterranean	This seeks to improve links (largely through improved rail and waterway systems) within a pre-existing busy corridor containing three of the top airports and four of the top seaports	350: 92 rail and 116 IWW (€70 billion)
Scandinavian–Mediterranean	This is the longest corridor, connecting Scandinavia to Germany, Austria, Italy and Malta	666: 167 rail and ERTMS; 204 maritime and MoS (€202.4 billion)
Rhine–Danube	This east–west link connects France, Germany, Austria, Czechia, Slovakia, Hungary, Croatia, Romania and Bulgaria	563: 141 rail; 65 IWW; 118 ports (€91.9 billion)

TEN-T Non-Corridor Themes

Objective	Connectivity	Projects
European Rail Management Traffic System (ERMTS)	This standardised signalling system replaces more than 30 different national systems	Deployed across all relevant corridors where relevant to support high-speed rail (over €20 billion)
Motorways of the Sea (MoS)	Aims to revive short sea shipping in Europe by increasing connectivity between EU ports	Covers 309 ports across and between four maritime arteries (Baltic, Western Europe, South West Europe and South Rast Europe)

Source: European Commission (2018).

Such a design was to refocus TEN-T on those projects with a clear European interest and not on those solely prioritising regional cohesion at a national level (Proost et al. 2011). Alongside these corridors are two horizontal measures: the European Rail Traffic Management System (ERTMS), which seeks to create a uniform, EU-wide rail signalling system; and Motorways of the Sea (MoS), which seeks to increase the utilisation of short sea shipping in the EU logistics system (see Table 2.3). Each of the corridors was assigned a coordinator to develop, plan work and provide momentum to the network integration process through acting as a forum for inter-state collaboration. The corridors are designed to be both multi- and inter-modal where possible. This also entails adopting a wide range of common standards such as the aforementioned ERTMS and traffic management systems. The aim is also to align TEN-T with the broader objectives of the EU's transport policy, notably with regard to themes of sustainability, safety and traffic management systems (EC 2009a). In 2018 the EU estimated that the EU27 needed to invest €500 billion in the core network between 2021 and 2030 (EC 2018a). Schade et al. (2015) estimate that failure to meet the TEN-T core network completion deadline of 2030 would lower growth by 1.8 per cent and lower employment prospects by about 10 million jobs.

The comprehensive network comprises a secondary network that feeds into the core network, with the intent that, by 2050, no EU citizen will be more than 30 minutes from the comprehensive network. The comprehensive network is made up of 95,700 km of road links, 106,000 km of railway links (including 32,000 km of high-speed links), 13,000 km of inland waterways, 411 airports and 404 seaports. The majority of these already exist, but over a quarter of both road and rail (mostly high-speed) networks have yet to be built. According to Aparicio (2017), the notion of the comprehensive network is to effectively place the rest of TEN-T into a state of limbo as it deals with the larger basic layer of infrastructure designed to ensure broad mobility.

ASSESSMENT

TEN-T was a policy with a moving objective. It was seen as a solution to an evolving common problem. First, it was to realise the benefits of scale from market integration. Then it evolved in to promoting cohesion. From there it evolved as a policy strategy to offer Europe a route out of its growth and employment problems. Finally, it came to be a central plank of a European desire to promote energy transition and sustainable transport systems. According to the European Commission (EC 2015), the EU claims success with regard to the TEN-T objectives, with nearly 80 per cent of both core and comprehensive rail systems being standardised in terms of gauge and electrification (see Table 2.4) – though less than 10 per cent had applied the ERTMS. With road systems, three quarters of the core network adhere to agreed standards though this falls to as low as 60 per cent for the comprehensive network. For IWW, compliance with EU standards is near universal, with all TEN-T seaports connected to TEN-T railways. This inter-modality is also evident in other sectors, with over 60 per cent of TEN-T airports connected to a TEN-T railway. However, what existed prior to TEN-T and what was stimulated by TEN-T is not clear. Thus claims that TEN-T acted as a stimulant to infrastructuring are uncertain. Nonetheless there have been some successes, not least as regards integrating the NTS of South, East and West Europe (EC 2020). Table 2.4 offers a summative assessment of the completion of core TEN-T projects across the EU27.

Over time, the programme has shifted away from an emphasis on hard systems towards the softer components of the ETS (see below), though physical bottlenecks and missing links have been key continuities (EC 2020). This reflects a failure of the policy where – according to Otsuka et al. (2017) – there was a temptation to focus on suprastructures over infrastructure. This suprastructure policy focus tended to ignore the core supporting role of embedded regional and local systems, and suffered from weak technical logic combined with poor assessment of its impact on economic and environmental systems (Aparicio 2017). Sichelschmidt (1999) argues this was symptomatic of a policy that introduced a set of biased incentives to get states to overinvest in infrastructure based on overstating European value added. Indeed Sichelschmidt concurs with Aparicio that the major issue was the failure of co-ordination over soft infrastructure systems.

The national focus of TEN-T led to an emphasis on the needs of state territorial strategy, with geo-strategic themes being a secondary consideration. The efficacy of geostrategy within TEN-T has to reflect the independent means of the supranational body. States otherwise will develop infrastructure on a pragmatic rather than a strategic basis. TEN-T will only be an overlaying strategic network where there is independent funding above the state (EC 2010b). Member states were (and still are) the power brokers over infrastructure – they have the final say and, if a TEN-T project does not coincide with their priorities, then it does not happen (Martellato 2011).

Table 2.4   *State of the TEN-T corridors in the EU27*

State	Percentage of Core Projects Completed (2016)			
	Road	Conventional Rail	High-Speed Rail	Inland Waterway
Belgium	99	71	100	87
Bulgaria	50	11	n/a	100
Czechia	55	63	0	84
Denmark	83	50	0	n/a
Germany	59	94	58	100
Estonia	34	3	0	n/a
Ireland	91	92	n/a	n/a
Greece	76	80	55	n/a
Spain	100	96	46	100
France	98	99	47	75
Croatia	60	5	n/a	33
Italy	81	70	41	66
Cyprus	n/a	n/a	n/a	n/a
Latvia	100	0	0	n/a
Lithuania	7	12	0	100
Luxembourg	53	85	n/a	100
Hungary	81	8	0	100
Malta	n/a	n/a	n/a	n/a
Netherlands	96	84	100	97
Austria	97	72	37	100
Poland	62	23	0	100
Portugal	100	95	0	24
Romania	45	4	0	91
Slovenia	100	6	0	n/a
Slovakia	39	20	n/a	100
Finland	72	44	100	100
Sweden	77	51	0	100

Source: EC (2020a)

As a result, bilateral programmes tend to be more effective for cross-border infrastructure than supranational programmes, especially when the Commission has no power to enforce cross-border projects. The ECA (2018) in its review of the TEN-T high-speed rail plans argued that the fact that states retained such power meant plans were not credible both in terms of time frame and the absence of any compulsion by states to develop such systems. There is low European value added within the high-speed system as states will prioritise their own objectives, with an absence of coordination, despite a commitment by states to honour the TEN-T regulation. There is also the problem that high-speed rail is not always necessary in all the places it has been prioritised.

TEN-T projects were also curtailed by state unwillingness to offer the EU substantial independent competences with regard to finance (Johnson and Turner 1997). While the TEN-T budget is small, when combined with funding from other EU sources – as well as loans from development banks such as the European Investment Bank (EIB) – this can rise to as much as a third of the capital allocated. However, there is a difference between what has been spent and what needed to be spent according to the Commission's ambitious plans (EC 2009). TEN-T has always been hindered by the scale of the finance needed and the general absence of any political commitment by states to fill the funding gaps within the prioritised projects. However in progressively narrowing down the ambitions of TEN-T, the EU was able to increase the efficacy of the strategy, raising the co-funding rate from around 5 per cent to up to 30–40 per cent for projects with a clear European dimension (i.e. cross-border or bottleneck projects). In 2020 it was estimated that €1.5 trillion needed to be invested in the two decades to 2030 (EC 2020). Throughout its development several alternative sources have been explored – such as Union Bonds and, more recently, the Connecting Europe Facility (CEF) – but all have been hindered by an unwillingness of the private sector and/or non-EU state bodies to offer finance in the necessary volume. As such, the state has remained the primary financier of such systems, retaining the focus on national needs in TEN-T. Thus TEN-T became – in many cases – an alternative source for supporting territorial systems rather than looking to align with the states' broader geostrategic interests. Consequently, bilateral programmes were more effective in developing cross-border projects.

Arguably, the greatest retardant of TEN-T projects has been that they are not a priority for many states given the competing demands on state budgets. The legacy of infrastructure nationalism remains strong within the EU, with states still seeking and retaining the right to shape their own NTS to their own priorities and interests. Transport systems are dominated by intra-state flows with, for example, domestic freight movements comprising over 90 per cent of the total volume of European freight flows (Eurostat 2019). This is also evident in passenger traffic, where most movements are local and where – in rail, for example – cross-border flows are only about 1 per cent of total flows. Only in aviation are intra-EU flows important. Thus the European dimensions of NTS are largely incidental to national transportation strategies, therefore sidelining TEN-T as a policy strategy as the needs of territorial strategy are predominant.

SOFT INFRASTRUCTURE AND THE TEN-T PROGRAMME

Given the problems with the 'hard' component of TEN-T it can credibly be argued that its soft infrastructural component is a greater driver in pushing for a more interconnected (if not integrated) transport system. These processes allow the co-ordinated management of NTS to align the rules of operation and engagement between systems to support and facilitate flows between them. This can cover a range of themes within the ETS; but – given the limited room – this chapter will limit itself to a brief exploration of the main shifts.

With the scaling back of TEN-T's physical ambitions, the European Commission sought to add impetus to the process via a stronger govern-ance system to focus efforts on the prioritised corridors (Aparicio 2017). This was enabled via the creation of new systems based upon dedicated project co-ordinators to bring stakeholders together as well as a new authority – the Innovation and Networks Executive Agency (INEA) – to push the development of TEN-T. Whilst the power remains with the states, these arrangements focused efforts on projects with a strong a European dimension and offered forums for the creation of bilateral agreements or memorandums of understanding (MoUs) between states. These project coordinators seek to draw up credible work plans, though not without member state approval (Öberg et al. 2018).

The soft infrastructure component of TEN-T is shaped not simply by the governance arrangements established for the corridors outlined above but also by the overlap between TEN-T and the EU Common Transport Policy (CTP). As TEN-T is market driven and the CTP is about creating the conditions for efficient transport markets, the link is intuitive – but not always explored. As TEN-T has evolved so it has become a more overt part of the CTP. The logic of the CTP in ending impediments to the free flow of traffic services between member states has a direct link to the rationalisation of TEN-T if – as expected – such conditions lead to increased traffic flows. Through such processes the missing border links and bottlenecks that are central to TEN-T are highlighted (Ponti et al. 2013). These themes (as identified in Figure 2.1) were also linked to the liberalisation of transportation services, stressing that in TEN-T themes of access, interconnection and interoperability were not simply realised through easier movement between states but also by increased competition between transport operators (see below) (EP 2014a, 2014b). This reinforced the logic of market-driven flows feeding through into rising infrastructure investment (EC 2001). This process also, according to Lehmkuhl (2002), highlighted how EU transport policy has shifted away from developing a supranational competence towards stimulating reform at the national level.

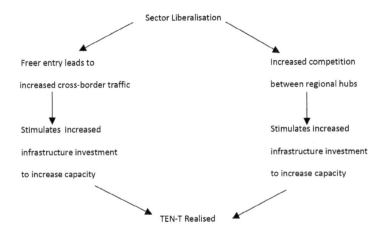

Figure 2.1   *The idealised link between transport liberalisation and TEN-T*

These processes of regulatory reform were also evident in attempting to promote those modifications that allowed existing infrastructure to be more effective by seeking to integrate its management (as is the case for aviation, rail and maritime) where fragmentation hinders intra-EU flows (such as in aviation and rail) or to promote its use where the resource is under-utilised (as in IWW) (EC 2011). Alongside these measures were attempts by the EU to alter the modal shift away from road towards rail (again reflected within TEN-T) and to promote safe infrastructure usage, notably with regard to roads (EC 2006). All these align with TEN-T's objective of enabling and adding velocity to transnational flows.

As the Commission wishes TEN-T to be market-led, the liberalisation process is central to the realisation of these infrastructures. The link between liberalisation and TEN-T is not clear-cut as the process tends to focus on opening up NTS to other (EU and non-EU) service suppliers. Whilst networks services are infrastructure-dependent, they do not really enter the infrastructure integration policy narratives directly. As such, liberalisation is about creating continuity across NTS to create a consistent set of network rules. This opens up the possibility of a transnational services environment and, through this, greater interaction between NTS to drive closer infrastructural integration. Another anticipated consequence of this process would be a re-infrastructuring of existing NTS, which would be upgraded to cope with the increased traffic and desire for added velocity to flows that results (see Figure 2.1). Through these processes there is an expectation that pressure to expand cross-border interconnections will increase. Most transport links (i.e. road and rail) are under state ownership, and infrastructure investment is driven by broader considerations than those that simply demonstrate responsiveness to traffic generated by service liberalisation. Rail intentionally focused on the TEN-T network for liberalisation based on the logic that this would improve services and speed through these core corridors. Nevertheless some states remain unwilling to open their networks to competition (Knieps 2013).

With regard to transport modes, the EU is keen to encourage intra-sector competition (where possible) between airports and sea/river ports to drive increases in investment. It also reflects a desire to increase competition between modes. Overall, this reflects how the EU sees a direct link between reform of the governance of NTS and the promotion of TEN-T. However, this association seems indirect at best as the link between the creation of uniform network service conditions and investment in TEN-T links remains lacking in evidence (EC 2018). Where there is evidence, it is limited and indirect, such as in the case of rail where liberalisation has increased pressure on states to upgrade and maintain systems (after decades of neglect). There is more direct evidence in aviation, where there is a need for an infrastructural response to rising air traffic (in the aftermath of liberalisation), placing a squeeze on airport capacity (EC 2018b). Overall, progress in liberalisation across these sectors has been patchy (Ponti et al. 2013), with different parts of transport policy being formed without any real reference to systemic needs (Granger and

Kosmider 2016). In part, this erratic progress has been shaped by the fact that states started at different points with regard to the maturity of their NTS (Finger et al. 2015).

TEN-T, in promoting free mobility, must be reconciled with state security. This implies reinforcement of external borders to create mutual trust between states based on the capability to screen both passenger and freight traffic entering areas of free inter-state mobility. This reflects a paradox: that the rationale for TEN-T can often lie within the de-infrastructuring of borders where the removal of border infrastructure has been expected to stimulate flows, leading to a need for more capacity at these core pinch points (Davis and Gift 2014). These, in turn, were a direct legacy of member states' legal obligations under the terms of the Single European Act. To avoid freight barriers at borders states have improved co-ordination and information exchange. However this has not secured obstacle-free movement of freight as borders remain key pinch points and processes can easily be disrupted, with some states often slow to communicate the emergence of new (often short-term) obstacles caused by strikes or other such disruptions where, for example, damage to perishable goods was significant (EC 2019). Thus, the removal of physical systems needs to be supported by regulatory systems to sustain flows and prevent divergence within the management of NIS that work to inhibit flows and go against SEM principles. These were reinforced by the terms of the Schengen Agreement, which was designed to enable the free flow of people across borders (adding both freight and passenger mobility). This again was supported by a process of information exchange between states.[13]

Thus, de-infrastructuring at borders – so as not to infringe state territoriality – has been supplanted by a virtual soft infrastructure system based on information exchange so that freer movement does not impede security and/or control whilst enabling the economic benefits of freer flows (Evrard et al. 2018). These processes push the state's borders out to the edges of the economic bloc. The fact that states retain the right to restore border control where there are security concerns (as was evident during the 2015 refugee crisis and the Covid-19 pandemic) raises the issue of incentives for states to improve capacity at borders to speed up and intensify cross-border flows. However this right to restrain flows arguably becomes more difficult with increasing intensity and speed (and disruption incurred by impediments) of cross-border flows (Evrard et al. 2018, Votoupalová 2018). This is especially salient as trust by some Northern states of other states capability to monitor borders is dubious to the extent that they are hesitant about allowing new entrants from CEE into the Schengen grouping (Zaiotti 2013). Expansion without trust is likely to impede incentives for fuller infrastructural integration.

The overlap between TEN-T and infrastructure criticality is an unexplored theme within the programme (EC 2006a).[14] By nature TEN-T should only involve those projects with an 'international impact' whose failure would have a multinational effect. However, as mentioned above, this was frequently not the case. This reflects that those infrastructures that are deemed international – and thus fall within the scope of EU action according to the principle of subsidiarity (such as regional hub seaports or airports) – are often state-based, with no direct physical, cross-territorial overlap (Hämmerli and Renda 2010). As such, as with TEN-T itself, these remain within the scope of state activity, with the EU seeking to operate as a conduit between affected states (EC 2012, 2013). This reflects the absence of the notion of a separate EU territoriality and that, as such, the state remains the primary territorialising agent. Supranational entities merely operate as facilitators of co-operation rather than as independent bodies.

THE EXTERNAL DIMENSION OF TEN-T

Whilst there are longstanding links between the EU's transport systems and those of neighbouring states, these links have been increasingly shaped by the European Neighbourhood Policy (ENP) – a strategy to promote political and economic stability in those states bordering the EU (Lippert 2007). Prior to the ENP, the external dimension to TEN-T was shaped by the prospect of enlargement. With the rise of 'enlargement fatigue', the extension of TEN-T to the bordering states has been shaped more by the needs of geopolitics than by future expansion plans; though ENP participation does not preclude enlargement (Smith 2005). As of 2020, there were 16 ENP partner states to the south and east of the EU (Browning and Joenniemi 2008). A broad examination of the diverse themes engendered within ENP is beyond the scope of this volume (see for example Kostanyan 2017). However, transport has emerged to become a central theme in the process of regional co-operation that lies at the core of the ENP. In part, this is driven as a legacy of the promotion of closer economic engagement; but it also offers an incentive for the better-performing states to be integrated into TEN-T. This was evident in the EU's move towards the development of a Single Transport Area, where the external component (especially with neighbours) is a central pillar to promote market integration as well as seeking more effective governance of transport flows between the EU and its neighbours (EC 2011).

To aid this process, the EC treats TEN-T corridors as integral to pan-European corridors (see below). These seek to connect non-EU European and Eurasian states to the TEN-T system. These ten corridors were identified as far back as 1994, though many of these components have now been formally integrated into the programme as the relevant states have acceded to the EU. For those states that are still outside the EU, the body remains committed to prioritising these networks as a basis for economic integration across the wider European region. A number of themes overlapping with TEN-T thus became prioritised within TENs, namely:

- Motorways of the Seas: seeking to link all major littoral countries within the European landmass as well as enhancing links to the Suez Canal towards the Red Sea.
- Northern axis: connecting the northern EEA with Belarus and Russia and beyond.
- Central axis: linking central EU states to Ukraine and the Black and Caspian seas with links to Eurasian states targeted and link to trans-Siberian rail and Russian inland waterways.
- South Eastern axis: linking the EU (via the Balkans and Turkey) to the Eurasian states, with links to the Maghreb (some states of North West Africa) and the Middle East.
- South Western axis: connecting south-western EU states with Switzerland and the Maghreb.

These have been subsumed within the Eastern Partnership Agreements (EaP), which set out a number of ambitious objectives, such as: the creation of a Common European Aviation area; integration of all states into the 'Blue Belt' maritime system;[15] improved cross-border processes; and moving towards common standards in rail systems. The EaP applies to six Eastern European/Eurasian states with the purpose of increasing uniformity of the treatment of flows across a broader area.[16] In aviation and maritime systems, the issue reflects longstanding interdependencies, with the EaP focusing on the spread of best practice in areas of security, sustainability and safety (EC 2011a); though, unlike with TEN-T, there is no sense that the EU seeks to shape modal patterns. The major form of EU influence will be through the provision of technical assistance on the development of prioritised corridors and possible funding from public and private bodies (such as the EIB), including the EU's Neighbour Investment Facility, which provides seed capital for mature projects (EC 2015).

Much of the problem behind the EaP transport strategy is that the quality of infrastructure of participating states is markedly divergent, especially with regard to capacity and reliability. Road transport systems in non-EU EaP states are lower in quality and capacity than in Western Europe, have a lower share of dual lane roads (about 20 per cent of total) and operate at lower average speeds (EC 2015). These differences are also evident in rail systems, which are also less developed. These differences matter as the primary flows of traffic are east to west along the designated corridors. Unlike the TEN-T projects, the majority of prioritised projects for the corridors involve road systems (75 per cent of the designated projects); the rest are mainly rail systems, with a single maritime project. Given its size and proximity to the EU, Ukraine is a focal point for much of the corridor activity. With much of the prioritised strategic corridors being single-carriageway highways, the focal point of the scheme is to upgrade these systems to raise capacity. This pattern is repeated with rail, where a large proportion of the networks integrated into the strategic corridor are single-track.

To support the transport dimension of the EaP, the EC (2020a) offers a maximum of €13 billion up to 2030, of which two-thirds will be dedicated to road systems. The focus is those projects that have lower levels of risk and are mature in their development. These EU funds are just 0.3 per cent of these projects' costs, with the main financiers being international financial institutions (81 per cent). Indeed, these bodies will remain the major financiers of these projects over the medium to long term. However inter-state co-operation has floundered due to insufficient funding and difficulties with Central Asian states over border crossings. According to the German Council on Foreign Relations, this has been compounded by high residual levels of corruption and relative political instability (DGAP 2019). This latter problem appears to have been driven by Russian proactivism in many of these states' affairs. However China – through its Belt and Road Initiative – is also being increasingly proactive in these states, viewing them as key conduits in this programme (see below).

To the south, transport links are based also upon the desire to move towards freer trade with all states bordering the Mediterranean. Not surprisingly, the extension of TEN-T to these regions is via the Motorways of the Sea theme. The MoS is seen as a catalyst to promote inter-modality and interoperability in all Mediterranean ports. This is set within the broader framework of the EU's EuroMed Strategy, which seeks to build links between the EU and its Southern neighbours for broader mutual geo-political objectives. Like the EaP, a primary focal point is the spread of best practice to enhance local soft infrastructure systems to aid system safety as a precursor to fuller physical interconnection. This also reflects that many EU ports were prioritised in their role as hubs for inter-continental flows, notably in the Iberian Peninsula and Southern France. In the shorter term, the challenge is to improve the exchange of data and digital infrastructure across all ports to aid the secure and reliable monitoring of maritime freight transport as well as the safety of such flows. With regard to road and aviation, the aim is to extend liber-alisation to all systems as well as the promotion of safety. This reflects that co-operation is based on mutual confidence in safety and security of 'bordering' NTS (EC/UfM 2013, 2015).

Beyond its neighbourhood, TEN-T has overlap with longer-standing inter-governmental initiatives developed by the United Nations Economic Commission for Europe. Formed in the aftermath of the Second World War, UNECE has sought to promote economic interaction and integra-tion across the continent through the promotion of inter-governmental co-operation and co-ordination on major inland forms of transportation infrastructure – namely road, rail and inland waterways (see below). This led to a series of multilateral initiatives which sought to commit states to upgrade and build inland transportation systems to common standards. The longer-term objective is to create a virtual international corridor system based on mutual interconnection and interoperability of national systems and the spread of best practice in system governance (Schipper 2008). Frequently states sign MoUs to form the bilateral links to create the corridors; these are less of a commitment and more a statement of intent. As such, there was little pressure to shape these corridors, though many of the rules – over time – were shaped by the TEN-T system. Indeed these roads development, like TEN-T, were to be market-led with states meeting much of their cost.

UNECE programmes were focused initially on Central and Eastern Europe; but as these states gradually acceded to the EU, so the projects linked to the programmes (such as the Helsinki corridors) became subsumed into TEN-T.[17] As a result, over time, the focal point of pan-European initiatives has been less to operate as a platform for EU expansion and more as a means of building bridges into Eurasia, and eventually to promote inter-continental connectivity between Europe and East Asia (UNECE/UNESCAP 2007). Over time the aim is to open up land-based routes between these continents which (due to cost advantages) are currently dominated by maritime flows that represent 95 per cent of Eurasian trade by volume and 70 per cent by value (UNECE 2012, 2020). There is currently only very limited rail traffic between the EU and Eurasia, and this is dominated by high-value flows enabled largely by the rise of block trains (i.e. those designed to carry containers). Despite nearly 300 bilateral road transport agreements between the EU and Eurasian states, road is also under-utilised and only tends to be used for intra-regional links.[18] As a result, road only tends to be utilised in those states which are peripheral to the main global maritime logistical channels (UNECE 2020).

These trans-continental links have been facilitated by UNECE (2012) under its Europe-Asia Transport Links (EATL) programme. They include 38 states and 311 projects covering nine road and rail corridors, 17 IWW, 52 river and 70 maritime time ports.[19] Of these, 188 projects were seen as high priority, at a cost of $78 billion. By the end of the first phase (in 2012) 53 per cent of the priority projects were completed, with progress in the development of enabling soft infrastructure being mixed with wide variation in the speed and efficacy of customs processes being evident.

The longstanding international E-road agreement (established in 1950) sought to foster improvements in national road systems by designating specific parts of national road systems as components of pan-European freight traffic corridors (Schipper 2008). This intergovernmental agreement (which was as much about security as economics) sought to define the minimum conditions under which national segments of this system should work and be developed as a means of providing continuity across the system. The agreement commits (currently 36) states to building, maintaining and upgrading their section of the E-Road network. E-roads were only the small top layer of the pan-European road system and were not always high-speed, high-capacity infrastructures (Schipper 2008). However, the uneven progress in developing E-roads reflects the desire for states to fragment despite a narrative driving integration with states wanting to control cross-border and internal flows.

Overlapping with the E-road strategy (as well as TEN-T) was the Trans-European Motorway (TEM) programme, which was launched in 1977 to facilitate upgrades in Central, Eastern and Southern European infrastructure as a means to enable their integration into the more developed Western European system. TEM was the backbone of the pan-European road corridors in Central and Eastern Europe and of the Transport Infrastructure Needs Assessment (TINA) exercise. The TEM narrative is explicitly built around co-operation rather than integration, though the latter maybe a consequence of the former. Importantly, TEM was more about traffic facilitation and national system harmonisation than creating a pan-European system per se. The TEM programme (which includes both EU and non-EU European states) created a framework for investment that would adapt to rising traffic flows but also improve the quality of transport services as well as seeking to push for the greater approximation of quality and quantity of high-capacity road systems. TEM includes 294 projects covering both road building and maintenance/upgrading, at a cost of over €100 trillion (UNECE 2020).

By 2015, 56 per cent (as measured by total length of network) of TEM had been completed, with a further 6 per cent under construction. Given that much of this was built prior to the programme being launched, this represents a very limited attainment by this programme. This limited success reflects issues of financing and planning inadequacies and the absence of transport strategies at national levels (UNECE 2011). This has been compounded by poor inter-state co-ordination, notably with regard to timing, inconsistency of road classification and rules (e.g. what is an expressway, what are speed limits, etc.), lack of realism in project development and poor data collection to monitor development (UNECE 2018a).

Rail has also been a focal point of UNECE activity, first through the E-rail network, which targets those segments of the participating 28 national systems that need to be built, upgraded and maintained to support pan-European mobility. As with the E-road system, the E-rail systems were extended to Eurasia as TEN-T was applied to Central and Eastern European states as they joined the EU. This programme has also been enhanced by the Euro-Asian rail transport corridors of the Organization for Cooperation of Railways (OSJD), which identified 13 links between Europe and Asia based on MoUs as a basis for co-ordinated action. Second has been the overlapping Trans-European Rail (TER) programmes (established in 1990) aimed at less-developed rail systems in, what were then, the more peripheral parts of Europe (Peters 2003). The objective was to use this as a basis for integration with Western Europe systems through the adoption of common practices agreed by the UN. The European rail system became fragmented as borders were redrawn after conflict, not just physically but also by divergences in standards as railway systems were upgraded and expanded (Schmidt and Giorgi

2001). By 2011, TER consisted of 191 rail projects, again with strong overlap with TEN-T. As with TEM, TER is based on national strategies and, as such, will be driven by inter-governmental co-operation. In 2020 TER involved 17 Central Eastern, South Eastern European and Caucasus states. Its aim is to promote a network based on interfaces between national rail backbones in each of the 17 states. Like TEM, the push is towards a market-based system in its development where the system emerges in anticipation of flows rather than simply being used as a strategic tool by states. However, this only applies to those segments considered as part of TER. With a strong focus on high-speed rail, there are questions as to TER's realism as a credible policy strategy.

A final aspect of UNECE's work within the EIS is its efforts within the IWW system via its E-waterway programme, which covers 37 states extending beyond Europe into Asia. The E-waterway system is dominated by two river basins (the Rhine–Danube and the Azov–Black Sea–Caspian) that make up nearly 80 per cent of the total UNECE IWW system. In the former, there is considerable overlap with the TEN-T programme. Covering both EU and non-EU states, UNECE has (since 1956) designated 29,000 km of IWW and over 400 ports as being of international importance. Of the designated IWW, the UN (2017) estimates that 6.8 per cent are missing links/bottlenecks where capacity is not as required by the system or where the connecting waterway simply does not exist. The main river systems of Europe are managed by designated commissions, of which there are four within the European region. UNECE operates as a means of developing co-operation and co-ordination both between these bodies and between the EU and UNECE itself (UNECE 2011b). These bodies interact to develop common rules for IWW, of which the main rules are set within the European Agreement on Main Inland Waterways of International Importance (AGN) (UN 2017). As such, UNECE operates as an effective forum for low-level integration between authorities to ensure harmonisation, and operates effective co-ordination between inland waterway authorities with an emerging system of legally binding rules on operation.

Pan-European systems have been hindered by the unevenness of development of these state-based systems in terms of their relative maturity across the corridors; their ability to be financed to allow the national system to reach the desired standard; and by wide variations in state application of the necessary rules and protocols to align national systems to support the development of corridors (UNECE/UNESCAP 2007). Bilateral protocols have only been patchily implemented, with the result that operators face high transit fees and long clearance times at borders. This has been especially evident as the lack of compulsion for states to adhere to these protocols, compounded by lack of time with regard to the pace of implementation, has led to lagged corridor development. Furthermore, many states have been slow to align border capacity and processes, reflecting a broad absence of co-operation and co-ordination along these corridors (UNECE 2011a). Finally, the liberalisation of domestic transport systems has also been very uneven, further reinforcing the poor condition of logistics systems, notably in Armenia and Georgia (World Bank 2019).[20]

THE EUROPEAN DIMENSION OF CHINA'S BELT AND ROAD INITIATIVE (BRI)

Much of the longstanding pressure for European infrastructural integration has come from the internal interaction between states. The development of large, ambitious plans for TEN-T has always come up against states' ability to deliver the investment to upgrade national systems to support the development of key links and hubs within TEN-T. However, Europe has become a focal point within the Belt and Road Initiative (BRI), which was launched in 2013 with an envisaged completion date of 2049 (ECFR 2015). The BRI is the planned large-scale investment by Chinese entities (mainly development banks) in overseas infrastructure systems to promote international connectivity between China and the western and southern hemispheres as well as its more immediate neighbourhood (Jones and Zeng 2019, Mayer and Zhang 2020). It has emerged, through the consolidation of a series of pre-existing investments, into a single coherent plan, and, as such, tends to be looser than the notion of a grand strategy as suggested by popular narratives (Hellström 2016, Jones and Zeng 2019). This is not a new Marshall Plan; the BRI is about China's geostrategic interests as it embeds itself into other states' territorial strategy through the infrastructure function (see for example ECFR 2015).

In the case of Europe, BRI-linked investment is driven by the need to have an effective disembarkation/landing point for Chinese exports that China can control and which can be used as a base for the penetration of the wider European market. This occurs through two channels: a Eurasian land bridge connecting the EU and China; and the Maritime Silk Road, where flows reach Europe through normal maritime routes but benefit from improved port facilities. As such, much of the EU-linked investment is focused on hubs within maritime channels, though connectivity to key inland hubs (notably Duisburg – see below) have also been prioritised (Garlick 2019). The aim is to increase frequency and reliability of flows whilst, as mentioned, increasing Chinese control of these flows. However Zeng (2017) argues that the EU is of secondary importance to China as it is too fragmented to constitute a formal power within the global system.

Of the 72 states that are part of the BRI, 24 are European/Eurasian and, of these, 13 are EU members all located in Eastern Europe, though the EU as a bloc has no plans to join.[21] These states tend to have less mature national transport systems, so the BRI is seen as an extra source of finance and know-how in NTS development (OECD 2018). For most states (especially those in the North and West EU), the links to the BRI is little beyond membership of the Asian Infrastructure Investment Bank (AIIB) (Dunmore et al. 2019). For the EU, the issue is how it aligns the BRI to the needs of TEN-T. The official Chinese government line is that the BRI is complementary to TEN-T. This alignment is due to the fact that core EU hubs for the BRI are also salient to TEN-T corridors (see below). Thus, whilst China approaches TEN-T in a project-by-project manner, it could align the BRI to connect to EU's priority core corridors. To further promote alignment, in 2015 the EU and China signed a co-operation agreement (the EU–China Connectivity Platform) which essentially sought to formally align the BRI with TEN-T, promoting co-operation in areas of technology and governance standards. The aim is to create soft infrastructural security on links between the two and to ensure any investment is compliant with EU norms. This allows the EU to begin to shift the BRI to more fully align with TEN-T and the rules that underpin it. The agreement could also help the process of regionalism by operating as a catalyst to narrow the infrastructure gap between EU states (EP 2016). This co-operation also extends to the creation of a new corridor within the western Balkans (see below). According to the European Think-tank Network on China (ETNC 2016), the EU–China Connectivity Platform reflects that the BRI is still a malleable concept that evolves with the tension placed upon it by host governments.

It is evident that China has positioned the Greek port of Piraeus as its bridgehead into the EU. It is the terminus for the BRI in the sense that it is where dedicated BRI infrastructure ends. It is also positioned for transshipment of Chinese products into Africa. This has led to the port becoming a European hub for multinational corporations (MNCs) whose value chains extend into China. Piraeus is the first major EU port from the Suez Canal, but is not the most accessible. The investment by COSCO (the

Chinese state-owned shipping and logistics operator) in port facilities in Piraeus might be important to Greece; but for the European system the impact is minimal as Piraeus is not a major hub in the European system (Van der Putten and Meijnders 2015). Despite this apparent peripherality to the EU logistical system, Piraeus has seen the highest rates of container growth of any European port (almost 21 per cent in the year to 2018) and is now Europe's fourth biggest container port, whereas it was outside the top 20 in 2007; though its traffic volume is still less than a third of Rotterdam's. However, this trend is typical of many Mediterranean ports that have experienced similar growth patterns (Eurostat 2019).

Investment in Piraeus has been followed by investment in other sea ports, namely Valencia and Bilbao (Spain), Rotterdam, Antwerp and the Italian port of Vado. There is also Chinese investment in the major Spanish port of Algeciras (for logistics development) and in Marseille (Angiolillo 2019). The link between these investments and the BRI (apart from Rotterdam, which is a key end point) is as yet unspecified, though they may be included at a later date. However, they are all important hubs within TEN-T. On top of this, there is longstanding Chinese interest in the Portuguese port of Sines, which is the nearest port in the EU to the Panama Canal. Furthermore, the ports of the North Adriatic Sea Port Authority (including Venice) have signed a memorandum of understanding to operate not only as hubs for Chinese traffic but also as part of a feeder system between Piraeus and Venice operated by COSCO. These ports have signed the 'Five Ports Alliance' to create a major terminal offshore through which Chinese goods will be landed and which – via these ports – will be shifted to major Western European markets. The aim is to increase competition for this traffic with both Northern and Southern ports (Wang et al. 2017).

Alignment with TEN-T also comes through the utilisation of Duisburg as an inland port hub for the BRI. It is being utilised as an end point of the Yuxinou Railway between central China and Germany; lowering the journey time between China's interior and Europe's interior from six weeks to two. By 2019, there were to be 39 direct rail services between China and Duisburg, up from five in 2017 (Li 2017). From Duisburg, freight can connect to the EU's IWW systems as well as its road and rail systems. This has been more about enabling services by simplifying soft infrastructure along the route rather than building new infrastructure. This allowed for the simplification of customs/borders processes that speeded transit flows. These trains need to change gauge twice throughout the route as they switch back and forth from the standard gauge operating in China and the EU to the Russian gauge between Kazakhstan and the Polish-Russian border (Dunmore et al. 2019). From these locations and intermediate stations in Poland, the plan is to speed flows to the Baltic region as well as landlocked states in the EU. In short, Duisburg is used as a hub for the rest of North West Europe. However, a legacy of this is that demand for traffic from Piraeus via the Orient–East-Med Corridor can be expected to decline. Baltic and North Sea ports could also see reduced traffic.

Integral to BRI-related activity has been the '16+1' initiative to stimulate economic co-operation between China and 16 Central and Eastern European states (11 EU states and five non-EU Balkan states). Whilst the EU states are more economically powerful and do more trade with China, it is the non-EU Balkan states that have received the bulk of the investment. Under the 16+1 programme, the Chinese government is seeking to develop high-speed rail links between Piraeus and Budapest (Hungary), with further links from the Black Sea towards Vienna (Austria) via Budapest and Bucharest (Romania). These are envisaged as connecting to the Turkish system, which in turn will connect to western China. The programme also involves China exporting its high-speed rail know-how to Bulgaria and promoting co-operation between ports on the Black, Adriatic and Baltic Seas. Hellström (2016) argues that this investment is driven by the fact that they have the least stringent infrastructure investment rules amongst European states.

A problem for the EU and the TEN-T project from the BRI is that market-led priority projects might find that competition for flows could be distorted by the rise of traffic through non-prioritised parts of the system. This could create unforeseen bottlenecks and capacity crunches. Moreover, the actual path and timing of flows are also difficult to predict (OECD 2018). Dunmore et al. (2019) suggest that not all rail systems are ready for point-to-point services between China and the entire TEN-T area, and that there is the danger (especially expressed within the 16+1 initiative) for the EU that some states' need for capital investment in infrastructure will create a division within the bloc if dependence by individual states on China emerges. That is, states could end up supporting Chinese geopolitical interests in return for investment that could, in turn, undermine the co-operative territoriality in the TEN-T programme. There are also concerns that China might use its 16+1 strategy to push its agenda and divide and rule between EU states to prevent the emergence of common EU positions that are disadvantageous to China (Amighini 2017). The development sub-sets of EU states within the 16+1 programme raises the prospect of misalignment between states in issues of the infrastructural mandate which are supposed to be aligned under the EU's systemic approach. For non-EU European states especially, the concern is that the BRI could lead to a geostrategic reorientation towards China and away from the EU. By offering finance, it could see states preferring co-operation with China over the EU if the Chinese geostrategy has a greater impact on territorial strategy than EU processes. This is most evident with regard to issues of security and the Chinese ownership of infrastructure. The BRI is also evidently a potential challenge to the efficacy of the European Neighbourhood Policy. However, as a group of states the EU can formulate a geostrategic response and co-operate with China to promote development in Eurasia as a clear point of mutual advantage. Chinese investment in the EU 'neighbourhood' could be a positive force if its BRI investments promote stability (EIU 2015). Despite this, Vergeron (2018) argues that the impact of BRI can be easily overstated as, between 2012 and 2017, China invested $15 billion in the 16+1 states, whilst European regional funding was $86 billion for Poland alone. However these funds are not only spent on infrastructure.

CONCLUSION

Whilst transport infrastructural integration has been a longstanding theme across Europe it is set against a background of the sustained salience of national systems. In terms of intra-EU mobility, the majority of passenger and freight traffic is national (originating and concluding in the same state), and states think of transport infrastructure in those terms. The international dimension of traffic is peripheral to state transportation strategy and – where it is salient – the process is more about interaction rather than integration. Cross-border infrastructure is only relevant for some users – and only then for part of the time. Thus, cross-border interactions are variable across modes and tend to be the exception rather than the rule. However such statistics do not reflect to what extent these internal flows are part of the process of external value creation – that is, national-based value chains to support international competitiveness or as part of value network for goods that are traded globally. Thus simply measuring traffic flows and using this to determine the efficacy of international systems is misleading.

Regionalism in NTS is rationalised by the desire to solve a common problem. If there is a problem, then it is how the fragmentation of NIS has impeded cross-border flows. In a relatively fragmented space such as Europe, isolating national transportation systems from each other becomes difficult where interactions have strong historical precedence. This process rationalises TEN-T as a policy strategy to promote the enablement of transnational flows. This inevitably draws attention to those processes that hinder the de- and re-territorialisation of flows. This implies a focus on cross-border systems, where this process is most evident. This means capacity at borders and ease of flows through this infrastructure. However, within the EU, the checking of these flows under the legacy of SEM has been away from borders towards mutually agreed soft infrastructure systems. As borders (especially within the Schengen area) become less important as a filtering mechanism, so the bottlenecks shift away from the interface between territorial systems and towards core trade corridors. However, the very nature of flows renders TEN-T more about national systems than international systems.

NOTES

1   Transport infrastructure is defined here as the multi-modal territorially fixed links (i.e. road, rail, waterways, airways) and nodes (ports, airports, rail stations, freight terminals, etc.) used for the transmission of passengers and freight flows between and within states.
2   As a unit of measurement, this refers to a single tonne of goods being transported a single kilometre. The figure quoted excludes goods transported between the EU27 and the rest of the world.
3   This measures passenger mobility through assessing a single passenger being moved a single kilometre.
4   The full list of states included can be found at www.oecdstat.org (date accessed 02/03/2020).
5   High-speed rail lines are designated as those that can run at over 250 km/h for at least some portion of the journey.
6   As of 2017, an extra 1600 km were under construction.
7   This number is inflated by the smaller states appearing to have large provision due to a few airports over a small area. Indeed the figure for Malta is 938 airports per 100,000 km^2.
8   Direct connectivity occurs through direct links between airports. Indirect connectivity occurs via a hub and spoke system.
9   Short sea shipping is the transport of goods through maritime channels over relatively short distances.
10 In practice, many projects consisted of a number of sub-projects along a defined geographic axis. The 30 prioritised in 2004 were in fact an amalgam of 188 projects.
11 In 2013, there were 438 TEN-T projects, of which 27 were cancelled. Of the remaining 411, 80 per cent were national only, and the remainder multinational.

12   Some 88 per cent of CEF is focused on the core network.
13   Though as of 2020 there were four non-EU states that participate in Schengen and five EU states that are excluded from the agreement.
14   Critical infrastructure refers to those physical structures whose failure or disruption could directly impact state territoriality.
15   The Blue Belt system seeks to harmonise (and thereby ease) customs procedures for maritime-based transport across the EU and its neighbours.
16   The six states are Armenia, Azerbaijan, Belarus, Georgia, Moldova and Ukraine.
17   The Helsinki corridors (also known as the Crete corridors) were ten multi-modal corridors designated in 1997 to promote infrastructural integration between Western and Eastern Europe.
18   In 2020 EU road transport agreements existed with Armenia, Azerbaijan, Belarus, Georgia, Kazakhstan, Kyrgyzstan, Moldova, Russia, Tajikistan, Turkmenistan, Ukraine and Uzbekistan.
19   The 38 states are Afghanistan, Armenia, Azerbaijan, Belarus, Belgium, Bosnia and Herzegovina, Bulgaria, China, Croatia, Cyprus, Finland, France, Georgia, Germany, Greece, Iran, Italy, Kazakhstan, Kyrgyzstan, Latvia, Lithuania, Luxembourg, Malta, Moldova, Mongolia, North Macedonia, Pakistan, Poland, Portugal, Romania, Russia, Serbia, Spain, Tajikistan, Turkey, Turkmenistan, Ukraine and Uzbekistan.
20   Armenia is ranked 116th and Georgia 124th out of 167 states in the World Bank's Logistics Performance Index.
21   In 2020 the EU states involved were Lithuania, Austria, Estonia, Malta, Poland, Croatia, Slovakia, Bulgaria, Latvia, Czechia, Romania, Greece and Hungary.

REFERENCES

Airports Council International (ACI) (2019). Airport industry connectivity report 2019. Available at https://www.aci-europe.org; date accessed 03/03/2020.

Amighini, A. (2017). *China's Belt and Road: A game changer?* Milan: Edizioni Epoké.

Angiolillo, F. (2019). Development through acquisition: The domestic background of China's Europe policy. Available at https://www.iai.it/en; date accessed 22/04/2020.

Aparicio, Á. (2017). The changing decision-making narratives in 25 years of TEN-T policies. *Transportation Research Procedia*, Vol. 25, pp. 3715–3724.

Badenoch, A., and Fickers, A. (eds) (2010). *Materializing Europe: Transnational infrastructures and the project of Europe*. Basingstoke: Palgrave Macmillan.

Browning, C. S., and Joenniemi, P. (2008). Geostrategies of the European neighbourhood policy. *European Journal of International Relations*, Vol. 14, No. 3, pp. 519–551.

Button, K. (1998). The good, the bad and the forgettable – or lessons the US can learn from European transport policy. *Journal of Transport Geography*, Vol. 6, No. 4, pp. 285–294.

Central Commission for the Navigation of the Rhine (CCNR) (2018). *Annual Report 2018: Inland Navigation in Europe. Market Observation.* Strasbourg: CNNR. Available at https://inland-navigation-market.org; date accessed 05/03/2020.

CIA (2019). *World fact book.* New York: Skyhorse Publishing. Available at www .cia.org; date accessed 20/02/2020.

Community of European Railway and Infrastructure Companies (CER) (2015). Broad-gauge infrastructure in northern and eastern Europe. Available at www .cer.be; date accessed 02/03/2020.

Davis, D., and Gift, T. (2014). The positive effects of the Schengen Agreement on European trade. *World Economy*, Vol. 37, No. 11, pp. 1541–1557.

Dunmore, D., Preti, A., and Routaboul, C. (2019). The 'Belt and Road Initiative': Impacts on TEN-T and on the European transport system. *Journal of Shipping and Trade*, Vol. 4, No. 1, pp. 10–27.

Economist Intelligence Unit (EIU) (2015). *Prospects and challenges on China's 'one belt, one road': A risk assessment report.* Available at www.eiu.com; date accessed 22/04/2020.

Eurocontrol (2017). European aviation in 2040: Challenges of growth. Available at www.eurocontrol.int; date accessed 03/02/2020.

European Commission (EC) (1994). *Proposal for a European Parliament and Council decision on community guidelines for the development of the Trans-European Transport Network.* Brussels: Commission of the European Communities.

European Commission (EC) (1998). Progress report on the 14 Essen Projects: Supplement to Transport Europe. Brussels: European Commission.

European Commission (EC) (2001). European transport policy for 2010: Time to decide. White Paper. Luxembourg: Office for Official Publications of the European Communities.

European Commission (EC) (2002). Revision of the Trans-European Transport Networks 'TEN-T' community guidelines. Available at http://europa.eu.int/ comm/transport/themes/network/english/ten-t-en.html.

European Commission (EC) (2002a). *Trans-European Transport Network: TEN-T priority projects.* Luxembourg: Office for Official Publications of the European Communities.

European Commission (EC) (2003). *A European initiative for growth: Investing networks and knowledge for growth and jobs. Final Report to the European Council.* Brussels: Commission of the European Communities.

European Commission (EC) (2006). *Keep Europe moving: Sustainable mobility for our continent.* Brussels: European Commission.

European Commission (EC) (2006a). European programme for critical infra-structure protection, COM(2006) 786 final. Brussels: European Commission.

European Commission (EC) (2009). Trans-European transport network: Implementation of the priority projects. Progress report. Brussels: European Commission.

European Commission (EC) (2009a). TEN-T: A policy review. Towards a better integrated Trans-European Network at the service of the Common Transport Policy. Green Paper. Brussels: European Commission.

European Commission (EC) (2010). Establishing a single European railway area. Communication from the Commission. Available at www.europa.eu.int; date accessed 26/02/2020.

European Commission (EC) (2010a). Europe 2020: A European strategy for smart, sustainable and inclusive growth. Communication from the Commission. Brussels: European Commission.

European Commission (EC) (2010b). *Consultation on the future Trans-European transport network policy*. Brussels: European Commission.

European Commission (EC) (2011). Roadmap to a single European transport area: Towards a competitive and resource-efficient transport system. White Paper on Transport. Brussels: European Commission.

European Commission (EC) (2011a). *The EU and its neighbouring regions: A renewed approach to transport cooperation*. Brussels: European Commission.

European Commission (EC) (2012). The review of the European Programme for Critical Infrastructure Protection (EPCIP), SWD(2012) 190 final. Brussels: European Commission.

European Commission (EC) (2013). On a new approach to the European Programme for Critical Infrastructure Protection: Making European critical infrastructures more secure, SWD(2013) 318 final. Brussels: European Commission.

European Commission (EC) (2015). Eastern Partnership regional transport study. Available at https://ec.europa.eu/transport; date accessed 09/04/2020.

European Commission (EC) (2018). Support study for the impact assessment accompanying the proposal for a regulation/directive on streamlining measures for swifter implementation of the projects of common interest on the Trans European Transport Network. Final Report, June 2018.

European Commission (EC) (2018a). The Trans-European Transport Network: An EU that delivers investments in smart, sustainable and safe mobility for jobs and growth. TEN-T Days, Ljubljana 25–27 April 2018. Available at ww.europa.eu.int; date accessed 24/03/2020

European Commission (EC) (2018b). Indicative TEN-T investment action plan. Available at www.europa.eu.int; date accessed 09/04/2020.

European Commission (EC) (2019). Evaluation of Regulation (EC) 2679/98 on the functioning of the internal market in relation to the free movement of goods among the member states, SWD(2019) 372 final. Brussels: European Commission.

European Commission (EC) (2020). Transport in the European Union: Current trends and issues. Available at www.europa.eu.int; date accessed 24/11/2020.

European Commission (EC) (2020a). Progress report on implementation of the TEN-T network in 2016–2017. Available at www.europa.eu.int; date accessed 24/11/2020.

European Commission/Union for Mediterranean (EC/UfM) (2013). Regional Transport Action Plan for the Mediterranean Region (RTAP) 2007–2013: Evaluation report. Available at www.europa.eu.int; date accessed 09/04/2020.

European Commission/Union for Mediterranean (EC/UfM) (2015). Regional Transport Action Plan for the Mediterranean Region (RTAP) 2015–2020. Available at www.europa.eu.int; date accessed 09/04/2020.

European Council on Foreign Relations (ECFR) (2015). 'One Belt, One Road': China's great leap outward. Available at www.ecfr.eu; date accessed 22/04/2020.

European Court of Auditors (ECA) (2018). A European high-speed rail network: Not a reality but an ineffective patchwork. Available at www.eca.europa.eu .int; date accessed 27/03/2020

European Parliament (2014). *EU road surfaces: Economic and safety impact of the lack of regular road maintenance.* Luxembourg: Publications Office.

European Parliament (EP) (2014a). *The cost of non-Europe in the single market in transport and tourism, I: Road transport and railways.* Brussels: European Parliament.

European Parliament (EP) (2014b). *The cost of non-Europe in the single market in transport and tourism, II: Air, maritime and inland waterways.* Brussels: European Parliament.

European Parliament (EP) (2015). Modal share of freight transport to and from EU ports. Available at http://www.europarl.europa.eu/studies; date accessed 04/03/2020.

European Parliament (EP) (2016). One Belt, One Road (OBOR): China's regional integration initiative. Available at http://www.europarl.europa.eu; date accessed 24/04/2020.

European Round Table of Industrialists (ERT) (1990). *Missing networks in Europe.* Brussels: ERT.

European Think-tank Network on China (ETNC) (2016). Europe and China's new silk roads. Available at http://www.iai.it; date accessed 24/04/2020.

Eurostat (2019). EU transport in figures. Available at http://epp.eurostat.ec .europa.eu; date accessed 25/02/2020.

Evrard, E., Nienaber, B., and Sommaribas, A. (2018). The temporary reintroduction of border controls inside the Schengen area: Towards a spatial perspective. *Journal of Borderlands Studies*, Vol. 35, No. 3, pp. 1–15.

Finger, M., Bert, N., and Kupfer, D. (2015). EU transport policy. *Transportation and Economy*, Vol. 75, pp. 4–9.

Garlick, J. (2019). *The impact of China's Belt and Road Initiative: From Asia to Europe.* London: Routledge.

German Council on Foreign Relations (DGAP) (2019). The future of EU's eastern partnership beyond 2020. Available at https://dgap.org/en; date accessed 09/04/2020.

Granger, R. J., and Kosmider, T. (2016). Towards a better European transport system. *Transportation Research Procedia*, Vol. 14, pp. 4080–4084.

Gutiérrez, J., Condeço-Melhorado, A., López, E., and Monzón, A. (2011). Evaluating the European added value of TEN-T projects: A methodological proposal based on spatial spillovers, accessibility and GIS. *Journal of Transport Geography*, Vol. 19, No. 4, pp. 840–850.

Hämmerli, B., and Renda, A. (2010). *Protecting critical infrastructure in the EU.* Brussels: Centre for European Policy Studies (CEPS). Available at www.ceps .eu; date accessed 02/04/2020.

Hellström, J. (2016). *China's acquisitions in Europe: European perceptions of Chinese investments and their strategic implications.* Stockholm: FOI.

High-Level Group on the Trans-European Transport Network (HLG-TEN-T) (2003). Report. Available from www.europa.eu.int; date accessed 08/03/2020.

International Transport Forum (ITF) (2013). *Spending on transport infrastructure 1995–2011: Trends, policies, data.* Paris: OECD.

International Transport Forum (ITF) (2019). *ITF transport outlook.* Paris: OECD.

Johnson, D., and Turner, C. (1997). *Trans-European networks: The political economy of integrating Europe's infrastructure.* Basingstoke: Macmillan.

Johnson, D., and Turner, C. (2007). *Strategy and policy for trans-European networks.* Basingstoke: Palgrave Macmillan.

Jones, L., and Zeng, J. (2019). Understanding China's 'Belt and Road Initiative': Beyond 'grand strategy' to a state transformation analysis. *Third World Quarterly*, Vol. 40, No. 8, pp. 1415–1439.

Knieps, G. (2013). Competition and the railroads: A European perspective. *Journal of Competition Law and Economics*, Vol. 9, No. 1, pp. 153–169.

Kostanyan, H. (2017). *Assessing the European Neighbourhood policy.* London: Rowman & Littlefield.

Larkin, B. (2013). The politics and poetics of infrastructure. *Annual Review of Anthropology*, Vol. 42, pp. 327–343.

Lehmkuhl, D. (2002). Harmonisation and convergence? National responses to the common European transport policy. *German Policy Studies/Politikfeldanalyse*, Vol. 2, No. 4, pp.1–27.

Li, Y. (2017). Belt and Road: A logic behind the myth. In Amighini, A. (ed.), *China's Belt and Road: A game changer?* Milan: ISPI, pp. 13–33.

Lippert, B. (2007). *The discussion on EU Neighbourhood Policy: Concepts, reform proposals and national positions.* Berlin: Friedrich-Ebert-Stiftung, International Policy Analysis. Available at https://library.fes.de/pdf-files/id/ 04737.pdf; date accessed 07/04/2020.

Maggi, R., Masser I., and Nijkamp P. (1992). Missing networks in European transport and communications. *Transport Reviews*, Vol. 12, No. 4, pp. 311–321.

Martellato, D. (2011). TENT-T priority projects: Where do we stand? *European Research Studies*, Vol. 14, No. 3, pp. 51–66.

Mayer, M., and Zhang, X. (2020). Theorizing China–world integration: Socio-spatial reconfigurations and the modern silk roads. *Review of International Political Economy*, Vol. 27, No. 1, pp. 1–30.

Mulley, C., and Nelson, J. D. (1999). Interoperability and transport policy: The impediments to interoperability in the organisation of trans-European transport systems. *Journal of Transport Geography*, Vol. 7, No. 2, pp. 93–104.

Nijkamp, P. (ed.) (1993). *Europe on the move: Recent developments in European communications and transport activity research.* Aldershot: Avebury.

Öberg, M., Nilsson, K. L., and Johansson, C. M. (2018). Complementary governance for sustainable development in transport: The European TEN-T core network corridors. *Case Studies on Transport Policy*, Vol. 6, No.4, pp. 674–682.

Organisation for Economic Co-operation and Development (OECD) (2018). China's Belt and Road Initiative in the global trade, investment and finance landscape. Available at www.oecd.org; date accessed 22/04/2020.

Organisation for Economic Co-operation and Development (OECD) (2019). Transport statistics. Available at www.oecd.org; date accessed 02/03/2020.

Otsuka, N., Günther, F. C., Tosoni, I., and Braun, C. (2017). Developing trans-European railway corridors: Lessons from the Rhine–Alpine Corridor. *Case Studies on Transport Policy*, Vol. 5, No. 4, 527–536.

Pellegrini, P., and Rodriguez, J. (2013). Single European sky and single European railway area: A system level analysis of air and rail transportation. *Transportation Research Part A: Policy and Practice*, Vol. 57, pp. 64–86.

Peters, D. (2003). Cohesion, polycentricity, missing links and bottlenecks: Conflicting spatial storylines for pan-European transport investments. *European Planning Studies*, Vol. 11, No. 3, pp. 317–339.

Ponti, M., Boitani, A., and Ramella, F. (2013). The European transport policy: Its main issues. *Case Studies on Transport Policy*, Vol. 1, No. 1–2, pp. 53–62.

Proost, S., Dunkerley, F., De Borger, B., Gühneman, A., Koskenoja, P., Mackie, P., and Van der Loo, S. (2011). When are subsidies to trans-European network projects justified? *Transportation Research Part A: Policy and Practice*, Vol. 45, No. 3, pp. 161–170.

Rodrigue, J. P., Debrie, J., Fremont, A., and Gouvernal, E. (2010). Functions and actors of inland ports: European and North American dynamics. *Journal of Transport Geography*, Vol. 18, No. 4, pp. 519–529.

Schade W., Krail M., Hartwig J., Walther C., Sutter D., Killer M., Maibach M., Gomez-Sanchez J., and Hitscherich K. (2015). Cost of non-completion of the TEN-T. Study on behalf of the European Commission DG MOVE, Karlsruhe, Germany.

Schipper, F. (2008). *Driving Europe: Building Europe on roads in the twentieth century*. Eindhoven: Technische Universiteit Eindhoven.

Schmidt, M., and Giorgi, L. (2001). Successes, failures and prospects for the common transport policy. *Innovation: The European Journal of Social Science Research*, Vol. 14, No. 4, pp. 293–313.

Schot, J. (2010). Transnational infrastructures and the origins of European integration. In Badenoch, A., and Fickers, A. (eds), *Materializing Europe: Transnational infrastructures and the project of Europe*. Basingstoke: Palgrave Macmillan, pp. 82–109.

Sichelschmidt, H. (1999). The EU programme 'trans-European networks': A critical assessment. *Transport Policy*, Vol. 6, No. 3, pp. 169–181.

Smith, K. E. (2005). The outsiders: The European neighbourhood policy. *International Affairs*, Vol. 81, No. 4, pp. 757–773.

Spiekermanfl, K., and Wegener, M. (1996). Trans-European networks and unequal accessibility in Europe. *European Journal of Regional Development (EUREG)*, Vol. 4, No. 96, pp.35–4.

TEN-T Expert Group (2010). Integration of transport policy into TEN-T planning. Final report of the expert group 2, 19 April 2010. Available at https://ec.europa.eu/transport/.

Turró, M. (1999). *Going trans-European: Planning and financing transport networks for Europe*. Oxford: Elsevier.

United Nations (UN) (2017). *Inventory of main standards and parameters of the E waterway network: 'Blue book'*. New York/Geneva: UN. Available at www.unece.org; date accessed 17/04/2020.

United Nations Economic Commission for Europe (UNECE) (2011). Master plan of the Trans-European Motorway (TEM) and Trans-European Railway (TER) Part 1: Main report, Available at www.unece.org; date accessed 16/04/2020.

United Nations Economic Commission for Europe (UNECE) (2011a). Master plan of the Trans-European Motorway (TEM) and Trans-European Railway (TER) Part 2: Annexes. Available at www.unece.org; date accessed 16/04/2020.

United Nations Economic Commission for Europe (UNECE) (2011b). White Paper on Inland Transport Available at www.unece.org; date accessed 17/04/2020.

United Nations Economic Commission for Europe (UNECE) (2012). Joint study on developing Euro-Asian transport linkages, Phase II: Expert group report. Available at www.unece.org; date accessed 15/04/2020.

United Nations Economic Commission for Europe (UNECE) (2018). TEM project strategic plan 2017–2021. Available at www.unece.org; date accessed 16/04/2020.

United Nations Economic Commission for Europe (UNECE) (2018a). 2018 Inland transport statistics for Europe and North America. Available at www.unece.org; date accessed 25/02/2020.

United Nations Economic Commission for Europe (UNECE) (2020). Euro-Asian transport linkages: Operationalisation of inland transport between Europe and Asia, Phase III. Available at www.unece.org; date accessed 15/04/2020.

United Nations Economic Commission for Europe (UNECE)/United Nations Economic and Social Commission for Asia and the Pacific (UNESAP) (2007). Joint study on developing Euro-Asian transport linkages. Available at www.unece.org; date accessed 14/04/2020.

Van der Putten, F. P., and Meijnders, M. (2015). *China, Europe and the maritime silk road*. The Hague: Clingendael, Netherlands Institute of International Relations.

Van der Vleuten, E., and Kaijser, A. (2005). Networking Europe. *History and Technology*, Vol. 21, No. 1, pp. 21–48.

van Exel, J., Rienstra, S., Gommers, M., Pearman, A., and Tsamboulas, D. (2002). EU involvement in TEN development: Network effects and European value added. *Transport Policy*, Vol. 9, No. 4, pp. 299–311.

van Weenen, R. L., Burgess, A., and Francke, J. (2016). Study on the implementation of the TEN-T regulation: The Netherlands case. *Transportation Research Procedia*, Vol. 14, pp. 484–493.

Vergeron, K. L. D. (2018). The new silk roads: European perceptions and perspectives. *International Studies*, Vol. 55, No. 4, pp. 339–349.

Votoupalová, M. (2018). Schengen cooperation: What scholars make of it. *Journal of Borderlands Studies*, Vol. 35, No. 3, pp. 1–21.

Wang, X., Ruet, J., and Richet, X. (2017). One Belt One Road and the reconfiguration of China–EU relations. Available at https://hal.archives-ouvertes.fr/hal -01499020; date accessed 24/04/2020.

Wiegmans, B., Witte, P., and Spit, T. (2015). Characteristics of European inland ports: A statistical analysis of inland waterway port development in Dutch municipalities. *Transportation Research Part A: Policy and Practice*, Vol. 78, pp. 566–577.

World Bank (2019). Logistics Performance Index 2019. Available at www .worldbank.org; date accessed 20/04/2020.

World Economic Forum (WEF) (2019). Global competitiveness report. Available at www.wef.org; date accessed 05/03/2020.

Zaiotti, R. (2013). Chronic anxiety? Schengen and the fear of enlargement. In Laursen, F. (ed.), *The EU and the Eurozone crisis: Policy challenges and strategic choices*. Farnham: Ashgate, pp. 161–176.

Zeng, J. (2017). Does Europe matter? The role of Europe in Chinese narratives of 'One Belt One Road' and 'new type of great power relations'. *JCMS: Journal of Common Market Studies*, Vol. 55, No. 5, pp. 1162–1176.

3. The European energy infrastructure system

INTRODUCTION

It has long been argued that energy represents the hidden dimension of European integration. Transnational infrastructural integration in the energy sector has been a longstanding theme in Europe as states sought to mutualise energy security through inter-governmental agreement (Lagendijk 2008, Kanellakis et al. 2013). Whilst the notion of energy security can be a rather amorphous concept, this chapter will seek to address the concept through the lens of the evolving European energy infrastructure system (Kruyt et al. 2009, Benson and Russell 2015). In so doing, when examining the main territorial and geostrategies aimed at attaining this objective, it will stress that energy security is not simply about possessing sufficient quantities of energy; it is also about obtaining it on terms that support the broader objectives of the infrastructure mandate as encapsulated within the 4 A's of energy security, namely: availability, accessibility, affordability and acceptability (Cherp and Jewell 2014). As well as examining the major sources of and trends in energy (including the infrastructure needed for their extraction, processing and distribution) the chapter will examine the forces shaping European regional energy infrastructuring – initially, the European Energy System (EES) and the challenges of energy security. Whilst examining the energy mix of the European states, the emphasis will be on gas and electricity infrastructures, which have been a major focus of transnational activity. Thereafter the range of policy programmes developed at the supranational level are explored as regards their ability to address the overlap between the states' territorial and geo-strategies. This will then extend to inter-governmental programmes/initiatives regarding pan-European energy infrastructures. Finally, the chapter explores the legacy of the latest energy transition for the process of infrastructural integration.

THE EUROPEAN ENERGY SYSTEM AND ENERGY SECURITY

In territorial terms, the notion of an energy system is based on the totality of energy resources within a territory (or collection of territories) that has the capability to extract, process and transport/distribute energy. The aim is for the energy system to reliably generate energy internally and/ or externally secure sufficient supplies to support desired levels of economic and social activity (Cherp 2012, Winzer 2012). Conventionally, the nature of this energy system has been formed around the utilisation of hydrocarbons as the main sources of energy. Historically this was based upon locally abundant sources: initially wood but later, with the onset of industrialisation, coal. Over time this has morphed into the increased consumption of other hydrocarbons (i.e. oil and gas). This initial transition placed adaptive pressure on energy infrastructure as many European states found their energy systems internationally stretched as oil and gas were more unevenly distributed across the globe.[1] Through this process an inevitable alignment occurred between the needs of states' territorial and geostrategies. Indeed, energy has been a main driver in state geostrategy throughout the latter half of the 20th century and into the formative decades of the 21st (Ostrowski 2020). This process – as addressed later on – is arguably turning full circle as the new energy transition (arguably) pushes states towards more locally sourced resources for their energy mix.

Within Europe, these nationally focused systems formed the concept of energy security around notions of self-sufficiency, with external dependence reflecting a potential territorial vulnerability (Bouzarovski et al. 2015). The strategic response to this vulnerability was, in part, to establish a regional dimension to national systems through inter-governmental agreement to create an interconnected EES (Braun 2011, Aalto and Korkmaz Temel 2014). Ultimately, the EES is based on the interconnection between national energy systems (NES) to ensure that – via energy flows across borders – each is able to ensure a secure supply relative to divergent needs across time and space, notably where a state's energy needs and generating capability are asynchronous. Thus the EES operates as a support rather than a replacement for NES; and, according to the Asia Pacific Energy Research Centre (APERC 2007), it acts not just to promote energy security within these systems but also as a valve to allow surplus energy to be moved between states. The creation of this regional system lies at the core of infrastructural integration within Europe.

The European Energy Mix and Balances

In 2018, members of the EU27 still depended on fossil fuels for nearly three-quarters of their energy consumption (EC 2020). This is only a minor reduction since 2000, when these fuels comprised 80 per cent of total energy consumption. This figure varies markedly between states (which retain sovereign over their energy mix), with the share for 2018 ranging from as high as 96 per cent (in the case of Malta) to as low as 33 per cent (in the case of Sweden). By 2019, nearly a third of the EU27's electricity was generated from renewables, up from 14 per cent in 2000. This too varies greatly, from as little as 9 per cent (Cyprus) to as much as 75 per cent (Austria and Lithuania) (EC 2020). By comparison, renewables provide 98 per cent of electricity in Norway (EC 2019).

The EU27's import dependency is 55 per cent, up from 46 per cent in 2000.[2] Again, this figure varies markedly between states, with some states' import dependency being as low as 4 per cent (Estonia) and others as high as 103 per cent (Malta) (EC 2020). Nonetheless all EU states are net energy importers. Of the non-EU European states, only Norway is a net energy exporter, with a net import dependency of nearly −600 per cent (EC 2019). Across the major primary fuels, EU import dependency was highest for oil (at close to 90 per cent), with three-quarters of all EU gas being sourced from non-EU states. The lowest level of import dependency was in solid fossil fuels (e.g. coal), where imports were around 44 per cent of total energy supplied. Of these imports, nearly two-thirds of the EU's natural gas came from two states – Norway and Russia. Crude oil was more evenly distributed, with Norway and Russia accounting for 42 per cent of imports; Russia was also the largest single supplier of hard coal (EU 2019a). Net imports rose by 15 per cent between 2000 and 2017 (EC 2020). Almost all of the EU's energy imports (99 per cent) are hydrocarbons; gas and oil comprise almost 90 per cent and hard coal much of the rest. As such, there are little net imports of either renewables or electricity. Where such imports do exist they tend to be driven more by conventional utilisation of hydropower between the Alpine and Nordic states, notably from sources generated in Switzerland and Norway.

In 2018, the EU27's total energy production was 636 million tonnes of oil equivalent (Mtoe), a reduction of 20 per cent from 2000. The total energy supplied was 1439 Mtoe, whilst total energy consumption was

1154 Mtoe (EC 2020). This underscores the energy deficit experienced by the EU whereby its production is outweighed by its consumption. By 2018, just over 75 per cent of the EU's primary energy was sourced from hydrocarbons, about 14 per cent was from renewables and 13 per cent was nuclear. This dominance of hydrocarbons in energy production represents a slight reduction since 2000, when the EU obtained 80 per cent of its primary energy from these sources (EU 2019a). The aim of the latest energy transition (see below) is to reduce the contribution of hydrocarbon primary fuels to the energy mix by almost 20 per cent by 2030. Of indigenous primary energy production, renewables were the single biggest contributor, comprising some 30 per cent of total production, just ahead of nuclear. When combined, hydrocarbons comprise some 40 per cent of indigenous EU energy production. In terms of consumption, oil (and petroleum products) is the largest energy source, comprising almost 35 per cent of total consumption, with gas and coal also widely consumed. Overall, hydrocarbons account for some 72 per cent of total consumption (EC 2019a).

THE EUROPEAN ENERGY INFRASTRUCTURE SYSTEM

In its formative stages, the integration of energy systems was enabled by transportation systems that allowed the movement of coal between energy-rich and energy-poor locations. However, the costs involved foreclosed on the prospect of long-distance transmission. Nonetheless, on a bilateral basis, states have been increasing the interdependence between NES. This has been evident across all states as their energy mix has become more diversified. The configuration of infrastructure within and between EU states reflects how states seek to manage their energy mix and balance through developing their own systems and integrating NES. In assessing its contribution to the EES, the chapter will split the focus between its three major networked components – namely oil, gas and electricity.

Crude Oil and Refined Petroleum Products Infrastructure

Oil industry infrastructure within the EU encapsulates a diverse set of facilities operating along the industry value chain involving exploration, production, transportation, refining, storage and retailing of crude oil and oil-based products. The heavily import-dependent European oil infrastructure system (about 90 per cent of EU oil is imported[3]) is based on creating capacity at the point of entry into the system at core refining/ storage hubs which can operate as bases to move crude oil (and refined products) around the European system. Most of the oil (about 80 per cent) arrives in crude form via the maritime system from the Middle East and, to a lesser extent, Africa (EC 2019a). The rest arrives via pipelines from two neighbouring states, Russia and Norway, via Norpipe (between Norway's North Sea field and the UK) and the Druzhba system between Southern Russia and various parts of Central and Eastern Europe (see below).[4] However the bulk of Russian and Norwegian oil for EU consumption still arrives by maritime channels as these suppliers use domestic pipeline systems to access their main maritime export terminals to convey crude product (EIA 2020). The dependence on the transportation system is reinforced by the distribution system for refined products (notably petroleum), which relies on road and rail systems to reach the end user (EP 2009). Of the EU states (as of 2019 and prior to the UK's departure), only four had any meaningful oil production capacity. This fell by around two-thirds with the UK's departure from the EU (BP 2019).

As mentioned, the EU oil-refining system is at the core of its oil infra-structure. The EU28 have about 14 per cent of global refining capacity, with the larger states (as well as smaller states with large ports) dominat-ing internal capacity.[5] Twenty states have meaningful capacity, with the larger states operating as hubs for the pan-EU system supplying those smaller EU states which have limited or no capacity. In 2018, there were 75 mainstream refineries across 22 EU states.[6] Below this are a small number of minor refineries, bringing the total to 87 across the EU, with Germany being the single largest refiner with nearly 16 per cent of total EU capacity. There is a widely acknowledged over-capacity within the EU refining system with there being a decrease in capacity of 95 million tonnes per annum between 2010 and 2018 as production was scaled back and 18 refineries either mothballed or closed (Concawe 2020). Capacity utilisation of the EU's refineries has oscillated between 78 per cent and 84 per cent, with 86 per cent seen as the threshold at which operations are deemed viable. Indeed the divergence between the production and consumption of refined products means that over 40 per cent of the EU's refined petroleum products are exported due to falling demand, increased non-EU competition and simple over-capacity (FuelsEurope 2019).

These refining capacities have been supported by the creation of a network of pipelines and other transportation links to support inter- and intra-territorial flows of refined oil products within and between EU states (Nivard and Kreijkes 2017). The EU's internal system is very limited. Whilst pipelines are the most efficient mode of delivery, low population densities can preclude their development. This is especially evident in the Nordic states. However, it is the northern states with large sea ports that dominate intra-EU petroleum trade. In the east, it is shaped by connections to the main east–west pipeline (see below). In the west, it is shaped by access to the main terminal ports. This is reflected in the salience of two Rotterdam-based pipelines that connect the port to both the Ruhr and Antwerp. Rotterdam's position as a core hub for oil transport is also reflected in its role within NATO's Central European Pipeline System.[7] National networks for the distribution of refined petroleum products differ widely across the EU. Generally, the larger states (both EU and non-EU) with large refining capacity have the more extensive networks; Germany, France and the UK each have around 5000 km of pipelines. This internal system is dominated by Germany's extensive oil infrastructure that connects its oil-importing ports to centrally located refineries. There are also southern links between the ports of Marseille and Trieste and German refineries via the South European Deutsche Transalpine Ölleitung crude oil pipelines. Other than Spain (which has about 3500 km of internal oil pipelines) and the Netherlands (which has 2500 km), these domestic networks tend to be sporadically developed, with ten EU states having no refined petroleum pipeline systems. Sometimes these 'national' networks are in practice highly localised networks reflecting the nature of the processing of crude into refined products as they often merely involve the transfer of material between neighbouring installations or even within an integrated refinery. They can, however, also involve transport between refineries and storage locations nearer concentrations of users.

A final component of the configuration of the EU oil infrastructure is the national system of oil-storage facilities required of member states. These are to hold emergency stocks of oil to bide states over in times of disruption to supply either due to external geopolitical issues or where there are disruptions to EU critical infrastructure. These facilities must have the capacity for up to three months' worth of supply held either by the supplier or by a designated non-state body. Whilst these stocks are held within states, the logic is that these storage facilities comprise a mutually supporting regional network where a shock is asymmetric or where a state does not hold its own stock within its own territory. There has been debate over the extent to which the high degree of stocks is needed and whether diversity of supply (both in terms of oil and non-oil supply) means that these holdings do not need to be as high. Indeed, the UK on its exit from the EU signalled its intention to water down these security of supply obligations due to a more benign oil supply environment.

Gas Infrastructure

Gas infrastructure comprises the facilities required to explore, extract, produce, transport, process, store and distribute gas (either in its natural or liquid state). Gas represents around a quarter of the EU's energy consumption. Though it is less dependent on gas imports than oil supplies, the EU still relies on imports for 70 per cent of its gas (mainly from Russia and Norway), despite there being extensive (though declining) indigenous sources. Around 80 per cent of Europe's imports arrive via the international pipeline system, with the rest via its expanding liquefied natural gas (LNG) facilities (see below). Though 17 EU27 states have some form of gas production, most of the bloc's gas lies within a single state – the Netherlands – which has two-thirds of EU resources (IEA 2019).

The EU's gas infrastructure is used to bridge the gap between production and consumption. Its extensive internal and importing gas infrastructure system is the most mature energy transmission system on the continent. The EU's gas system has been developed gradually over the past 80 years, with much of it based around the discovery of gas in the Netherlands in the 1960s. This was the catalyst for morphing the series of regional and national networks that were fairly isolated from each other into a more integrated and extensive Europe-wide system. This process continued as there were discoveries in the UK and Norway in the 1970s and 1980s as well as increased dependence on Russian gas in the aftermath of the oil crises. The use of gas was also extended through the development of internal gas systems to peripheral parts of the EU, notably Ireland and Greece. These have been supported by increased investment in LNG facilities (see below). In some places (notably the Nordic states) gas interconnections remain under-developed due to a long-term desire to switch away from hydrocarbons. The EU's gas infrastructure system varies in intensity across the region, with it being especially intensively developed in those places with multiple entry points for gas imports, notably in North West Europe and in the eastern parts of the bloc. Very few of the gas pipelines are for long-distance transmission as the internal system is designed to allow distribution to points proximate to point of production due to the cost of transmission (Högselius et al. 2013).

By 2018, there were 225,000 km of gas pipelines within the EU27, the UK and Switzerland. At its core, the EU's gas transmission system is based around more than 20 major pipeline systems that have been developed over decades. All states have gas pipeline infrastructure, though the extensity/intensity of its development does vary markedly between states according to size and population density. Much of this capacity is based around Western and Northern European states as flows from the Netherlands, the UK and Norway enter the system. Interconnection between national systems is relatively high, allowing for the relatively easy flow of natural gas between states (Dieckhöner et al. 2013). According to the European Network of Transmission System Operators for Gas, as of 2019, there were 86 interconnection points between national systems within the European Economic Area (EEA) and the UK and Switzerland (ENTSO-G 2019). These interconnectors can be reversible to allow flow in either direction, though many are unidirectional due to the nature of demand.[8] These interconnectors are also important in the development of hubs where a number of separate gas flows coalesce, creating a high intensity of trading, and are core to the creation of competition between multiple sources of gas. These interconnectors are especially evident at the borders of western and eastern Germany as well as Austria. The degree of interconnection has evolved with the evolution of the EU, with newer members being slower to integrate into the EU gas grid and this has become a theme of the Trans-European Energy Networks (TEN-E) programme (see below).

These interconnectors form part of an extensively developed pan-European system for intra-EU movement, storage and processing for both internally and externally sourced gas supplies. These cross-border capacities vary markedly between states with these flows being highest from the Dutch system. These extensive flows between systems reflect the increased utilisation of gas for electricity generation. Despite the high degree of interconnection, there is a feeling that more is needed to fully secure Europe's energy supplies. In 2019 around 75 per cent of gas consumed within Europe did so within a liquid market (i.e. one that can be moved across borders to meet spatial variations in demand). Interconnection between LNG facilities and the EU transmission system needs development as over 40 per cent of this capacity cannot be accessed by neighbouring states. Without such interconnections, the system would reach capacity limits in two decades (IGU 2019). However, there is doubt over continued expansion, with three planned connectors cancelled over the past five years as demand for gas falls as states shift away from hydrocarbons. This has led to calls for a refocusing of the European gas system towards the transmission of biogases (see below).

A further core component of the EU gas system is the network of storage facilities that are integral to the security of supply. Storage reflects that gas demand is temperature dependent and that there is a need for storage to reflect peaks and troughs in demand alongside the need for secure supplies at all times of the year. Initially part of vertically integrated gas businesses, these have been disintegrated so as to allow for better security through competition between suppliers. Their role in ensuring market balance is key and, since liberalisation, there has been an expansion in storage capacity. However, as gas prices have fallen so some of this capacity has been mothballed or even closed. This has been aided by better interconnection, allowing gas to flow more freely between states and also facilitating the wider use of LNG which has also negated the need for storage. This has led to the exploration of these facilities being converted to alternative fuels such as hydrogen (see below). As of 2018, the EU27 had 156 underground gas storage facilities, with around half of this capacity in four states – France, Germany, Italy and the Netherlands (ENTSO-G 2018). Most of this capacity is held for commercial purposes, though some states (notably Italy) hold some stock for strategic purposes (EC 2015). These storage facilities tend to be placed underground within disused fields, aquifers and so on; though, like pipeline systems, they are expected to have to adapt to the shift towards lower use of hydrocarbons in the EU energy mix. This storage capacity is under-utilised, with around 7 per cent of average volume of gas used being stored; this fall in gas storage as a share of overall consumption is seen as a long-term trend (EC 2017). As a result, there has been some closure of storage sites. To counter this, some states are compelling some operators to store more gas, though this comes at the expense of cross-border flows.

The final aspect of the EU's evolving gas infrastructure system is the increased use of LNG that enters via maritime transmission channels. LNG infrastructure in the EU is based on port terminals that have a regasification capacity to return gas to its natural state from the liquid form it is held in during transmission. From here the gas enters the European transmission system. LNG use grew by over 10 per cent per annum between 2000 and 2017, with about half sourced from Qatar and Algeria; the former is the largest single source, supplying around a third of imports

(BP 2019). This has diversified the form and structure of Europe's gas supply. In 2018, LNG comprised around 14 per cent of the EU's (plus the UK) gas imports, with Spain alone accounting for a quarter of this total. The EU's LNG system has enough capacity to meet around 45 per cent of its gas consumption, though in some parts of Eastern Europe the demand for LNG systems is driven more by a desire to diversify sources of supply away from dependence on Russia. For this reason, the development of LNG infrastructure has been a core theme within TEN-E (see below). As of 2019, the EU27 had 24 large-scale LNG terminals which served as entry points to the transmission system (ENTSO-G 2019). Almost all of these are in Western Europe. As more LNG capacity comes online, so the expected sources of supply are likely to increase (EC 2016). Despite this rise in the use of these LNG terminals, they have conventionally had low utilisation rates (on average around 30 per cent per year between 2010 and 2020), though this does not seem to have hindered plans to increase the EU's LNG import terminal capacity. This capacity has been increased since 2010, with six states generating LNG capacity for the first time. However the viability of investment in such capacity oscillates with the price of gas. However, as mentioned, as these facilities remain under-utilised, the need for more facilities is questionable.

Electricity Infrastructure

The EU's electricity system comprises the national generating, transmission and distribution systems that enable the supply of electrical power within and between European states. These systems tend to exhibit a high degree of maturity across the EU (and other connected Western European states) (WEF 2019). Not surprisingly given their level of economic development, the EU27 states are both large producers and consumers of electricity, accounting for about 12 per cent of global generating capacity. About 40 per cent of the EU's electricity comes from hydrocarbons, around a quarter is nuclear and about 35 per cent comes from renewable sources such as hydroelectric power (BP 2019). Most states can meet the vast majority of their electricity needs through domestic sources, with Germany sourcing 99.8 per cent of its consumption through domestic generation, Czechia 99.9 per cent and Slovakia 99 per cent. Overall 20 EU states generate over 95 per cent of their consumption domestically. The real outlier is Croatia, which generates less than 30 per cent of its electricity consumption domestically. Italy only generates around three-quarters and Lithuania just over 55 per cent from domestic sources (ENTSO-E 2018).

The EU27's (plus the UK) installed capacity for electricity generation has expanded by almost 50 per cent between 2000 and 2017. Production is spread unevenly across the EU, with two states (France and Germany) accounting for nearly 40 per cent of total EU generating capacity. The share of electricity exported varies widely between EU states. Of the EU27 (plus the UK) in 2017, seven states exported more than 10 per cent of their generating capacity. However more states (14) export less than 5 per cent of their total. Indeed for Finland this figure is as low as 0.1 per cent. Eight states import more than 10 per cent of their consumption, whilst 11 import less than 5 per cent (ENTSO-E 2018). As a result, there is a large movement of electricity exports between those states that dominate EU generating capacity and other EU states. The exports from these larger generating states is more than 2–3 times that of the next nearest state (EIA 2020). Somewhat paradoxically, all exporters are also importers of electricity, reflecting the integration of national electricity grids and the flows across borders. According to ENTSO-E (2018), no EU state exported more than 10 per cent of its annual generation to neighbouring states, whilst 11 imported more than 10 per cent of their annual consumption from other European states. Ten EU states are net exporters of electricity, whilst the rest are net importers.

The EU has the largest internationally interconnected electricity grid, with each state responsible for maintaining its integrity by balancing supply and demand within its own systems. This reflects a long-term trend (since the 1930s) of states seeking to integrate national generating and distribution systems (Van der Vleuten and Kaijser 2005). This is enabled by interconnectors between national systems that – in the case of Denmark and Austria – can be up to 40 per cent of installed generating capacity. Interconnection tends to be highest where markets are mature, where energy use is especially intense and where inter-state economic activity is clustered. Almost all of the EU's electricity is self-generated, with there only being extra-EU exchanges between those states (usually Alpine and/or Nordic) where one state has a surplus of hydroelectricity. With the UK's exit from the EU (and its series of interconnectors with a number of EU states – see below) this is likely to change. On a daily basis, it is estimated that up to 12 per cent of the electricity consumed by an average user was imported. Some states – as they operate as de facto 'electronic highways' – import more electricity than they consume as they are transit points in the EU system as the energy moves on to more distant locations (notably Denmark and Latvia). In addition, Norway's vast hydroelectric reserves operate as a substantial backup for EU (especially Nordic) and non-EU states.[9] By 2020, all EU states were expected to reach a (rather arbitrarily determined) 10 per cent interconnection ratio (Table 3.1), but by the end of 2019 only 17 had attained this objective. The EU has increasingly positioned these interconnectors as tools to enable it to meet its renewable energy targets. The system has no central control, but systems are closely coordinated (ENTSO-E 2019). Despite longstanding interconnections energy remains a deeply national affair, with the mix of fuels used for generation reflecting historical preferences as well as the political economy of energy within any given state.

Table 3.1   Interconnection ratios (2020)

Interconnection Ratio	European State
Less than 5 per cent	Iceland, Cyprus
Between 5 and 10 per cent	Spain
Between 10 and 15 per cent	UK, Portugal, Italy, France, Greece, Bulgaria, Germany
More than 18 per cent	Denmark, Norway, Sweden, Finland, Estonia, Latvia, Lithuania, Poland, Czechia, Slovakia, Slovenia, Croatia, Romania, Hungary, Serbia, Bosnia, North Macedonia, Montenegro, Kosovo, Austria, Switzerland, Belgium, Netherlands, Luxembourg, Ireland

Note: The interconnection ratio is the share of the exchange capacity as a share of total generating capacity, where the exchange capacity is the maximum amount of electricity that can be exchanged between states without compromising the security of supply of the respective systems.
Source: ENTSO-E (2019)

Connectors were initially seen as a backup for national grids, with states tending to use them as emergency valves to either meet shortfalls or export surplus. These security concerns have more recently been supported by economic and social welfare arguments, lowering the need for reserve capacity and supporting lower energy prices (Jacotett 2012, Puka and Szulecki 2014). For states, grid interconnection lowers the cost of meeting domestic energy demand and – in effect – replaces the need for more investment in indigenous generation infrastructure (Hawker et al. 2017). Consequently, interconnection is a political decision. It is about offshoring energy security with trusted partners and lowering self-sufficiency, with national generation becoming a regional resource ensuring that spare capacity can be used for mutual benefit (Zachmann

2013). Other states use interconnection as a lower cost pathway to decarbonisation, though again this could be problematic if wholesale prices fall as a result of interconnection. This means that interconnection could have a legacy of curtailing domestic investment in such systems. The benefits of interconnection, or any extension of the process, depend on a number of factors, including the cost of imported energy, the strategic objective of the link and who benefits from it and how (Poyry 2016). For operators, links are legitimated by the power of price differential between NES. For states, security, cohesion and welfare concerns are paramount (Mezősi et al. 2016). There are sceptics regarding the value of electricity interconnectors due to the cost to consumers of providing electricity; the replacement of cheap, dirty electricity from other EU states which displaces cleaner internal sources; and, finally, that the interconnection (though lowering prices) could – as mentioned – limit investment in domestic generation (Aurora Energy Research 2016). These will have to be militated by the necessary supporting policy measures.

The EU system also has sub-regional systems based on long-term grid interconnections such as Nord Pool of the Nordic states and the Pentalateral Energy Forum in Central Europe (Schubert et al. 2016). These arrangements exist alongside those that the EU has evolved from the simple sharing of capacity in times of emergency to longer-term cross-border trade in electricity. These are largely multiple bilateral initiatives to align systems, though they are often not strong enough to offer full interconnection due to congestion. Whilst the states drive this process, the TEN-E programme (see below) has become a factor within the process (IEA 2016).

The vulnerability of interconnection was highlighted by pan-European blackouts of 2006 (Van der Vleuten and Lagendijk 2010). To the EU, this reinforced a notion that its grid needed further centralisation of governance. Van der Vleuten and Lagendijk (2010) argue that the response proved that the decentralised system works well enough. This raises issues with regard to the governance of critical infrastructure systems. Already electricity – as well as gas – has strong inter-governmental collaboration to secure these systems against events and processes (caused both by humans and occurring naturally), indicating that centralisation is not necessary (Zachmann 2013, IEA 2016). Indeed, the natural response of states in emergencies is to isolate themselves to protect their domestic systems and minimise the risk of 'infection' to other systems. The designers of the European system had long seen the risk of a cascading failure and had already established principles to deal with such a problem;

something that worked as supply was sustained for most users (Van der Vleuten and Lagendijk 2010a).

THE TRANS-EUROPEAN ENERGY NETWORKS (TEN-E) PROGRAMME

TEN-E reflects longstanding EU interest in energy infrastructure, though its actions in fostering systems integration have been a poor second to the bilateral (and often multilateral) interconnection initiatives noted above. Indeed states retain control of this domain, with energy security largely driven by states and their interactions with commercial entities (Haghighi 2008). However the EU was keen to push the idea that a national system to meet solely national needs was antiquated where there was high import dependency and large variations between states as regards energy supply and demand (Johnson and Turner 1997). In seeking to treat national systems as sub-systems of a European system, the EU has sought to intensify pre-existing interconnection and increase cross-border capacity through wider co-operation and co-ordination between states as a means of diversifying supply – in both primary (mainly gas) and secondary (mainly electricity) sources – from both inside and outside the bloc (EC 1993, Andersen et al. 2016, Szulecki et al. 2016). In so doing, the EU argues that energy needs to be treated as an EU-wide resource that should be moved easily across the region according to state-based variations in supply and demand (Helm 2001, Wettestad et al., 2012). In this context, the absence/under-development of energy system integration is a strategic weakness not only in terms of exposing states to the vulnerability of dependence on a single supplier but also from the inability to access cleaner sources of energy located at distance from potential points of use (Crisan and Kuhn 2016, EC 2019b).

TEN-E confirms that – in energy infrastructure at least – it is the states and their needs that drive the process of interconnection and integration (Helm 2014).[10] As such, the development of TEN-E sees the EU operate as a forum for co-operation and co-ordination to enable inter-governmental/inter-operator agreed projects to support the interconnection of national systems. The EU seeks to steer these processes towards developing those projects that are most clearly aligned to attaining the objectives of the Energy Union – namely security of supply, sustainability and competitiveness (EC 2010a, Alemany Rios 2015, Szulecki et al. 2016, Leal-Arcas and 2015a, Ringel and Knodt 2018). Consequently – as identified in Table 3.2 – the TEN-E programme has become streamlined, concentrating on developing a number of energy corridors (which operate as an amalgam of territorially consistent projects) that are most effective in supporting the objectives of the Energy Union (EC 2011, 2013). To this end, TEN-E seeks to mitigate the weaknesses of the system that have poor east–west and north–south connections (Johnson and Turner 1997, 2007). The long-term aim is to create energy highways across the EU. These should aid the flow of energy across the system, enabling it to be moved across and between states to ensure consistency of supply and to ensure that all states have access to the 'right' forms of energy – namely those that promote decarbonisation.

Table 3.2   The Energy Union and the infrastructural mandate

Infrastructure Mandate	EU Energy Union Theme
Security	Promote security through interconnection of national systems and diversify supply
Competitiveness/growth	Enable access to reliable supply to sustain activity but also allow for competition of rival sources across networks to access cheapest source of energy
Sustainability	Develop networks to enable access to renewable sources no matter where generated; move renewable energy through system and future proof system
Cohesion	Remove isolated islands that have under-developed energy systems or lack diversity of supply

Project choice is through a multi-scalar process, with operators (via industry bodies ENTSO-E and ENTSO-G) drawing up a list of potential projects within a Ten-Year Development Plan (based on predicted demand). From this list the EU, alongside the operators, identifies projects of common interest (PCIs) to show funding gaps and where support is best utilised. This also seeks to give impetus (as well as limited finance – see below) to PCIs by reforming and reframing the soft infrastructure systems surrounding such projects (such as permits and other regulations). Thus, at the national level, PCIs enjoy preferential status with regard to regulatory approval. Between 2013 and 2020, the EU identified 248 PCIs, 33 of which are core to the enablement of the Energy Union (EC 2013). This list had to be altered in 2015 (notably in light of Russia's cancellation of the South Stream Pipeline), which streamlined the PCIs in energy to 195. It is estimated that the cost of these PCIs within operators' Ten-Year Development Plan (up to 2030) is €200 billion (EC 2010).

Based on this, there is an estimated gap of around €100 billion in required energy infrastructure investment.

Of the funds available under the Connecting Europe Facility (CEF), TEN-E received €4.8 billion between 2010 and 2020, around 16 per cent of the total (EC 2019d). CEF funding will only be offered where the project has extensive pan-European benefits but marginal viability under the agreed system of regulation. This supports 173 actions across the EU's energy network. In 2017, the supported PCIs were split as follows: 110 electricity and smart grids, 53 gas, six oil and four cross-border CO_2 network projects. This limited funding reflects that these PCIs are overwhelmingly financed through a mix of debt, own resources, state help and regulated revenues; the EU is largely incidental to this financing process. TEN-E envisages that the costs of developing a PCI should fall to the beneficiary of the project. National regulators agree amongst themselves how cost is to be allocated, though if they cannot agree the EU Agency for the Cooperation of Energy Regulators (ACER) makes the decision. TEN-E support is focused on those PCIs where such revenues would be insufficient to the extent that they would inhibit project development. Thus the focus is more on legacy systems that limit transit and where systems are of variable development so that there were problems with diversity of supply. Thus TEN-E was often used to fund under-developed systems and to promote security and diversity of supply, with over 80 per cent of funding being directed towards gas and electricity infrastructure and oil attracting less support (Crisan and Kuhn 2016). These PCIs across the three major industry sectors are outlined below, with gas and electricity dominating (see Tables 3.4 and 3.5).

Oil Corridors

Oil – despite being a major source of energy for the EU – is less of an issue for the TEN-E programme. Part of this reflects that much of it is externally sourced and that the major internal infrastructure is commercial refineries. States take responsibility for internal storage and transmission of refined oil products, much of which occurs through the transport system. Thus oil is arguably more of a beneficiary (albeit indirect) from TEN-T than it is from TEN-E. Indeed oil pipelines represent less than 1 per cent of the estimated capital spend required by the EU energy system between 2020 and 2030 (EC 2018). Nonetheless oil does feature within TEN-E through the promotion of corridors that enable landlocked states to access oil, especially where there are currently limited supply options.

To this end, actions regarding oil within TEN-E are limited to seeking to diversify the connections for Central and Eastern European states so they are less reliant on the Druzhba pipeline. This is a geostrategic project to ensure that – if Russia decides to redirect flows of oil away from this system – these states do not face supply issues as oil can reach them through alternative routes. The targeted corridors are highlighted in Table 3.3.

Table 3.3   TEN-T oil pipeline priorities

Priority Project	Project Objectives
Oil supply connections in Central Eastern Europe (OSC)	The project aims to promote the interoperability of CEE oil pipeline network so as to increase security of supply and lower environmental risks.
Link between Czechia and Germany	The project aims to connect the Druzhba system and the German refinery system.
TAL plus pipeline	This project connects Adriatic terminals with Central Europe through the establishment of a link between Trieste and Germany.
Adamowo–Brody pipeline	This is to connect the Ukraine to Poland, thereby connecting two pan-European systems.
Pomeranian pipeline	This connects Gdansk in Poland (and maritime-delivered crude) to Central Europe.
Bratislava–Schwechat pipeline	This links Slovakia to the Western oil system via the Schwechat Refinery in Austria.

Source: EC (2013)

Gas Interconnectors/Projects

TEN-E in gas has targeted a number of corridors that enable it to meet its strategic objective of diversifying supply (see Table 3.4) (EP 2009). These focus on adding to pipeline capacity to ensure sources from external suppliers (notably North Africa and Eurasia) are able to fully integrate into the European system (EC 2020). The aim is to ensure that all forms from all sources (including LNG and North Sea gas as well as Eurasian and North African sources) are able to be accessed by all EU states so all member states will have access to at least two supply sources (Johnson and Turner 1997). A core underpinning geostrategic theme for TEN-E was the desire to rid Eastern EU states of a legacy of dependence on Russian gas (Kandiyoti 2015). To this end, TEN-E has prioritised the North–South Interconnection project to enable wider access to LNG facilities and also to make existing pipelines bi-directional. In the case of LNG, TEN-E has promoted the development of facilities in Eastern Europe as well as improving pipelines for better access across the EU to regasification facilities (King & Spalding 2018). It is estimated by the EC (2015) that, of the energy investment needed up to 2030, gas is – at best – able to finance some 23 per cent of the desired total. Even then this is surrounded by uncertainty due to the unknown future levels of demand (Chatham House 2016).

In 2017 TEN-E had 53 gas projects that are PCIs, including 42 in transmission, five focusing on LNG and another five involving underground storage (ACER 2019). Across the prioritised corridors, more than 80 per cent is to be invested in NSI East and NSI West, with the Southern Gas Corridor (SGC) and the Baltic Energy Market Interconnection Plan (BEMIP) comprising 15 per cent and 4 per cent respectively. With regard to LNG, the PCIs are mainly proposed facilities in Greece, Cyprus, Poland, Ireland and Croatia – though an extension to the Zeebrugge facilities in Belgium was also included (now completed). Beyond these links it is proposed to ensure that those states with good pre-existing but underutilised LNG facilities are able to increase utilisation rates by being able to move gas between sub-regional systems via the NSI West and BEMIP gas priority corridors.

Prioritised Electricity Interconnectors

TEN-E in electricity was motivated by three factors: first, to kick-start investment in electricity systems which, according to Zachmann (2013), had fallen to historic lows so as to meet anticipated increases in demand; second, to foster access to renewables; third, to develop a single market in energy. To this end, TEN-E sought to promote wider and deeper electricity system interconnection to facilitate the sharing of national generating capacity. The logic was to allow states with surplus capacity to sell electricity to states with a deficit (Nies 2009). The knock-on effect was to lower the necessary investment in extra-generating capacity at the state level, with Newbery et al. (2018) identifying that the process could save up to 2–3 per cent on generating costs. This priority within TEN-E in electricity reflected that some national grids developed in isolation from others and from the wider European system. Such 'islands of generation' became a strategic vulnerability in limiting diversity and security of supply across the EU, especially if such disconnectivity not only limited access to the main European grid but also to non-domestic supplies, notably of African solar power which transits through Spain (Zachmann 2013). To add impetus to this interconnection process, the EU set itself the 10 per cent electricity exchange objective mentioned above, which it seeks to expand to 15 per cent by 2030 (EC 2020). Such expanded interconnections underlines that the ties between energy security and the Internal Energy Market (IEM) are treated as complementary in electricity (see below); in other contexts they are seen as potentially contradictory (Zachmann 2013). For the European electricity system to meet the afore-mentioned objectives, the system's technological capabilities also need to be enhanced through the development and deployment of smart grids to manage flows, as well as investment in storage capabilities. Over the longer term, the objective is to prepare a platform of electricity highways able to cope with decentralised generation that accompanies the shift towards renewable energy and the need to transmit this electricity over long distances.

Table 3.4   *The TEN-E gas projects*

Project	Themes/Aims
Southern Gas Corridor (SGC)	To facilitate diversification of resources at regional level by sourcing gas from suppliers in Eurasia and the Middle East. This is to be enabled by the development of infrastructure for the transmission of gas from the Caspian Basin, Central Asia, the Middle East and the Eastern Mediterranean Basin to the EU to enhance diversification of supply.
North–South interconnections in Central Eastern and South Eastern Europe (NSI East Gas)	To develop interconnecting infrastructure between and within the Baltic Sea region, Adriatic and Aegean Seas, eastern Mediterranean Sea and Black Sea, and for enhancing diversification and security of supply.
North–South interconnections in Western Europe (NSI West Gas)	To link resources in Northern Europe to users in the south by increasing capacity in key points of this corridor to facilitate better access to external supplies and in enabling LNG plants and storage facilities to connect into the European system.
Baltic Energy Market Interconnection Plan in gas (BEMIP Gas)	To develop infrastructure (interconnecting and internal) to end the isolation of the Baltic region so as to diversify and secure supplies and remove single supplier dependency.

The cost of developing an electricity infrastructure to support the above objectives depends on the dispersion of the generation capacity. As states ramp up investment in renewable generation – and electricity production becomes more dispersed – so costs increase as all parts of the EU will need to be connected to ensure continuous flows. As renewable generation can be intermittent, investment in capacity is necessary beyond the need to ensure supply when flows from any single source cannot be secure. Between 2021 and 2030, there is an estimated requirement for €142 billion for electricity PCIs, an increase from the €139 billion needed to be spent up to 2020 (EC 2010). About 35 per cent of these costs are for offshore projects due to the size and type of technology used. As such, 50 per cent of funding is for the NSI-West corridor, 32 per cent for the North Seas Offshore Grid (NSOG), 10 per cent for NSI East and 8 per cent for BEMIP (EC 2018).

In 2018 (and feeding into the EU's PCIs), the ENTSO-E proposed 186 projects up to 2030 of an estimated investment of €114 billion. There are both transmission and storage projects (ENTSO-E 2018). Based on this the EU's electricity PCI list is developed. The 2018 energy PCI list included 110 electricity projects based around the corridors, of which 89 were transmission (46 interconnectors and 43 internal state systems). These developments are based around four regional groups which align with the project corridors identified in Table 3.5. These regional groups are North Sea, North South Interconnection Western Europe, North South Interconnection Eastern Europe and Baltic States. The groups bring local expertise to the projects. By the end of this period, the attainment of electricity PCIs should mean that all states meet the 10 per cent interconnection target. The rest are smart grids (six) and storage (13) (ACER 2019). Within the latest plans for TENs, the main themes are reflected within Table 3.5. PCIs within smarts grids are focused on Central and Eastern Europe.

TEN-E ASSESSMENT

Despite research arguing that TEN-E was an effective device for infrastructure developments (EC 2018b), its record has arguably been more mixed, especially when energy policy remains the preserve of the member states. In part, this is due to the fact that the pressures to integrate already existed with interconnection being a longstanding feature of NES. What TEN-E does offer – in retrospect – is to steer the development of ongoing interconnectivity to meet the needs of the Energy Union (most notably the Internal Energy Market) as well as its broader territorial aims (see Table 3.2). Whether bilateral inter-governmental interconnectivity systems would have delivered this anyway is a moot point. Nonetheless

TEN-E's purpose is to add momentum to the development of those cross-border projects that would have the greatest impact on European territoriality whilst still being commercially viable.

Table 3.5   TEN-E electricity projects

Priority Corridor	Interconnection Themes/Aims
North Seas offshore grid (NSOG)	The aim of this corridor is to promote the development of an integrated offshore electricity grid and related interconnectors in the North Sea, Irish Sea, English Channel, Baltic Sea and neighbouring waters to transport electricity from renewable offshore sources to centres of consumption and storage (notably in Alpine and Nordic states as well as CEE) .It also seeks to increase cross-border electricity exchange between eight EU states, the UK and Norway.
North–South interconnections in Western Europe (NSI West Electricity)	The aim is to promote interconnection between Northern EU countries and the Mediterranean EU states. In particular the aim is to integrate electricity from renewable energy sources and reinforce internal grid infrastructures to promote market integration in the region.
North–South interconnections in Central Eastern and South Eastern Europe (NSI East Electricity)	The aims are to promote stronger interconnections and internal lines in north–south and east–west directions so as to integrate 'isolated' energy islands into the pan-European grid. This process seeks to promote diversity of supply, complete the IEM, integrate renewable generation and, over time, enhance storage capacities.
Baltic Energy Market Interconnection Plan in Electricity (BEMIP Electricity)	To integrate and enhance pre-existing sub-regional links in the Baltic into the larger regional systems and end relative isolation of these states. This is through enhancement of internal sub-regional connections but also extending these links across contiguous states, including working towards the integration of renewable energy in the region.

Source: EC (2017)

It has been widely accepted that many of the main limitations to project development have come from administrative issues. Cross-border projects can take up to 20 years with local authorities to cease their development at any point (Battaglini et al. 2012, ENTSO-E 2018). These planning and administrative problems have also been common within the PCIs (EC 2018a). These have been compounded by persistent funding gaps in TEN-E (especially within electricity), with operator plans and EC-identified needs differing by almost €50 billion in the period up to

2020. These gaps have not been filled, despite increased investment by operators. Moreover this has been a period where both the US and China have significantly increased investment in electricity systems. Despite detailed EU or ENTSO-E plans, there is no binding commitment by national operators to meet the financing needs of any given project. Hence the Ten-Year Development Plans are frequently delayed. This decentralised planning allows state-based operators to defer projects if they are simply not interested in them. For projects with high spillover between states, co-operation and coordination only tend to happen where the mutual benefits are very high. This – and the level of funding from the EU – means that the practicalities of the programme were always outweighed by its ambitions (Zachmann 2013). The European Court of Auditors (ECA 2015) was critical of TEN-E PCIs as there seemed to be no real assessment of how any individual project fitted into its energy strategy. Moreover, the EU gave all projects equal weighting within its objectives and was allowed – under TEN-E regulations – to prioritise projects within any given corridor. In addition, by using a long list of projects, the EU often loses sight of the objective of the corridor.

In 2017, 47 out of 173 PCIs in energy were expected to be completed by 2020 (EC 2017a). More than half of these 173 PCIs were facing delays due to commercial uncertainty or permitting processes (ACER 2019). Since 2013, some 30 PCIs have been completed, with another 75 expected to have been completed by 2022. As of 2019, 45 per cent of electricity PCIs were still at this stage and only 21 per cent under construction. For gas, three-quarters were either being considered or were subject to the permitting process, with just 15 per cent under construction. With regard to the 10 per cent interconnection target, three of the EU27 states had not met this threshold by 2020 (see Table 3.1). This was down from ten in 2017. Though the longstanding energy isolation in Iberia and parts of Eastern Europe remains, there has been progress in the Baltic (EC 2019b). This reflects that investment in the EU electricity grid has not been forthcoming, with an extra €150 billion needed by 2030. By 2019, just 17 states had met the 10 per cent target. Part of the problem lies in a regulatory process that favours public service operators over privately developed interconnectors as it wants revenue returned to the system rather than to private investors. There has been progress in the diversification of gas supply, with all but one of the EU27 states possessing at least two independent sources. By 2022/23, all states bar two will have access to at least three independent sources. This has been enabled by expansion of LNG facilities, with the EU seeking to expand this access to 23 states by 2022. There was also a debate as to whether the speed of progress within energy markets since 2013 still renders the TEN-E (as currently configured) relevant. The accelerated push towards decarbonisation and decentralisation should cause a rethink on PCIs, especially with regard to support for gas. This reflects a desire to focus less on interconnection and more on smart grids (Giannelli and Fischer 2019).

Ultimately TEN-E is limited as it was not seen as necessary by many states. Energy infrastructure is planned on the national scale and funding is directed accordingly. States feel perfectly able to develop their own systems as they want, and can be suspicious of excessive dependence on non-domestic sources. Thus there was no great pressure to add a stronger supranational competence to the TEN-E process. This was evident from the existence of mechanisms that states use to allow space within the system to cope with a capacity gap by rewarding domestic suppliers for creating generating capacity which is turned on in exceptional circumstances. States support this in various ways, and in 2017 there were 13 states with such mechanisms (Hawker et al. 2017). In part, these reflect state perception of the risks of interconnection as were exposed in the 2003 and 2004 blackouts. On top of this, states also used these mechanisms for risk perception. In short, states are moving back towards self-sufficiency, a process reinforced by the latest energy transition (see below).

INFRASTRUCTURAL INTEGRATION AND THE INTERNAL ENERGY MARKET

The IEM is very much positioned as the soft infrastructural component in the development of a European Energy System. Thus, whilst a full discussion of the IEM is beyond the scope of this chapter, there is the need to explore the implications of EU-wide market integration to enabling co-operative territoriality (Siddi 2019). The fuller integration of NES represents a scaling up of the system to drive better national system security. The link between freer energy markets and energy security is not traditionally intuitive as many states equate plural supply structures with diminished control of NES. This control was conventionally necessary within the usual geopolitical approaches to energy security (Siddi 2019). Indeed the IEM process could also be counterintuitive if market integration acts as a deterrent to physical interconnection (notably in gas). For the EC, pluralistic supply structures are a rational choice for member states, lowering the risk of supply disruptions by allowing the creation of an integrated energy system (Prontera 2017). Of course, with EC power in energy being limited, the drive towards the IEM – through three sets of legislation between 1996 and 2009 – is (arguably) the most effective tool at its disposal to support energy security by committing pre-existing bilateral/multilateral inter-governmental agreements in energy to a common framework (IEA 2016). This process is thus driven by the nature of the relationship between the states and the EU, where the main thrust of energy security remains at the national level with there being exemptions to the process should it imperil any state's infrastructural mandate. The IEM sought to enhance inter-operator and inter-regulator co-operation towards systemic integration through the creation of the European Networks of Transmission System Operators for Electricity and Gas (ENTSO-E/G) and the Agency for the Cooperation of Energy Regulators (ACER).

For the EC, the logic and opportunity of the IEM will drive the interconnection of national and regional systems. The rationale is that pre-existing links are of insufficient capacity to enable the free flow of gas and electricity between states. Moreover, better interconnection enables security at lower cost by mitigating the need for the state to build domestic infrastructure to guarantee supply. This is important given the wide variation in energy resources (especially electricity) between states. States tend to use interconnectivity as a 'valve' to maintain national system integrity rather than seeking to treat pan-EU generating capacity as a 'common' resource with interconnectors working within the paradox of connecting closed systems (Glachant and Ruester 2014). These were based on monopoly systems of control where the single supplier imported to merely support its domestic position. These system connectors were seen as second best to sole national systems of self-sufficiency and were option of last resort rather than representing a valid strategic option of supply.

The development of the IEM meant moving the interconnectivity of NES beyond a process of mutual securitisation towards market-driven interdependence. Whilst the IEM does not erode this mutualisation of security, it offers new opportunities for its enablement and diversifying supply sources. Whether such a system is better than existing bilateral inter-governmental deals is a matter of conjecture (at this time). For the EU, these bilateral deals were based on national monopolies working to mutually secure their positions, with the result that interconnectedness between national systems did not work in the interest of the broader

European user (IEA 2005). Open markets (notably with third party access to system interconnectors) leading to energy flows between high- and low-cost locations should militate against the need for monopolistic control over NES to develop inter-system connections (Nies 2009).

The EU also set the terms for infrastructure construction, ensuring that infrastructuring does not reinforce market control, preclude new entrants and limit diversity. This has to be reconciled with the desire of infrastructure developers to ensure that enough product flows through the systems to generate return. Not surprisingly, operators saw EU involvement in system interconnection as unnecessary as this was something they were already doing bilaterally (Lagendijk 2008). Thus liberalisation needed to focus on the ease of exchange between systems rather than ease of access by third party businesses which would increase the cost of co-ordination between national systems and undermine energy security. Indeed Lagendijk argues that competition within the electricity system led to the erosion of goodwill between states to the extent that when one system faced blackout issues other states decided to isolate it rather than support it. This was done to protect their own systems rather than support a neighbouring sub-system (Siddi 2019).

Whilst the IEM has been successful in promoting regulatory convergence, creating a framework for co-operation between states on common rules and developing new infrastructures (ACER 2017), in other areas it has been mixed. Pollitt (2018) argues that the benefits of the IEM are difficult to assess but are likely to be small. Electricity is less traded than other primary fuels, though rising in the ENTSO-E area from 6 per cent in 1976 to 15 per cent by 2015. The ECA (2015) argues that whilst interconnection exists, it is short of the requirements to ensure IEM objectives. According to ACER (2017), some interconnections are not being used to full capacity as they are tied to bilateral agreements and therefore not available to third parties. Furthermore, only about half of connecting capacity is being made available to the market, creating congestion at crossing points. A clear gap identified by the ECA (2015) is the lack of systemic analysis of cross-border gaps within the energy system. The infrastructure for the IEM largely emerges at the sub-regional level, but this can often be difficult to develop due to asymmetric needs for links. Though price reduction effects do not appear to be significant, there is some evidence of convergence (EC 2019). States are also frequently reluctant to allow energy prices to be solely determined by supply and demand. Resistance to liberalisation remains strong, with many member states still reluctant to trust market integration as a security tool. This is especially evident amongst Eastern European states driven by vulnerabilities and dependence on Russian gas. According to Boersma and Goldthau (2016), this has replaced liberalisation with securitisation with increased control via diverse supplies and control over these supplies being the desired strategy for many states. Hawker et al. (2017) note that a lack of confidence in the IEM to deliver security of supply is evident from the aforementioned capacity mechanisms developed by states which have the potential to distort markets, with the result that system investment is state- rather than market-driven. Across the EU there is a largely uncoordinated patchwork of these capacity mechanisms, reflecting that states see security as an issue for them and not for regional markets. This reinforces the notion that states seek to limit market failures within NES (Prontera 2017). Thus states seek to retain control through national energy champions which could potentially emerge as multinational energy conglomerates as they fulfil their objective to deliver national energy security.

EXTRA-EUROPEAN TERRITORIAL ENERGY INFRASTRUCTURE

As mentioned above, by virtue of it being a large net importer of energy, the EU is a major player within the global energy system (Goldthau and Sitter 2015). This is based on longstanding and extensive links between itself and third party (mainly primary) energy suppliers. Whilst states differ on ideas of openness to these links and how they should inform energy security, expanding such links is central to the EU's energy strategy as it develops infrastructures to diversify supply without creating (or reinforcing) dependence. The logic of such a strategy is to create a resilient energy system with sufficient capacity in external links to ensure no (or minimal) disruption should any single link become subject to disruption (natural or otherwise). This implies the expansion not just of littoral points of access for energy but also transmission through the fixed links of inter-continental pipeline systems. The risk of disruption also reflects a strategic vulnerability, despite its market power. Thus there is a paradox in the development of these large-scale systems, namely that the long-term objective of EU states is to render them redundant via self-sufficiency. Energy dependence works both ways as the EU is dependent on imports but this dependence is attractive to suppliers. This gives the EU power over rival suppliers as they become dependent on this market, with an inability to quickly switch between markets as the necessary infrastructure is largely absent and cannot be built quickly (Dannreuther 2016). This reflects that energy infrastructure investment needs security of demand (Goldthau and Sitter 2015).

These transcontinental energy systems reflect an alignment of state and corporate interests, with multinational consortia (a mix of state-owned and commercial entities) driving their development. The EU (as an institutional system) only begins to really get involved in these systems (largely through the application of IEM) when they enter its 'territory', though states have often pushed back on applying such conditions. This suggests there are limits to the extent states will pursue supranationalism in energy systems. This reflects the retention of the EES as an essentially state-based system, with security and the energy mix national competences (Szulecki 2017). These systems are shaped by inter-governmental agreement to allow access and transit for these fixed energy systems. The need to develop links for security can often pit states against each other as they deal with third parties. This was evident not only with the South Stream pipeline but also with Nord Stream 2, which pitted the supply security of Western states against that of Eastern Europe, where supply is less secure (de Jong and Van de Graaf 2020). Europe does not speak with one voice, despite the objectives of Energy Union. Indeed these objectives can run up against state interests where the EU seeks to apply them to non-EU suppliers, which then places infrastructure development in jeopardy.

Oil

As mentioned above, as oil mainly arrives via maritime systems, the pan-European/transcontinental pipeline systems only deliver up to 20 per cent of the total imports. These are through two pipeline systems: Druzhba and Norpipe. The Druzhba system dates from the early 1960s and transports oil from Russia, the Urals and the Caspian region to Mozyr in Belarus, where it splits: the northern route serves refineries in North West Europe, while the southern route moves oil towards the Balkans. TEN-E has sought to develop further links in the Druzhba system (see above), especially for landlocked states in Eastern Europe. The current capacity is 1.2–1.4 million barrels per day (bpd), but can rise to a maximum 2 million barrels. Norpipe transports oil from the North Sea fields and has a capacity of up to 45 million barrels per annum. However, with the UK leaving the EU, this pipeline system is now wholly outside the EU. From the UK, oil is transhipped via maritime channels into the

European refinery system. There are other pipeline systems in the EU neighbourhood, but these tend to be used to transport oil from the point of extraction to the nearest port.

Gas

Without doubt the most salient intercontinental/pan-European energy systems are those delivering gas to the EU. There are four main gas corridors into the EU:

- the North East corridor from Russia
- the North Western corridor from Norway and the UK
- the South West corridor from North Africa
- the South East corridor from the Caucasus.

In total the EU has 30 cross-border gas interconnection points between itself and third states. Six of these are from the North Sea and four are from North Africa. The rest feed gas either directly or via third parties from the states of the former Soviet Union (Austvik 2016) including the Nord Stream (which is a direct link between Russia and Germany); the Northern Lights (Yamal), which transits via Belarus; and the Brotherhood and Soyuz pipelines (which both transit via Ukraine). These pipelines are at the crux of a complex system that moves gas from East to West Europe. The problem of transit through third states has led to the development of either bypassing routes (such as the Blue Stream and TurkStream systems which move gas to Europe via Turkey) or direct links such as Nord Stream and Nord Stream 2 (Morningstar et al. 2019).

The EU's dependence on Russian gas reflects longstanding links that evolved parallel to the Cold War when the latter had the gas whilst the former had the technology to enable its transmission (Högselius 2012, Dannreuther 2016). The links reflect path dependencies within the global energy system and the EU wants to avoid infrastructure lock-in with Russian gas (Raines and Tomlinson 2016). In 2018, 11 EU27 states depended on Russia for 75 per cent of their gas. This dependence has been a primary driving factor behind the Energy Union, especially after the supply disruptions in 2006 and 2009 and the fear that these risks could re-emerge. The 2009 Ukraine–Russia dispute highlighted the vulnerability of 15 (mainly Eastern EU) states to the disruption of gas flows from Russia. These states suffered from a lack of diversity of supplies and had to draw upon stores of gas to cope (Andersen et al. 2016).

The dispute led to the development of two new pipelines that sought to access supplies direct from Russia rather than via the unstable Ukrainian links. These were the Yamal pipeline between Russia and Poland (and on to Germany) and the aforementioned Nord Stream and Nord Stream 2. The latter create direct links between Germany and Russia (bypassing Poland). Russia relies on Germany (as the EU's largest gas market) to generate the market to scale up its energy production. Johnson and Derrick (2012) argue that bypassing transit (notably EU) states risks splintering Europe and exposing the vulnerability of Eastern EU states dependent on Russian gas imports. Direct access from Russia to already energy-secure states and reinforcing their diversity makes the less secure even more vulnerable. This allows Russia to use energy infrastructure as a geostrategic weapon. The EU believes fragmentation weakens its power; Russia argues the risk was not with them but the transit states; hence the need for extra capacity that bypassed these states (Bozhilova and Hashimoto 2010). This impact can be militated by increasing west to east gas flows via more systemic interconnection, as prioritised within TEN-E (Yafimava 2018, Hancher and Marhold 2019). The EU has also sought to militate against this power by seeking to lock Russia into its liberal energy regime. However this has not been successful (Goldthau and Sitter 2015, Prontera 2017, Schmidt-Felzmann 2019).

To reduce this dependence on Russian gas, the Southern corridor is being developed. This is a multi-pipeline system supplying South Eastern EU states with gas from the Caspian region via the Trans-Anatolian Pipeline (TANAP) connecting Turkey to the Caucasus (via the South Caucasus Pipeline). This is linked to the Trans Adriatic Pipeline (TAP), which connects to the Balkans and on to Italy (Aoun 2015) .The aim is to allow and expand access to Caspian gas to enable it to comprise up to 20 per cent of EU needs by 2020. Siddi (2019) doubts the strategic value for the Southern corridor as it would not allow significant diversification; it represents less than 3 per cent of total EU consumption. This is compounded by the fact that the pipeline's capacity cannot easily be expanded; and there is also the rising competition for this gas, notably from China. Russia's response to this was the aforementioned TurkStream pipeline as it sought to defend its position and then use TAP to gain access to the EU market (Amirova-Mammadova 2017). The EU is also seeking to build more capacity in the Mediterranean, but Algerian gas production is in decline.

Not all states are equally vulnerable or sensitive to the threat, with many Western states merely treating Russian gas as one part of the energy mix (Judge and Maltby 2017). Pardo Sierra (2010) argues that some states (notably Germany, France and Italy) are more amenable to Russia and see it as a strategic partner; but, unsurprisingly, the CEE states see Russia differently (Yorucu and Mehmet 2018). Though there is an argument (as mentioned above) that Russia has little interest in under-mining customer sentiment in its major markets, its dependence on this market is too great. There is a ratcheting up of extra-EU infrastructure as part of EU strategy, but states (especially Northern states) are less concerned with more choice and diversity of supply. Russian gas enters the energy mix without creating dependence. Indeed this dependence is not what it was as the EU has sought to build the infrastructure to diver-sify supplies from southern Eurasia and North Africa, as well as through building facilities to facilitate LNG supplies. Judge et al. (2016) argue that much of the analysis understates the complexity of the EU–Russia relationship, with the mutual economic benefits of energy trade super-seding day-to-day geopolitical disputes. Moreover, the infrastructure deployed and developed by both entities represents a large sunk cost which has generated path dependence within the energy relationship (Dannreuther 2016, Sharples 2016).

Electricity

As of 2016, the EU had 82 electricity connectors with non-EU states. However these do not involve long-distance transmission and are with non-EU Western European states (Switzerland, the UK and Norway), states in the former Soviet Union, and Turkey and Morocco, connecting to the nearest segment of the EU grid. The EU treats non-EU Western European states as part of the EU interconnection as they only have links with other EU states and not with other non-EU states (EC 2017b). Of especial note in this ongoing process of interconnection are the plans for the Euro-Mediterranean grid, which will promote long-distance transmission of electricity across the Mediterranean via a high-voltage line between Tunisia and Italy. In part, the plan is to enable EU states to access solar power-generating capacity in North Africa. The extra-EU generation and supply of renewables have had little discernible impact thus far (ENTSO-E 2019), with early initiatives such as Destertec (based on linking solar power in North Africa to Europe) having been stillborn (Nies 2009). There is also a planned link between Libya and Greece for much the same purpose, as well as a plan to end the energy isolation of Cyprus through links with Israel. These links are to help isolated parts of the EU to have secure supply from non-EU states to end islands of under-development of electricity systems where connection to non-EU neighbours are a complement to support EU links.

Over the longer term, transcontinental links between China and the EU are being explored, exploiting China's capability with high-voltage direct transmission technology (Ardelean and Minnebo 2017). Such strategies reflect not merely China's desire to export its know-how in long-distance transmission and its capacity in the manufacture of renewable energy infrastructure but also to exploit European innovation in green technology. This forms part of a wider Global Energy Interconnection (GEI) initiative promoted by China to link national electricity grids to marry rising global demand for energy through a global renewable energy system by 2070 (Ardelean and Minnebo 2017, Huang 2020). Given the limited cross-border trade where connections are already in place, there does seem reasonable grounds that the plan for the GEI is over-ambitious (Downie 2019).

ENERGY TRANSITION AND EUROPEAN ENERGY INFRASTRUCTURE

The immediate legacy of energy transition for the EES is a shift away from infrastructure based on/driven by hydrocarbons and towards an energy system that enables generation through renewable sources. As with any transition, this process of refocusing the energy system is envisaged to take place over an extended period of time. As of 2017, around 14 per cent of the EU's energy came from renewables (EC 2020). The aim within the Energy Union (as mentioned above) is to increase this to 32 per cent by 2030 – against a backdrop of increased energy use overall. This was via an interim target of 20 per cent by 2020 (EC 2019). By 2019, most EU27 states were on track to meet this target, though how (and when) is at their discretion (Siddi 2016). In terms of usage, renewables comprised (in 2017) around 30 per cent of electricity generation, about 20 per cent of heating and cooling, and about 6 per cent of transport energy consumption (EC 2019). Measured by EU production, renewables are marginally the largest single source, at nearly 30 per cent (up from less than 13 per cent in 1990); of course this hides the EU's high import dependency and high consumption of hydrocarbons. Of the EU's renewable energy generation, nearly three-quarters is wind and hydroelectricity. Solar is just less than a quarter, with the rest (geothermal, thermal, tide, wave, etc.) being marginal to the energy mix.

The broad geostrategic logic of the energy transition is to further lower import dependence in the EU energy mix. Whilst this logic is not universal for all states, it does exist alongside a more consensual view with regard to the value of sustainability within energy systems and international commitments by states to limit climate change. However as energy security is a national issue, there is the potential for the transition to reinforce the aforementioned fragmentation as descaling of generation enables states to develop their own renewable generation to further free themselves from energy imports at both extra-EU and intra-EU level. States have the ability to alter their own mix to shape their own security, so can secure their own interests first (Pérez et al. 2019). This is also compounded by some states actively resisting the shift towards renewables for political (as well as security) reasons (Handke 2018). This has led to divergent pathways between states with regard to energy transition. As many Eastern European states do not have the right conditions (for example, obsolete infrastructure) and/or finance for mass generation of renewable power, they will turn to indigenous resources to promote security (Boie et al. 2014). These are often 'dirty' hydrocarbons (notably coal). The states pushing renewables are less price-sensitive in terms of consumers but also see the spread of renewables as a commercial opportunity (EP 2009a).

For the EU, these renewable resources need to be seen as an EU-wide asset and that – whilst there is some degree of the distributed generation within a renewable system – this does not militate against the need for large-scale energy systems as there is still a need for this energy to be transported from point of generation to point of consumption. Thus – within the context of the TEN-E programme – seeking to ensure that interconnection allows uneven renewable generation to be spread throughout the EU (notably to those states where both wind and solar power are not as available) is a core priority. The ability of this to happen depends upon the rate of interconnection by businesses and the desire by states with a high renewable energy potential not to focus on narrow national interests in the development of renewable energy infrastructure. Furthermore, the EU argues against national retrenchment in renewables as intermittency of supply (without large-scale storage) could mean that abundance can easily turn into scarcity, leaving national systems vulnerable. For example, growth in wind power has caused problems when strong winds overload systems. The lack of connection means that some places can have low (even negative) prices during strong winds due to the generation of excess energy and need interconnections to spread their overload to other systems. Such fluctuations will not be spatially consistent, so interconnection will still allow states to access renewable generation even if their own sources (at any point in time) leave them vulnerable. Thus, according to the European Commission, an EU-wide renewable system would be more effective and stable than a disaggregated one. Notions that such co-operation at technical and economic levels could deepen integration are speculative as these problems are compounded by the planning systems that limit easy transnational grid development where interconnection decisions remain at the national level. Reflecting on this multitude of processes Pérez et al. (2019) argue that this creates two Europes: one that remains wedded to hydrocarbons and the other that is undergoing advanced transition.

This proposed scaling up of the transition process at the European level goes against the decentralising logic of the renewable energy transition in which disaggregated energy production increases in salience through the rise of new forms of generation such as prosumers – where users can be both consumers and producers of electricity (Egyedi and Mehos 2012). However Scholten et al. (2020) disagree with this, arguing that the shift towards renewables is likely to be a catalyst for the scaling up of regional systems to create 'supergrids' due to the cost of losses in long-distance transmission. In practice, the renewable energy system is likely to involve multi-scalar generation (Tagliapietra et al. 2019). Where scaling up is rationalised within the EES, so there is a push to develop intensive interconnection to allow all states to access renewables. There is already a belief that the characteristics of renewables are already causing issues, with Boie et al. (2014) estimating that 80 per cent of interconnection bottlenecks are due to the demands of renewable energy. As this process develops not only will interconnection capacity need to increase, but the shift towards non-hydroelectric renewable sources requires that areas of high solar power potential (notably Iberia) and wind power (the North Sea) are fully connected to the rest of the European grid. This is to allow those states with low renewable energy potential to add these sources to their energy mix. This trend also means a renewed need for action on storage. According to Boie et al., efforts on formal energy integration are still far too fragmented, and co-ordination on issues such as planning still piecemeal.

A legacy of this energy transition is that it has the ability to render much of Europe's pre-existing infrastructure systems redundant, especially those based on the use of hydrocarbons (Agora Energiewende 2019). Once built, energy systems have lifetimes measured in decades

(IRENA 2018). This varies from 20 years for wind farms to 80 years for a gas transmission grid. For the EC (2015) this potential obsolescence of key components of its energy system is one of the major problems it faces in the shift towards decarbonisation. Thus one of the key objectives in this process is 'future proofing' the energy infrastructure system (see below). This reflects that energy systems can involve significant sunk costs that could be irretrievable if a way is not found to redeploy such systems during and after transition (IRENA 2018). Thus the transition is not simply about transforming the energy mix; it is also about transition infrastructuring allowing it to be redeployed to support the move towards renewables. This is inherent in the interconnection process, which seeks to allow access to renewables without sacrificing pre-existing systems (EC 2019). Thus states can meet renewable targets without the need for widespread new investment in generation. It also offers a potentially cheaper process of transitioning and does not involve a widespread reinvention of generation (Agora Energiewende 2019). This should also facilitate the potential advantage of states accessing renewables (rather than hydrocarbons) during times of peak demand (EP 2009a). PricewaterhouseCoopers (PwC 2010) argue that the cost of refocusing the energy system towards renewables is quite small (about 2–3 per cent of GDP) but that the main barriers are regulatory and institutional (see also EC 2019c).

Gas is expected to become an increasingly important back-up for generating electricity (as well as a key transition technology) as the EU switches towards renewables. This means the system may have to be adapted for new types of gases (Kotek et al. 2019). Whilst individual states are encouraging and starting the use of alternative gases, these are still a small share of the energy mix (EC 2020). The utilisation of pre-existing infrastructure for low carbon gas could save €76 billion to €125 billion between 2018 and 2050. However these gases tend to be more localised (in terms of production and consumption), and thus do not require the large-scale transmission systems in place for natural gas (Dutton et al. 2017). This risks further fragmenting the system (Newbery et al. 2018). The widespread use of alternative gases does face problems linked to availability, costs, emissions and utilisation of pre-existing systems. This could cause short-term problems. As the span on energy infrastructure is up to 50 years the system could be redundant before the end of its lifespan due to the energy transition. The effect could be that investment (to meet current needs and strategies) could be deterred due to the fear of such redundancy (Dutton et al. 2017).

The decarbonisation agenda sees a declined use of natural gas, but existing gas storage could also be transferred to alternative gases. In some cases, this transfer could be easy, while in others some degree of adjustment might be needed (EC 2020). These uncertainties are higher for hydrogen than for other alternatives gases (such as biomethane). Whilst these gases could use pre-existing transmission systems, it is widely accepted that substantial investment in generating capabilities will be needed (IGU 2019). This is likely to be especially high if these gases are to be generated from renewable electricity to ensure their carbon neutrality. This suggests their generation needs to be close to these resources or have ready access to them (Frontier Economics 2019).

CONCLUSIONS

As with transport, there has been a longstanding process of informal integration within the energy sector. This has been based around notions of states seeking to address issues of energy security. Despite the EU's desire to increase the level of supranationality within the network of national systems that is the EES, it is still the states and their interaction that drives the process. It is states that decide on issues such as the energy mix and who to connect with to meet the requirements of national energy strategy. States are also still given considerable discretion (through devices such as capacity mechanisms) with regard to their NES within the EU's legislative activity to create an IEM. Whilst the EU saw the formalisation of NES integration as recognition that energy security was a common problem that needed a common strategy, states sought to preserve their discretion in such areas. As such they tend to treat systemic integration as an adjunct to territorial strategy rather than as a common geostrategic concern amongst states. Arguably, the greatest impact of supranationalism on this process is through acting as a forum for co-operation and co-ordination between states to address areas of common concern. Activism in energy infrastructure by the EU through the TEN-E programme has had limited efficacy upon such systems where the major drivers remain the interaction between states and the global energy system.

NOTES

1   Energy infrastructure comprises a diverse collection of assets, from the
     facilities used to extract primary material (such as coal mines and oil plat-

forms) to those used to store, refine, process and distribute these materials in crude or processed form (such as oil refineries/storage and power stations), to those dedicated channels/infrastructure used to convey these processed resources to the final user. These stages involve strong overlaps not only between transport and energy sectors (notably maritime channels) but also the dedicated pipelines systems that move energy resources within and between states.

2 Import dependency is the average of the share of a state's energy consumption that is sourced from outside the state's borders and could include imports from other EU states.

3 This represents about 60 per cent of the EU's total energy imports.

4 With the UK leaving the EU, Norpipe is now entirely non-EU.

5 Available data did not exclude the UK at the time of collection.

6 A mainstream refinery is one that operates above a certain capacity, in this case 2.5 million tonnes per annum.

7 This is one of several pipelines used to deliver fuel to support military resources throughout Europe.

8 Around 75 per cent of the EU's consumed gas operates within flexible markets where bidirectionality allows flows to be moved across space.

9 The UK also has an interconnector with Norway.

10 Whilst the Treaty of Lisbon (the EU's constitutional basis) made the internal energy market (IEM) and energy efficiency issues of EU competence, in practice power still lies with states.

REFERENCES

Aalto, P., and Korkmaz Temel, D. (2014). European energy security: Natural gas and the integration process. *JCMS: Journal of Common Market Studies*, Vol. 52, No. 4, pp. 758–774.

Agency for the Cooperation of Energy Regulators (ACER) (2017). Annual report on the results of monitoring the internal electricity and gas markets in 2016. Available at www.acer.europa.eu; date accessed 22/06/2020.

Agency for the Cooperation of Energy Regulators (ACER) (2019). Consolidated report on the progress of electricity and gas projects of common interest – 2019. Available at www.acer.europa.eu; date accessed 17/06/2020.

Agora Energiewende (2019). European energy transition 2030: The big picture. Ten Priorities for the next European Commission to meet the EU's 2030 targets and accelerate towards 2050. Available at www.agora-energiewende.de; date accessed 08/07/2020.

Amirova-Mammadova, S. (2017). *Pipeline politics and natural gas supply from Azerbaijan to Europe.* Wiesbaden: Springer.

Andersen, S. S., Goldthau, A., and Sitter, N. (eds), (2016). *Energy Union: Europe's new liberal mercantilism?* London: Palgrave Macmillan.

Aoun, M. C. (2015). *European energy security challenges and global energy trends: Old wine in new bottles?* Rome: Istituto affari internazionali.

Ardelean, M., and Minnebo, P. (2017). *A China-EU electricity transmission link: Assessment of potential connecting countries and routes.* Luxembourg: Publications Office of the European Union.

Asia Pacific Energy Research Centre (APERC) (2007). A quest for energy security in the 21st century. Institute of Energy Economics, Japan. Available at https://aperc.or.jp; date accessed 27/05/2020.

Aurora Energy Research (2016). *Dash for interconnection: The impact of interconnectors on the GB market.* Oxford: Aurora Energy Research.

Austvik, O. G. (2016). The Energy Union and security-of-gas supply. *Energy Policy*, Vol. 96, pp. 372–382.

Battaglini, A., Komendantova, N., Brtnik, P., and Patt, A. (2012). Perception of barriers for expansion of electricity grids in the European Union. *Energy Policy*, Vol. 47, pp. 254–259.

Benson, D., and Russel, D. (2015). Patterns of EU energy policy outputs: Incrementalism or punctuated equilibrium? *West European Politics*, Vol. 38, pp. 185–205.

Boersma, T., and Goldthau, A. (2016). Wither the EU's market making project in energy: From liberalization to securitization? In Andersen, S. S., Goldthau, A., and Sitter, N. (eds), *Energy Union: Europe's new liberal mercantilism?* London: Palgrave Macmillan, pp. 99–113.

Boie, I., Fernandes, C., Frías, P., and Klobasa, M. (2014). Efficient strategies for the integration of renewable energy into future energy infrastructures in Europe: An analysis based on transnational modelling and case studies for nine European regions. *Energy Policy*, Vol. 67, pp. 170–185.

Bouzarovski, S., Bradshaw, M., and Wochnik, A. (2015). Making territory through infrastructure: The governance of natural gas transit in Europe. *Geoforum*, Vol. 64, pp. 217–228.

Bozhilova, D., and Hashimoto, T. (2010). EU–Russia energy negotiations: A choice between rational self-interest and collective action. *European Security*, Vol. 19, No. 4, pp. 627–642.

BP (2019). BP statistical review of world energy. Available at www.bp.com; date accessed 12/05/2020.

Braun, J. (2011). EU energy policy under the Treaty of Lisbon rules: Between a new policy and business as usual. Available at www.ceps.eu; date accessed 28/05/2020.

Chatham House (2016). Europe's Energy Union: Foreign policy implications for energy security, climate and competitiveness. Available at www.chathamhouse.org; date accessed 27/05/2020.

Cherp, A, (2012). Defining energy security takes more than asking around. *Energy Policy*, Vol. 48, pp. 841–842.

Cherp, A., and Jewell, J. (2014). The concept of energy security: Beyond the four As. *Energy Policy*, Vol. 75, pp. 415–421.

Concawe (2020). Refineries map. Available at https://www.concawe.eu/refineries-map; date accessed 20/05/2020

Crisan, A., and Kuhn, M. (2016). The energy network: Infrastructure as the hardware of the Energy Union. In Andersen, S. S., Goldthau, A., and Sitter, N.

(eds), *Energy Union: Europe's new liberal mercantilism?* London: Palgrave Macmillan, pp. 165–182.

Dannreuther, R. (2016). EU–Russia energy relations in context. *Geopolitics*, Vol. 21, No. 4, pp. 913–921.

de Jong, M., and Van de Graaf, T. (2020). Lost in regulation: Nord Stream 2 and the limits of the European Commission's geo-economic power. *Journal of European Integration*, Vol. 42, No. 1, pp. 129–145.

Dieckhöner, C., Lochner, S., and Lindenberger, D. (2013). European natural gas infrastructure: The impact of market developments on gas flows and physical market integration. *Applied Energy*, Vol. 102, pp. 994–1003.

Downie, E. (2019). Powering the globe: Lessons from Southeast Asia for China's global energy interconnection initiative. Available at www.energypolicy .columbia.edu; date accessed 26/11/2020.

Dutton, J., Fischer, L., and Gaventa, J. (2017). Infrastructure for a changing energy system: The next generation of policies for the European Union. E3G Report. Available at www.e3g.com; date accessed 17/07/2020.

Egyedi, T. M., and Mehos, D. C. (eds) (2012). *Inverse infrastructures: Disrupting networks from below.* Cheltenham, UK and Northampton, MA, USA: Edward Elgar Publishing.

Energy Information Administration (EIA) (2020). International energy outlook. Available at www.eia.gov; date accessed 13/05/2020.

European Community (EC) (1993). Treaty of Maastricht, article 3n and 3t, Title II. Provisions amending the treaty establishing the European Economic Community with a view to establishing the European Community. Brussels. Title XII, Trans-European networks, Article 129b, c, d.

European Community (EC) (2010). Energy infrastructure priorities for 2020 and beyond: A blueprint for an integrated European energy network, COM(2010) 677 final. Brussels: European Commission.

European Community (EC) (2010a). The revision of the Trans-European Energy Network Policy (TEN-E): Final report. Available at www.europa.eu.int; date accessed 03/06/2020.

European Commission (EC) (2011). A growth package for integrated European infrastructures. Available at www.europa.eu.int; date accessed 03/06/2020.

European Commission (EC) (2013). Guidelines for trans-European energy infra-structure as regards the Union list of projects of common interest. Brussels: European Commission.

European Commission (EC) (2015). The role of gas storage in internal market and in ensuring security of supply. Available at www.europa.eu.int; date accessed 18/05/2020.

European Commission (EC) (2015a). A framework strategy for a resilient Energy Union with a forward-looking climate change policy. Available at www .europa.eu.int; date accessed 03/06/2020.

European Commission (EC) (2016). EU strategy for liquefied natural gas and gas storage. Available at www.europa.eu.int date accessed 18/05/2020.

European Commission (EC) (2017). Follow-up study to the LNG and storage strategy. Available at www.europa.eu.int; date accessed 28/05/2020.

European Commission (EC) (2017a). Communication on strengthening Europe's energy networks, COM(2017) 718 final. Available at www.europa.eu.int; date accessed 05/06/2020.

European Commission (EC) (2017b). Electricity interconnections with neighbouring countries: Second report of the Commission Expert Group on electricity interconnection targets. Available at www.europa.eu.int; date accessed 30/06/2020.

European Commission (EC) (2018). *Investment needs in trans-European energy infrastructure up to 2030 and beyond.* Luxembourg: Publications Office of the European Union.

European Commission (EC) (2018a). Evaluation of the TEN-E regulation and assessing the impacts of alternative policy scenarios. Available at www.europa.eu.int; date accessed 17/06/2020.

European Commission (EC) (2018b). The role of trans-European gas infrastructure in the light of the 2050 decarbonisation targets. Available at www.europa.eu.int; date accessed 17/07/2020.

European Commission (EC) (2019). Energy balance sheets: 2017 data. Available at www.europa.eu.int; date accessed 07/05/2020.

European Commission (EC) (2019a). EU energy in figures 2019. Available at www.europa.eu.int; date accessed 11/05/2020.

European Commission (EC) (2019b). Fourth report on the state of the Energy Union. Available at www.europa.eu.int; date accessed 26/05/2020.

European Commission (EC) (2019c). Renewable energy progress report. Available at www.europa.eu.int; date accessed 10/07/2020.

European Commission (EC) (2019d). Investing in European networks: The Connecting Europe Facility. Available at https://ec.europa.eu/inea/sites/inea; date accessed 10/11/2020.

European Commission (EC) (2020). EU energy in figures. Available at www.europa.eu.int; date accessed 01/12/2020.

European Court of Auditors (ECA) (2015). Improving the security of energy supply by developing the Internal Energy Market: More effort needed. Available www.europa.eu.int; date accessed 24/06/2020.

European Network of Transmission System Operators for Electricity (ENTSO-E) (2018). Electricity in Europe 2017. Available at www.entsoe.org; date accessed 20/05/2020.

European Network of Transmission System Operators for Electricity (ENTSO-E) (2019). Statistical factsheet 2018. Available at www.entsoe.org; date accessed 20/05/2020.

European Network of Transmission System Operators for Gas (ENTSO-G) (2018). Ten-Year Network Development Plan: Infrastructure report. Available at www.entsog.org; date accessed 04/06/2020.

European Network of Transmission System Operators for Gas (ENTSO-G) (2019). The European gas network. Available at www.entsog.org; date accessed 15/05/2020.

European Parliament (EP) (2009). An assessment of the gas and oil pipelines in Europe. Available at http://www.europarl.europa.eu; date accessed 13/05/2020.

European Parliament (EP) (2009a). Infrastructure for renewable energies: A factor of local and regional development. Available at http://www.europarl.europa.eu; date accessed 13/05/2020.

Frontier Economics (2019). The value of gas infrastructure in a climate-neutral Europe. Available at frontiereconomics.com; date accessed 14/07/2020.

FuelsEurope (2019). Statistical report 2019. Available at https://www.fuelseurope.eu; date accessed 12/05/2020.

Giannelli, E., and Fischer, L. (2019), Reassessing the EU's energy infrastructure needs: How to ensure better spending by revising the 'TEN-E' regulation. *E3G Blog*. Available at www.e3g.com; date accessed 17/06/2020.

Glachant, J. M., and Ruester, S. (2014). The EU internal electricity market: Done forever? *Utilities Policy*, Vol. 31, pp. 221–228.

Goldthau, A., and Sitter, N. (2015). Soft power with a hard edge: EU policy tools and energy security. *Review of International Political Economy*, Vol. 22, No. 5, pp. 941–965.

Haghighi, S. (2008). Energy security and the division of competences between the European Community and its members. *European Law Journal*, Vol. 14, No. 4, pp. 461–82.

Hancher, L., and Marhold, A. (2019). A common EU framework regulating import pipelines for gas? Exploring the Commission's proposal to amend the 2009 Gas Directive. *Journal of Energy and Natural Resources Law*, Vol. 37, No. 3, pp. 289–303.

Handke, S. (2018). Renewables and the core of the energy union: How the penta-lateral forum facilitates the energy transition in Western Europe. In Scholten, D. (ed.), *The geopolitics of renewables*. Cham: Springer, pp. 277–303.

Hawker, G., Bell, K., and Gill, S. (2017). Electricity security in the European Union: The conflict between national capacity mechanisms and the single market. *Energy Research and Social Science*, Vol. 24, pp. 51–58.

Helm, D. (2001). The assessment: European networks – competition, interconnection, and regulation. *Oxford Review of Economic Policy*, Vol. 17, No. 3, pp. 297–312.

Helm, D., (2014). The European framework for energy and climate policies. *Energy Policy*, Vol. 64, pp. 29–35.

Högselius, P. (2012). *Red gas: Russia and the origins of European energy dependence*. London: Palgrave Macmillan.

Högselius, P., Åberg, A., and Kaijser, A. (2013). Natural gas in cold war Europe: The making of a critical infrastructure. In Högselius, P., Hommels, A., Kaijser, A., and Van Der Vleuten, E. (eds), *The making of Europe's critical infrastructure: Common connections and shared vulnerabilities*. Basingstoke: Palgrave Macmillan, pp. 27–61.

Huang, Q. (2020). Insights for global energy interconnection from China renewable energy development. *Global Energy Interconnection*, Vol. 3, No. 1, pp. 1–11.

International Energy Agency (IEA) (2005). *Lessons from liberalised electricity markets*. Paris: IEA/OECD.

International Energy Agency (IEA) (2016). Electricity security across borders. Available at www.iea.org; date accessed 28/05/2020.

International Energy Agency (IEA) (2019). World energy report. Available at www.iea.org; date accessed 14/05/2020.

International Gas Union (IGU) (2019). Global gas report 2019. Available at www .igu.org; date accessed 19/05/2020

International Renewable Energy Agency (IRENA) (2018). Renewable energy prospects for the European Union. Available at www.irena.org; date accessed 09/07/2020.

Jacotett, A (2012). Cross-border electricity interconnections for a well-functioning EU internal electricity market. Available at https://www.oxfordenergy.org/ publications; date accessed 21/05/2020.

Johnson, C., and Derrick, M. (2012). A splintered heartland: Russia, Europe, and the geopolitics of networked energy infrastructure. *Geopolitics*, Vol. 17, No. 3, pp. 482–501.

Johnson, D., and Turner, C. (1997). *Trans-European networks: The political economy of integrating Europe's infrastructure.* Basingstoke: Macmillan.

Johnson, D., and Turner, C. (2007). *Strategy and policy for trans-European networks.* Basingstoke: Palgrave Macmillan.

Judge, A., and Maltby, T. (2017). European Energy Union? Caught between securitisation and 'riskification'. *European Journal of International Security*, Vol. 2, No. 2, pp. 179–202.

Judge, A., Maltby, T., and Sharples, J. D. (2016). Challenging reductionism in analyses of EU–Russia energy relations. *Geopolitics*. Vol. 21, No. 4, pp. 751–762.

Kandiyoti, R. (2015). *Powering Europe: Russia, Ukraine, and the energy squeeze.* Basingstoke: Palgrave Macmillan.

Kanellakis, M., Martinopoulos, G., and Zachariadis, T. (2013). European energy policy: A review. *Energy Policy*, Vol. 62, pp. 1020–1030.

King & Spalding (2018). LNG in Europe 2018: An overview of import terminals in Europe, Available at www.kslaw.com; date accessed 18/05/2020.

Kotek, P., del Granado, P. C., Egging, R., and Toth, B. T. (2019). European natural gas infrastructure in the energy transition. 16th International Conference on the European Energy Market (EEM), Ljubljana 18–20 September. IEEE, pp. 1–6.

Kruyt, B., van Vuuren, D. P., de Vries, H. J., and Groenenberg, H. (2009). Indicators for energy security. *Energy Policy*, Vol. 37, No. 6, pp. 2166–2181.

Lagendijk, V. C. (2008). *Electrifying Europe: The power of Europe in the construction of electricity networks.* Amsterdam: Aksant.

Leal-Arcas, R. and Alemany Rios, J., (2015). The creation of a European Energy Union. *European Energy Journal*, Vol. 5, No. 3, 24–60.

Mezősi, A., Pató, Z., and Szabó, L. (2016). Assessment of the EU 10 per cent interconnection target in the context of CO_2 mitigation. *Climate Policy*, Vol. 16, No. 5, pp. 658–672.

Morningstar, R. L., Simonyiolga, A., Khakova, O., and Markina, I. (2019). European energy security and transatlantic cooperation: A current assessment. Atlantic Council Global Energy Issue Brief, June. Available at www .atlanticcouncil.org; date accessed 01/07/2020.

Newbery, D., Pollitt, M. G., Ritz, R. A., and Strielkowski, W. (2018). Market design for a high-renewables European electricity system. *Renewable and Sustainable Energy Reviews*, Vol. 91, pp. 695–707.

Nies, S. (2009). *At the speed of light? Electricity interconnections for Europe.* Paris: Institut français des relations internationales (IFRI).

Nivard M and Kreijkes M (2017) The European refining sector: A diversity of markets. Available at https://www.clingendaelenergy.com; date accessed 12/05/2020.

Ostrowski, W. (2020). The twenty years' crisis of European energy security: Central and Eastern Europe and the US. *Geopolitics*, pp. 1–23.

Pardo Sierra, O. (2010). A corridor through thorns: EU energy security and the Southern Energy Corridor. *European Security*, Vol. 19, No. 4, pp. 643–660.

Pérez, M. D. L. E. M., Scholten, D., and Stegen, K. S. (2019). The multi-speed energy transition in Europe: Opportunities and challenges for EU energy security. *Energy Strategy Reviews*, Vol. 26, p. 100415.

Pollitt, M. G. (2018). The European single market in electricity: An economic assessment. EPRG Working Paper 1815, Cambridge Working Paper in Economics 1832. Available at www.eprg.group.cam.ac.uk; date accessed 19/06/2020.

Poyry (2016). Cost and benefits of GB interconnection. Report for National Infrastructure Commission. Available at www.nic.org.uk; date accessed 21/05/2020.

PricewaterhouseCoopers (PwC) (2010) 100% renewable electricity: A roadmap to 2050 for Europe and North Africa. Available at www.pwc.com/sustainability; date accessed 10/07/2020.

Prontera, A. (2017). Forms of state and European energy security: Diplomacy and pipelines in South-Eastern Europe. *European Security*, Vol. 26, No. 2, pp. 273–298.

Puka, L., and Szulecki, K. (2014). The politics and economics of cross-border electricity infrastructure: A framework for analysis. *Energy Research and Social Science*, Vol. 4, pp. 124–134.

Raines, T., and Tomlinson, S. (2016). *Europe's Energy Union: Foreign policy implications for energy security, climate and competitiveness.* London: Chatham House for the Royal Institute of International Affairs.

Ringel, M., and Knodt, M. (2018). The governance of the European Energy Union: Efficiency, effectiveness and acceptance of the Winter Package 2016. *Energy Policy*, Vol. 112, pp. 209–220.

Schmidt-Felzmann, A. (2019). Negotiating at cross purposes: Conflicts and continuity in the EU's trade and energy relations with Russia, pre-and post-2014. *Journal of European Public Policy*, Vol. 26, No. 12, pp. 1900–1916.

Scholten, D., Bazilian, M., Overland, I., and Westphal, K. (2020). The geopolitics of renewables: New board, new game. *Energy Policy*, Vol. 138, pp. 111–159.

Schubert, S. R., Pollak, J., and Kreutler, M. (2016). *Energy policy of the European Union.* Basingstoke: Macmillan.

Sharples, J. D. (2016). The shifting geopolitics of Russia's natural gas exports and their impact on EU-Russia gas relations. *Geopolitics*, Vol. 21, No. 4, pp. 880–912.

Siddi, M. (2016). The EU's Energy Union: A sustainable path to energy security? *International Spectator*, Vol. 51, No. 1, pp. 131–144.

Siddi, M. (2019). The EU's botched geopolitical approach to external energy policy: The case of the Southern Gas Corridor. *Geopolitics*, Vol. 24, No.1, pp. 124–144.

Szulecki, K. (ed.) (2017). *Energy security in Europe: Divergent perceptions and policy challenges*. Cham, Switzerland: Springer.

Szulecki, K., Fischer, S., Gullberg, A. T., and Sartor, O. (2016). Shaping the 'Energy Union': Between national positions and governance innovation in EU energy and climate policy. *Climate Policy*, Vol. 16, No. 5, pp. 548–567.

Tagliapietra, S., Zachmann, G., Edenhofer, O., Glachant, J. M., Linares, P., and Loeschel, A. (2019). The European Union energy transition: Key priorities for the next five years. *Energy Policy*, Vol. 132, pp. 950–954.

Van der Vleuten, E., and Kaijser, A. (2005). Networking Europe. *History and Technology*, Vol. 21, No. 1, pp. 21–48.

Van der Vleuten, E., and Lagendijk, V. (2010). Interpreting transnational infrastructure vulnerability: European blackout and the historical dynamics of transnational electricity governance. *Energy Policy*, Vol. 38, No. 4, pp. 2053–2062.

Van der Vleuten, E., and Lagendijk, V. (2010a). Transnational infrastructure vulnerability: The historical shaping of the 2006 European 'blackout'. *Energy Policy*, Vol. 38, No. 4, pp. 2042–2052.

Wettestad, J., Eikeland, P. O., and Nilsson, M. (2012). EU climate and energy policy: A hesitant supranational turn. *Global Environmental Politics*, Vol. 12, No. 2, pp. 67–86.

Winzer, C. (2012). Conceptualizing energy security. *Energy Policy*, Vol. 46, pp. 36–48.

World Economic Forum (WEF) (2019). Global competitiveness report 2019. Available at www.wef.org; date accessed 20/05/2020.

Yafimava, K. (2018). Building new gas transportation infrastructure in the EU: What are the rules of the game? Oxford Institute for Energy Studies OIES Paper NG 134. Available at https://ora.ox.ac.uk; date accessed 03/07/2020.

Yorucu, V., and Mehmet, O. (2018). *The southern energy corridor: Turkey's role in European energy security*. Cham, Switzerland: Springer.

Zachmann, G. (2013) Electricity infrastructure: More border crossings or a borderless Europe? Bruegel Policy Contribution, No. 2013/05, Brussels.

4. European information infrastructure

INTRODUCTION

Like other infrastructures, the notion of European-ness within information infrastructures is born of interconnectivity between national systems driven by ongoing processes of technological and commercial change. These have helped create a narrative of a borderless global system (which is largely illusory) but have also increasingly enmeshed a state's information infrastructure with its territorial objectives (MGI 2016). At the European level, the focal point of action lay within creating a common information area which is focused on enabling operators to create pan-European strategies to service national markets. Thus, as much as there is a narrative with regard to the European-ness of information infrastructure, the state remains the focal point of the information infrastructure evolution. This chapter will focus on the development of European broadband infrastructure.[1] In so doing, it will explore the dimension of co-operative territoriality between European states as they evolve national systems within the context of a rapidly evolving global information economy. Initially this chapter will examine national broadband systems before moving on to co-operative efforts (often via the EU) to support the development of national information infrastructure (NII) through the creation of the aforementioned common information area and the (now largely redundant) Trans-European Telecommunications Networks initiative (TEN-Telecom). The chapter then moves on to examine co-operative efforts to facilitate a network of NIIs that complement the territorial state's strategic objectives of cohesion and security.

THE EUROPEAN INFORMATION INFRASTRUCTURE SYSTEM

As with other European systems, the building blocks of the European information infrastructure system (EII) are the national systems that have developed along their own unique trajectories. Arguably, no other infrastructure system has assumed greater political, economic and social significance over the past two decades than the rapidly evolving information infrastructures. These infrastructures have become key points of territorial strategy as the digitisation of economic, political and social activity reshapes the state's infrastructural mandate (Turner 2020). Narratives surrounding policy initiatives such as the information society – by, for example, promoting access to essential public services through the NII or by enabling wider access through communal points of access, the creation of user groups, etc. – have underlined how states see the territorial penetration of these technologies as a means of shaping and influencing civil society (Mann 2012). In short, the NII is a channel for infrastructural power, where its efficacy as a means of asserting territoriality depends not simply on universality of access but also on effective utilisation by all socio-economic groupings within a territory (Gruber et al. 2014, OECD 2017, Briglauer and Gugler 2019).

The assertion of sovereignty over NII occurs against a context of a need for these systems to interconnect within other NIIs through intergovernmental agreement (Irion 2013, Taylor 2020). The framework for this interconnection is through co-operative forums, notably the International Telecommunications Union (ITU). These set the standards for interaction and interconnection of national systems to ensure both hard and soft infrastructure systems of NII are interoperable to allow for seamless interconnection. This allows for voice and data traffic to move from one jurisdiction to another without infringing territorial rights. For European states, Shahin (2011) argues that the co-operative framework provided by the European Conference of Postal and Telecommunications Administrations (CEPT) is a more effective means of conveying the states' interests within the ITU. This inter-governmental co-operation in evolving EIS is extended through a further range of official standards bodies such as European Telecommunications Standards Institute (ETSI), the European Committee for Standardization (CEN) and the European Committee for Electrotechnical Standardization (CENELEC).

This underscores that supranationalism – as noted below – has a very limited role within EIS evolution.

When compared to other regions, the EU+4 states have generally mature information infrastructure systems (Dutta and Lanvin 2019). This maturity is demonstrated by the extensiveness of usage across a population (as measured by fixed and mobile broadband subscriptions), the ability to absorb new technologies and (as noted below) the speed of the underlying infrastructure. Crude indices such as the World Economic Forum's assessment of telecommunications infrastructure (WEF 2019) offer some degree of comparison between NII but do tend to understate intra-group variances which are evident between Western and Eastern Europe, with the former showing higher levels of NII maturity. Moreover, such measures of NII development are based merely on measures such as information and communications technology (ICT) adoption and offer no real reference to underlying physical systems. Though again, when this is measured via a proxy such as internet download speed, the same type of variation between states appears (World Population Review 2020).

Across European OECD states, total access paths to telecommunications (including narrow and broadband lines) have risen from 10 million in 1996 to nearly 40 million in 2018 (OECD 2019). By 2019, these states had on average 35.4 subscriptions per 100 inhabitants, varying from 47 per 100 inhabitants in Switzerland to just over 20 per 100 inhabitants in Poland (OECD 2019). These penetration rates show a very close positive correlation with GDP per capita. Within the EU27, 88 per cent of households had access to broadband in 2019, up from 46 per cent in 2008. Switzerland and Norway have near universal penetration (Eurostat 2020). Internet access for households is 90 per cent for the EU27, up from 59 per cent in 2008. Broadband penetration for EU27 enterprises is slightly better, with 96 per cent of all businesses having access to this technology.[2] For EU+4 states (across all fixed and mobile access technologies), broadband coverage rose to near universality in 2019 (99.9 per cent of all households). This extra coverage is driven by the pervasiveness of satellite access in areas where fixed and mobile access may be limited (EC 2019). Of course, broadband is differentiated not simply by access technology but also by speed (see below). The aim is to increase broadband speed to increase the effectiveness of its penetration. By 2018, 95.5 per cent of the EU27's population had download speeds of at least 2 Mbps, 81.8 per cent had at least 30 Mbps and 57.2 per cent had at least 100 Mbps (EC 2019).

Fixed Broadband

Across the EU+4, 97 per cent of households have access to fixed broad-band, with 22 of these states having a penetration above 95 per cent (10 states being above 99 per cent), though in four Eastern European states this rate was below 90 per cent (EC 2018).[3] The share of EU+4 house-holds actually taking up this technology is 78 per cent (EC 2020). For faster next-generation (NGA) fixed access (speeds of at least 30 Mbps), the coverage is 86 per cent of households (up from 48 per cent in 2011), with a take-up rate of 41 per cent.[4] In 11 EU+4 states coverage is over 90 per cent of households, though such high rates of access are lagging in some large states (notably Poland and France) where only around two-thirds of households are covered. Ultrafast broadband (100 Mbps) covers 60 per cent of EU+4 households, with take-up of 26 per cent (EC 2020). This varies widely across the EU+4, with the Benelux states having over 90 per cent penetration, compared to less than 1 per cent in Greece. In terms of fibre to the premises (where the final link between network and the home is upgraded to deal with faster speeds rather than using pre-existing systems), this rose from 10 per cent in 2011 to 30 per cent in 2018. Again, this masks wide variations between EU+4 states, with some states (Latvia, Sweden and Spain) having access to this in over 70 per cent of households whilst in some larger states (notably Germany) the figure is less than 10 per cent. This is an indicator of broadband where the EU+4 compares poorly to its major competitors (OECD 2019). In terms of enterprises, 92 per cent have fixed broadband subscriptions, with 44 per cent having a fast broadband subscription. Access to fixed broad-band is universal amongst large-scale enterprises, though 9 per cent of small and medium-sized enterprises (SMEs) lacked such a subscription (as of 2019). Moreover, 75 per cent of large enterprises have fast fixed broadband, compared to only 40 per cent of SMEs (OECD 2019).

Cohesion is a major theme within fixed broadband strategies, with a presumption that market-led initiatives would leave rural areas under-served. Across the EU+4, in 2019 rural coverage was on the whole lower than urban areas by an average of around 10 per cent (EC 2019), a slight reduction from 2017. Seven EU+4 states have rural fixed broadband coverage of 99 per cent; these are states with a high share of their total population within urban areas. Across the EU+4, 10 per cent of households are not covered by any fixed networks and 41 per cent have no NGA access. In some Eastern European states (notably Poland) rural access to fixed broadband is as low as 50 per cent of households

(EC 2019). This differentiation between rural and urban provision of fixed broadband is sharpened when access to NGA is considered, where average coverage for rural areas is over 30 per cent lower than for urban areas. This gap is only slowly narrowing, with 12 states having less than 50 per cent coverage of NGA networks (EC 2019).

Mobile Broadband

Mobile broadband is seen by the EU as largely secondary to fixed broadband as, in 2018, less than 10 per cent of households accessed the internet solely through mobile technologies, though this rises to over a third in Finland and falls to as low as 0.04 per cent in the Netherlands. Moreover, mobile data traffic is a tiny share of total internet traffic (less than 6 per cent), and is not expected to rise to much more than 10 per cent by 2022. Despite this, across the EU+4 states, mobile broadband is reaching universal coverage, with 99 per cent of households able to access some form of enabling technology (EC 2019).[5] Indeed there is no state with less than 95 per cent penetration of mobile broadband; 19 EU+4 states have at least 99 per cent coverage and five have universal coverage (EC 2019). However network capability across these states can vary markedly due to localised conditions and varying standards. For the EU27, the portion of individuals who use the mobile technology for internet access on the move rose from 32 per cent in 2012 to 73 per cent in 2019. If Norway, Switzerland, the UK and Iceland are added then the average rises to over 75 per cent. The share of enterprises offering their employees mobile devices for internet access is just over 70 per cent.

With regard to the main forms of mobile broadband, across the EU+4 over 94 per cent of households have access to fourth-generation (4G) mobile technology (up from 85 per cent in 2017), with a 96 per cent take-up across households. The take-up of 4G technology represents a 60 per cent increase over a five-year period to 2019 (EC 2020), though the rate of increase has plateaued as near universality is reached. Whether the better 4G penetration matters or not depends on the extent to which it is a platform for migration towards fifth-generation (5G) technologies. In 2019, the EU's readiness for 5G (measured by assigned spectrum as a percentage of total harmonised 5G spectrum) was just 14 per cent, though this had risen to 21 per cent by 2020 (EC 2020). Rural 3G mobile coverage was just over 93 per cent in 2019, and rural 4G coverage just over 96 per cent. In the case of 4G, this represents an acceleration of coverage in a 12-month period. Only one state, Cyprus, has 4G coverage below 80 per cent. In the five years from 2014 to 2019, 4G coverage in rural areas rose from 38 per cent to 98 per cent (EC 2019).

STATE BROADBAND STRATEGIES

What constitutes information infrastructure is evolving with techno-logical change, network expectations and a desire to sustain the rel-ative position of a state's NII to comparable economies (Broadband Commission 2019). Such pressures have meant that, despite a consensus that commercial forces should be the driver behind NII evolution, states have played a prominent role in seeking to steer these processes to ensure that market-led development continues to support and enable, and not threaten, their territorial strategy (Lacey 2011). To this end, all EU+4 states have longstanding national broadband strategies to plot the migra-tion of their respective NIIs towards ever-advanced fixed and mobile broadband systems that are both intensively and extensively developed across their respective territories.

In many cases, these strategies involve little direct activism (except where territorial cohesion is a core objective – see below), merely offering political support or enacting key enabling soft infrastructure to allow commercial processes to mature (Garcia Calvo 2012). Evidence suggests that such strategies have a direct and positive impact on broad-band roll-out (Broadband Commission 2013). This underlines that plans are focused on state–industry coordination to meet a set series of often non-statutory targets, frequently across a diverse range of indicators (such as human capital requirements, accessibility and affordability). Early evidence suggested that these state-driven plans increased fixed broadband penetration by 2.5 per cent and mobile broadband penetration by 7.4 per cent (in the five years to 2017), with a commitment to com-petitive markets offering further stimulation (OECD 2017). However progress in the realisation of these strategies is hindered by several issues – namely, lack of awareness, capability, skills and coordination between assorted stakeholders.

National broadband strategies emphasise universal access to broadband as a core strategic priority, with most establishing targets for broadband access based upon specified levels of geographic coverage and/or targets for average transmission speeds (OECD 2011); though some states also set targets for adoption. Thus within all plans there is a desire to provide a catalyst for access through the provision of public services and other necessary services from the centre required by civil society (OECD

2017). Indeed, infrastructure development and eGovernment remain the two core themes of all EU+4 state broadband strategies.[6] This underpins direct state involvement in infrastructure to ensure no or limited emergent digital divides by promoting universal access and a requirement for the population to access such infrastructure via the conduit of essential public services. Thus state involvement is common in building infrastructure in areas that would be under-served if left purely to commercial logic.

The EU's Digital Agenda for Europe (DAE) set non-binding (aspirational) targets for EU states reflecting targets above what it is believed the market on its own would achieve (EC 2010). Such targets are based on the assumption that there are economic, social and political gains to be had from stimulating the supply of broadband. These were a reflection of longstanding strategies by states to promote the development of broadband (often framed within more broadly defined information society strategies) across their territories based upon benchmark figures of universal NGA coverage and 50 per cent ultrafast access by 2020 (EC 2014). That these targets are non-binding has meant that some states – notably France, Germany and the UK (which was still an EU member at the time of the plan) – have sought more protracted periods for the attainment of universal broadband access or have looser objectives. The attainment of these objectives lies at the state level with ability to attain any set objective dependent upon territorial features (such as pre-existing state of the network, distribution of population, etc.) as well as the available finance to support the roll-out where market-driven processes do not possess the capability to deliver targets unaided (notably in less populated rural areas) (EC 2019). Despite this, there has been little direct state action in deployment save the roll-out into rural (and other under-served) areas, where any actions had to comply with EU law on subsidies (see below) (EC 2017). Thus discretionary actions within national broadband strategies reflects that alignment with supranational frameworks is attractive insofar as they support the creation of a 'common information area' to allow for scaling up of regional markets as enablers of maturing national information systems (see below).

The use of targets is by no means accepted by all as the best method of developing broadband. Briglauer et al. (2016) suggest that such strategies can create path dependencies within NII evolution and lead to a situation whereby competitive dynamics are distorted and market-led investment deterred. The speed of perceived deployment might not be the best strategy as it might lead to inefficient choice of technology, or the market simply might not be ready for deployment. Thus targets might focus on supply of broadband for its own sake rather than its demand. Moreover, the use of the DAE to set uniform targets (albeit voluntary) runs the further risk of not fully comprehending the varied impacts that broadband technology can have in different territories. There are, for example, gaps between Western and Eastern European states with regard to readiness of take-up (Briglauer et al. 2016). Thus there is concern about a push for ultrafast broadband before many states' subscriber bases are ready. There is also a risk of moral hazard where the private sector, which is expected to drive the development and attainment of these targets, waits and expects state funds to support its realisation, with the result that – even accepting the possibility that the monies may have arrived anyway – the attainment of these objectives is delayed.

In practice, lack of any compulsion within these targets, as well as their flexible nature, has meant large lags in their attainment, reflecting the different starting places of states with there being no one size fits all policy. Some states are pursuing demand-side policies and others supply-side measures; others focus on transparency, and many more on regulatory/organisational measures. In practice, many pursue two or more of these actions (EC 2017a, 2017c). Of the EU+4 states, 16 follow their own discretionary policy. Only half of EU27 states follow the DAE targets, thus underlining its discretionary nature. Those states have more faith in the ability of markets to meet the desired level of broadband penetration at a speed civil society is able to take up. As such, these states focus on creating a fair market as a precursor to penetration. Where pre-existing conditions are less favourable there tends to be more state action (Bourreau et al. 2020).

There is an industry consensus that whereas once the EU+4 states were leading the field in mobile deployment, they have increasingly fallen behind other OECD states, notably the US and South Korea, in 4G deployment and take-up as well as download speeds (OECD 2019). Moreover these leading OECD states are making advancements with regard to the roll-out of 5G mobile technology (EC 2020a). This has become a major theme within national broadband strategies which now proactively seek to add further momentum to the mass migration of users towards ever more advanced mobile technologies, especially 5G (OECD 2019a). Readiness for 5G at the state level is measured as the share of the spectrum allocated to 5G that has been assigned. As of 2020, 17 of the EU27 member states had allocated some of the spectrum; four had allocated at least 60 per cent. The roll-out is urban led, with a number of cities being prioritised for 5G through either trials or commercial services

(OECD 2019a). As of March 2020, there were 138 EU cities running 191 5G trials or services. European trials are localised on national basis to agreed EU-wide standards. The strategy is to create a European 5G network on the basis of these systems integrating over time via regulatory and limited financial support (OECD 2019a). However only 17 of the EU+4 states have 5G roadmaps and an average 20 per cent of the 5G spectrum allocated.

By 2020 deployment of the technology was expanding with services launched in 13 states (EC 2020a). This was expected to rise to over 80 service offerings by the end of 2020 (ETNO 2019), though a divide between Western (especially the Nordic states) and Eastern Europe in terms of readiness remains evident (inCITES 2020). With Europe still lagging behind the US, Japan and South Korea, it is believed that market fragmentation between states (and the consequent relative absence of scale economies) acts as an impediment to the roll-out of 5G. This should act as a further catalyst for the creation of a digital single market (Institut Montaigne 2019). The EC (2017a) estimated that the cost of the deployment of 5G would be €56 billion in 2019, though this varies markedly from state to state (due to geography, demographics, etc.) as each seeks to 'densify' their networks with a larger number of towers to ensure effective penetration of 5G. To support the launch of 5G, European states have been co-operating on services along designated cross-border corridors. These bilateral agreements are mainly along cross-border motorways as a means of testing driving-based services that utilise this technology. The European corridors being trialled feature motorways across a total of 29 states, though some of these were still at the proposal stage at the time of writing (2020). These corridors were motivated by a desire to create a system that was 'boundless' – one that allowed interoperable and interconnected systems to emerge from islands of trial projects. These cross-border projects are formed around public–private partnerships (PPPs); some are driven by inter-state co-ordination (notably in the Nordic region), whereas in others the EU has taken on a facilitatory role through its research and development initiatives. Table 4.1 outlines the six cross-border 5G initiatives funded by the EU as at 2020. These are all driven by the perceived application driver of computer-aided mobility and involve a mix of modes and states, though all are based around PPP consortia.

Table 4.1   *Cross-border corridor projects in Connected and Automated Mobility (CAM)*

5G Link	States	EU Funding Project under Horizon 2020
Metz–Merzig–Luxembourg	France, Germany and Luxembourg	5GCroCo
Rotterdam–Antwerp–Eindhoven	Netherlands and Belgium	5G-Blueprint
Porto–Vigo and Evora–Merida	Portugal and Spain	5G-MOBIX
Tromso–Kolari – E8 'Aurora Borealis'	Norway and Finland	Not applicable
Helsinki–Turku–Stockholm Gothenburg-Oslo–Copenhagen Nordic Way2	Finland, Sweden, Norway and Denmark	Not applicable
Munich-Bologna – Brenner Corridor	Germany, Austria and Italy	5G-CARMEN
Thessaloniki–Sofia-Belgrade	Greece and Bulgaria	5G-MOBIX
Tallinn–Riga–Kaunas – Via Baltica (E67) –Lithuanian/Polish border	Estonia, Latvia and Lithuania	5G-Routes
Kaunas–Warsaw – Via Baltica	Latvia and Poland	Not applicable
Perpignan and Figueras	France and Spain	5GMED

Source: 5G-IA (2020)

Whilst these agreements are inter-state, it is still very much the private sector that leads their development. This state-based action is largely facilitatory, which ensures that any state support is compliant with EU regulations (5G-IA 2020a). The EU can offer facilitatory support in areas such as spectrum allocation, regulation and finance, but these are local projects focused on those states with the highest degree of NII maturity to allow effective interworking across borders (5G-IA 2020). Some projects can be supported through the Connecting Europe Facility (CEF) with EU involvement extending to allow synergies to be realised both across these projects and other Trans-European Network (TEN) sectors, notably transport. This requires frameworks for co-operation between states, operators and users.

Overall, the importance of national broadband strategies and the role of states in seeking to promote interconnection between emergent infrastructures underscore the role of states within the development of the EIS. Such interconnections reflect longstanding inter-governmental links between evolving NII that started with simple interconnection agreements between states to manage cross-border telecommunications traffic. State deployment and development strategies reflect where the power lies in the development of the NII. The state remains the core focal point within the EIS. However regionalism plays a salient role within its development, notably through the creation of the Common Information Area (see below). More proactive measures formed at the supranational level are largely peripheral forces in the development of the EIS, as has been evidenced by the evolving nature of the Trans-European Telecommunications Networks (TEN-Telecom) programme (see below).

SUPRANATIONAL ACTION TO SUPPORT NII EVOLUTION

Whilst NIIs are the core building blocks of the EII, there have been sustained efforts by the EU to formalise the informal integration into the broader process of EU integration. This integration is focused more on the operator level than the consumer level where national preferences/ demarcations remain. The EU Commission has the power to offer limited support for national programmes through a number of themes. Some are regulatory, but it also has limited funds through assorted programmes to support NII development – notably its research and development (R&D) programmes, Common Agricultural Policy (CAP) and the CEF. These actions are largely facilitatory both in terms of changing the underpinning soft infrastructure of the systems to facilitate the evolution of NII and through direct interventions in information infrastructure development through dedicated initiatives. These actions reflect an overlapping consensus between states on the need to speed up the evolution of NII. The EU mixes regulatory and developmental initiatives to support the development of EII.

The logic of supranational action is based on a desire to use these forums for co-operation and co-ordination across NIIs where there are common problems or areas of mutual concern. Across the EU, these problems are largely based on how fragmentation of an EII based upon national systems can erode the ability of a European information industry to attain the desired scale to compete on a global scale, but also for its impacts upon end user prices and access to technology. There are also concerns with regard to how an area where the EU was once a leader has become an area where it is now falling behind its major rivals both in terms of fixed and mobile broadband communications (EIB 2020). Beyond these multi-faceted competitive/growth concerns with regard to the evolution of EII, there are also ongoing concerns about territorial cohesion. This reflects a concern that information infrastructures will develop unevenly both across space and socio-economic groups. This runs the risk of market-driven NIIs reinforcing pre-existing socio-economic divides or even creating new divisions based upon ability to access NII. Finally, there is emergent commonality between states on the security of their respective NIIs. As information infrastructures have become embedded within economic and security structures, so a 'cyber-risk' based on the vulnerability (both actual and perceived) of NII has emerged as a common area of concern, reflecting the designation of NII as critical infrastructures.

Creating the Common Information Area

The extension of the principles of the Single European Market to telecommunications since the late 1980s established a broad inter-state consensus that investment in NIIs should be driven less by the monocentric system based on national monopolistic incumbents and more by one based upon polycentric activity (Turner 2018). Thus NIIs would evolve from being based upon a single infrastructure towards multiple competing infrastructure systems, with direct state control replaced by regulatory systems. These systems would seek to steer this investment towards meeting the competing territorial objectives of the state embedded within the NII, notably with regard to the sustenance of the public service dimension (i.e. security and cohesion) alongside the shift to competition (Cave et al. 2019). The logic of EU action was to co-ordinate the opening of NIIs based on common principles to facilitate the interoperation of national markets to allow for the widest choice of services and providers across all markets (Henry 1993, Clifton et al. 2010). The underpinning narrative of liberalisation has not been the erosion of national markets but of the creation of EU-wide service markets that operate within and between national markets. The logic was to reduce the cost of cross-border traffic flows to allow for the creation of an environment that can create EU-wide services, with the consequent benefits of scale driving roll-out at the state level.

The logic of this market-driven approach for NIIs was that rising traffic on the back of service liberalisation would stimulate infrastructure investment (Lemstra and Melody 2014). There was a belief that as firms accessed pre-existing infrastructure they would gradually increase their involvement towards building their own dedicated high-capacity system, with network congestion operating as a market indicator (Cave 2006, 2014). However in Europe there was a belief that this may limit investment as pre-existing owners seek to deter such investments.[7] There is scant evidence that this works (Falch and Henten 2018). Indeed, even as far back as 2001, it was evident that any hope that liberalisation would prove a catalyst for renewed broadband investment was being challenged as EU investment in NIIs was not keeping up with major rivals (notably the US and East Asian states) (Cave and Prosperetti 2001). It was felt that too liberal access to infrastructure had deterred investment by incumbents (Falch and Henten 2018). Cave et al. (2019) argue that the liberalisation process was better at lowering inefficiencies within the system than it was in providing a platform for the upgrade of NIIs. They also suggest that the commonality of regulation is difficult when NIIs are at different states of maturity with regard to technology, degree of liberalisation, market structure, etc. As a response, many states have replaced the regulatory approach to infrastructure development with a developmental approach where states are proactive in broadband deployment. This was evident from both the prevalence of national broadband strategies (see above) and by the level of government support for broadband roll-out in a manner that enables the territorial strategy (Melody 2013, Falch and Henten 2018).

The legacy of the national focus in the EII and the resistance to an EU-wide operating base has been the sustained importance of incum-bents within the respective NIIs. In the fixed broadband market, the market share of incumbents fell by only 10 per cent between 2006 and 2018, from 50 per cent to 40 per cent (EC 2019). Market fragmentation means that many users remain dependent upon a single supplier. In the EU, just under half of new entrants depend upon an incumbent's network. Whilst unbundling of networks has (to some degree) lowered the power of incumbents, they still remain the single most powerful force within national markets.[8] Grajek and Roller (2012) argued that monopolies have been replaced by oligopoly structures within national markets and systemic fragmentation remains rife. Whilst national markets remain the basis for the retail system, the operation of European telecommunications remains too fragmented for European champions to emerge, thereby limiting the lowering of cost at the EU level via prevention of realisation of scale (Cave et al. 2019).

The legacy of this lack of direct link between liberalisation and NII upgrades and the sustained fragmentation of the system drove two core initiatives from the EU to improve inter-state co-ordination. The first was the European Electronic Communications Code (EECC), which sought to plot a path towards more advanced infrastructures whilst maintaining territorial cohesion (EC 2018). Briglauer et al. (2017) – in their assessment of the EECC – argue that whilst the measure is a step in the right direction for improving investment in high-speed infrastructures (through facilitating co-investment) there remains room for improvement due to the complexity of the process. Included in the EECC was the Broadband Cost Reduction Initiative (BCRI), which aimed to speed up development of very high-speed networks by simplifying the administrative process associated with their development. This includes allowing for the joint use of infrastructure, which is seen as a key catalyst in NII development within a polycentric system. Under the BCRI operators of all networked infrastructure (not just telecoms) must consider reasonable requests to access their facilities.

The second initiative was the Digital Single Market (DSM) programme, which sought to address systemic fragmentation by promoting measures to ensure the mobility of all resources to allow online activities to develop harmoniously throughout the EU (based on agreed common rules, coordinated enforcement and lower barriers to access). The objective is to create an EU-wide digital ecosystem based on internationalised national systems drawing on a common EU-wide digital resource base allowing both users and operators to move seamlessly between national markets (EPC 2010). The logic of the DSM of NII investment is that open markets will allow users to understand (and demand) the benefits of faster broadband infrastructure. However it is up to operators to provide this, and for users to trust it. As such, much of the DSM is about providing an underpinning soft infrastructure that stimulates trusted cross-border flows (EC 2013, 2017b). The ongoing (and oft-mentioned) lack of a single operating environment is blamed for the absence of pan-EU operators, with operators still focused on national markets. For operators, the process of national jurisdiction in regulation does not account for the needs of international operators, and the absence of co-ordination and co-operation was limiting a pan-EU service environment. The DSM's agenda is that what co-operation and coordination as does exist between states does not go far enough to address the common needs of the territorial states. These are driven by absence of a uniform service environment which presupposes absence of a NII investment. This was also created by divergent implementation of pre-agreed rules (EP 2018). Whilst there are expected to be substantial efficiency benefits from the realisation of the DSM – around €180 billion (EP 2018) – its impact on infrastructure is more ill-defined other than a belief that as traffic rises infrastructure investment naturally follows. The position is that these measures exist alongside the EECC measures so that traffic can be enabled by lower risk investment in infrastructure. This also underlines the importance of the supporting European Gigabit Society initiative (see below) (EC 2016).

The lack of consistency between national systems has been a long-standing issue with regard to the development of NII. This was a major driver in the formative variants of the eTEN programme (formerly TEN-Telecom – see below). There is a concern that this process is being repeated in 5G systems where there is a desire for rapid roll-out of this technology, but states are deploying different approaches in the development of governance that will shape its progress (Institut Montaigne 2019). French think tank Institut Montaigne (2019a) argues that this fragmentation has meant that the EU has fallen behind in developing standards for 5G but that no state really wants to change this. These prevent EU operators from enjoying the same scale economies that are open to other economies. Through its 5G action plan, the EC seeks to establish a set of co-ordinated actions to ensure consistency of approach, notably with regard to the harmonisation of spectrum allocation, technology utilised and standards adopted (EC 2016a). On top of this the EC seeks to influence the pace at which this technology is deployed by aligning national pathways for 5G deployment. The theme is familiar with regard to enabling the scaling up of provision. This process is expected to be aided by a co-ordinated rather than piecemeal introduction of 5G services (EC 2016a). The EU argues that failure to do this will deter deployment of this technology and of the supporting infrastructure to facilitate the links between local and backbone networks through the dense installation of 5G cell equipment. For the European Round Table for Industry (ERT 2020) this process requires a regulatory structure that allows for network sharing deals.

EU Information Infrastructure Initiatives

As with the other sectors, the EU gained competence in the development of the TEN-Telecom programme in 1993. Unlike the other sectors, the EU's actions on the EII took place during what turned out to be a period of rapid change for information infrastructures. As such, the holistic plans proposed by the EU since then have been of limited direct efficacy in the development of the EII. The initial TEN-Telecom programme was a 'bottom-up strategy' focused not on physical infrastructure per se but on a number of small-scale projects linked to generic services and applications (Rand Europe 2008). As such, its role was largely facilitatory, focusing on user-driven applications and services, notably those (such as data exchange between public administrations) that supported and enabled the SEM (Johnson and Turner 1997, Turner 1997). Over time this has been expanded to include a wider range of public service applications with stronger local/national relevance. Efforts on the physical system were focused on promoting the harmonisation of pre-existing digital networks and expanding access to such systems and offering support for early broadband trials (Johnson and Turner 2007).

Over time TEN-Telecom became a flanking policy (and was rebranded eTEN) for a series of holistic development plans – such as eEurope and, more latterly, the Digital Agenda for Europe – to facilitate broadband roll-out as an enabler of the development of a broadly based EU-wide ICT ecosystem (Turner 2001, Falch and Henten 2018). The eTEN programme stresses the broader information society themes involved in the holistic initiatives, with a focus on content delivery rather than broadband deployment. The consequence was support for the deployment of trans-European e-services of public interest in the following areas: government, health, inclusion, learning and services for SMEs. The impact of the programmes (both TEN-Telecom and eTEN) was limited with deployment not scaling up in a satisfactory time frame (EC 2004). This indicated early on that the EU's intervention was of limited impact upon the EII. This was often due to the fact that projects were of limited size and that synergies with other flanking programmes were not exploited (Rand Europe 2008).

The Digital Agenda for Europe had an infrastructure component, namely through setting the goal of universal broadband by 2020 where all had access to at least 30 Mbps and where 50 per cent of the EU's population had access to at least 100 Mbps (EC 2010, Gruber et al. 2014). These targets for universal broadband access by 2020 required – given the pace of roll-out and reticence of private sources – a need for further state involvement; they also reflected the limited appetite for and capacity of supranational involvement. Thus there needed to be means of allowing compliance with state aid rules to allow state finance to drive broadband penetration within any given territory (Falch and Henten 2018, Feasey et al. 2018). These targets are in practice mere suggestions, but their success has been hindered not only by state limitations but also by sustained cohesion problems and the inability of low-intensity user bases to attract investment (Briglauer et al. 2016).

The latest initiative on the co-ordinated development of broadband is the European Gigabit Society programme which seeks to build upon the DAE to set targets for increasingly advanced connectivity throughout Europe (EC 2016). To this end, it has suggested improved connectivity for key public services, households and mobile services by 2025. The targets are access speeds of up to 1 gigabit per second (Gbps) for main public service users (such as education establishments, transport hubs, health care providers, research centres) and digitally intensive businesses. It also seeks download speeds of up to 100 Mbps for households (with an open-ended commitment to upgrade to 1 Gbps). The final dimension is the widespread deployment of 5G wireless technology for major urban centres and transport arteries. In 5G, the European Commission is seeking to promote co-ordination between separate national systems to ensure no new fragmentation emerges during deployment phases (EC 2016a). This is based on co-operation on spectrum harmonisation. This policy fits alongside and supports (and where necessary enables) national broadband plans, especially where enabling such plans through subsidies and inter-operator collaboration and infrastructure sharing could possibly run contrary to EU single market rules. This requires €500 billion in investment by 2025, of which there is an estimated deficit of around €155 billion (EC 2016a).

With limited funds, the promotion of these objectives is to be attained via the EC supporting state-driven activities, especially with regard to territorial cohesion (see below). Within the CEF, funding for the EII is directed not only towards the development of transnational 5G corridors (see above) but also for connectivity to promote cohesion and interconnecting all parts of the EU via high-capacity cables, notably submarine cables for island states. This reflects that the CEF has two pillars: the first for digital service infrastructures and the second for connectivity. Total funding of around €1.05 billion is peripheral to the total needed (at least €500 billion) to upgrade the EU's digital infrastructure (EC 2019b). The main focus is on the EU using its limited funds not as grants but as equity funding to stimulate commercial investment, especially in those locations where funding would be difficult to obtain. The CEF has been extended to all EU+4 states as well as Serbia. The funds are used to spread the development of digital public services.

Territorial Cohesion

The promotion of territorial cohesion is a state-level function with states within their respective national broadband strategies focusing on offering universal coverage for their evolving NII. In practical terms this universality can often mean stimulating provision in those parts of the territory (frequently rural and peripheral but also including some urban areas) where market forces alone would lead to an under-provision of broadband infrastructure and services (OECD 2018). This reflects that states see the penetration of broadband infrastructure as a core enabler of growth in those peripheral regions where there can be low population densities, uneven population dispersion, difficult geography and/ or economically disadvantageous localities (OECD 2017a). To enable this process, the EU has sought to reconcile such support with its competition laws through its policy on state aid regarding broadband. The EU's primary motivations in terms of cohesion are driven by a desire to limit any emergent digital divide between states to the extent that it could inhibit the EU's ability to operate as a cohesive bloc (Kyriakidou et al. 2011). The digital divide therefore is not simply an issue within states but also one between states created by the unevenness of broadband penetration. In the EU, this is normally based on an east–west divide, though this divide is not straightforward as some Eastern nations (such as the Baltic states) have high broadband penetration and some Western states are lagging behind. However in dealing with the digital divide between states the EU supports localised projects, blurring the boundaries between inter- and intra-state digital divides.

Whilst states drive the majority of funding, the EU offers limited financial support through its regional and agricultural systems. These funds are also supported by lending facilities from the European Investment Bank (EIB) and the European Fund for Strategic Investment (EFSI). These have also been enabled by funds from the CEF (EC 2019b). These latter devices are less direct subsidies and more about supporting private investment in broadband roll-out in NIIs by limiting their risk and offering some degree of support by taking an equity stake within a project. However their proactive role in promoting cohesion is minimal. Indeed EU support – when compared to the support offered to other sectors – accounts for little over 1 per cent of the total investment believed to be required to upgrade the EIS (EC 2020). Indeed, there is a strong belief that the market can by and large deliver the EII, with state action (either by individual states or the EU collectively) merely seeking to steer the process to its territorial aims. Thus arguably the greatest contribution of the EU is through the aforementioned state aid regulation rather than direct action. Since its original conception, what constitutes the digital divide has been evolving with shifting technology. Moreover it is evident that gaps are narrowing both within and between states. The move towards mobile broadband and the near ubiquity of the technology has focused efforts less on infrastructure and more towards take-up as a driver of increased capacity broadband systems.

Security

Issues of state security have become increasingly prominent within information infrastructure systems (Liaropoulos 2011). Narratives surrounding critical infrastructure have underlined how information infrastructure has become embedded within other infrastructure systems (such as military and key economic systems) as well as its increasingly prominent role within socio-economic and political activity generally (Rinaldi et al. 2001). Like territorial cohesion, security remains a state-based competence. However the EU has established supranational frameworks to enable co-ordination and co-operation between states to promote greater consistency in terms of cybersecurity strategy (EC 2020b). This has been enabled largely through the creation of the European Network and Information Security Agency (ENISA; now the European Union Agency for Cybersecurity). This operates a forum for the exchange of views and to spread best practice throughout EU states, and has allowed for a common equipment certification process. It is not an operational agency. States remain sole responsibility for any criminal or economic and political security issues.

   ENISA (2020) reported that in 2019 there were 153 security incidents reported to national regulatory authorities across 26 EU and two European Free Trade Association (EFTA) states. Of these cases, only a fraction was due to malicious actions. Indeed only 1 per cent of lost user hours (and 5 per cent of total registered incidents) was due to incidents of malicious intent. Most security incidents are caused by system failure, natural events or human error. Actions with malicious intent account for 10 per cent of fixed telephony and 14 per cent of internet incidents. For mobile telephony and broadband, malicious intent is 3 per cent of incidents in both. In terms of trust services, there was an 80 per cent rise in cases between 2018 and 2019 (though this is put down to increased awareness). Again this is largely driven by system failure. Only 9 per cent were deemed a result of malicious attacks. At the level of citizens, within the EU+4, 39 per cent experienced security issues; in the UK and Denmark this was as high as 50 per cent, with phishing and pharming the most common problems.[9] These security concerns are rising amongst all users. At the level of the enterprise, users are making citizens aware of their obligations with regard to securing IT systems (EC 2020).

It is security at the national level which is the immediate common concern, with the number of cyber-attacks on EU state systems (such as cloud providers and other key infrastructure) rising, and many of the attackers being either state or state backed. The commonality of concern is reflected within the EU's security strategy (EC 2020b). There is also the fear that as the system decentralises there will be greater exposure to threats. The response has been increased levels of co-operation between states offering intelligence sharing (OECD 2019a). To this end, the EU is looking to further develop co-operation between states through structures such as a proposed Joint Cyber Unit to offer mutual assistance in cases of disruption to an NII. To enable and support this, in 2016 the Network and Information Systems (NIS) Directive sought commonality on the security of networks so as to support the evolving internal market for communications services. This applies to operators of specific 'essential services', digital service providers operating across borders. The directive also establishes a co-operation framework for common security issues. These measures have to reflect the different maturity of information systems across the EU as well as national sensitivities and budget constraints (Markopoulou et al. 2019). However the European Court of Auditors (ECA 2019) argued that the legislative framework was incomplete and compounded by uneven transposition of legislation into national law.

The link between security and the NII has been highlighted by the emergence of 5G technology and choice of infrastructure provider. This has become controversial given the centrality of this technology to a new generation of services and of the potential risk of disruption to national systems should this be disordered. States have co-operated to establish common frameworks for risk assessment in 5G deployment. This toolbox seeks to create a set of harmonious conditions for 5G cybersecurity (ENISA 2020a). These cross a range of issues from strategic and technical measures to ensure 5G infrastructure is secure. This includes undertaking risk profiles of providers and ensuring system physical security. Again, there is no compulsion for states to adopt these measures; merely that they agree to best practice (EC 2020c). In part, these common security frameworks are a measure to overcome fragmentation in the national systems of 5G deployment. The Institut Montaigne (2019a) infers that this security risk derives directly from the fact that that no EU-based/ trusted supplier has the scale economies of the main non-EU 5G providers (notably the Chinese company Huawei – see below). Therefore system fragmentation has – unintentionally – created a security risk.

This fragmentation is reflected in the divergent approaches of EU states on the utilisation of equipment from Huawei (which has alleged links to the Chinese military). France and Germany have rejected an outright ban and Spain – which depends on Huawei equipment – sees the equipment as safe. There is more hesitancy (under US pressure) in Eastern Europe, though Hungary is an outlier as it has friendly relations with China (Institut Montaigne 2019a). Many of these states do not want to allow their infrastructure to be built by a firm believed to be under foreign state interference. The choice of infrastructure provider is a decision that is left to the state; the EU has no direct influence over individual states and their choice of what can be seen as high-risk providers. However the EU admits it is not good practice to rely on a single provider (EC 2019a). How much of a security concern this process is reflects the extent to which any equipment has to meet state approval prior to installation, though there is only so far this can go. To partially mitigate this process, there is an EU-level push towards harmonisation of approvals to ensure mutual security and standards of 5G systems.

DIGITAL SOVEREIGNTY

Whilst states are sovereign over their own NII, the trend towards digital sovereignty reflects more that flows of data within and from outside a territory are subject to rules reflecting that a state's/region's preferences as to how this data and other digital assets are treated. Thus states will seek total control over all stored and processed data located within their territory, including who can access it and to where it can be transferred (Digital Summit 2018). The notion of digital sovereignty presupposes increased autonomy of any state from any other state it relies on for at least part of its information system, whether data itself or the technology that underpins data flows (Taylor 2020). The essence of digital sovereignty is for states to seek to ensure that all data collected within a state/ region is processed/stored within that region and not moved out without due consent and safeguards in the host state. This issue has increased in salience as a reflection not merely of the power of data in state security but also of the emergence of a global cloud architecture. The global cloud system means that data can be stored beyond the territory where it has been created and could be used with no regard to its potential security implications (EP 2020). There is also concern over divergence of interest between host and home states regarding data. The host of the data has no territorial interest in the data, and so has no interest in regulating it. The host merely has control over infrastructure (OECD 2018a).

There is an emergent concern that the EU cloud infrastructure system has become dominated by US businesses, which hold over 90 per cent of total Western data in storage (Burwell and Propp 2020). There is also a fear that cloud providers may be subject to third country regulations as well as uncertainty as to the compliance of overseas suppliers with EU regulations. That the EU should question the security of US business operations reflects concerns over the US surveillance of EU data once it is out of EU jurisdiction, as identified in the WikiLeaks scandal that high-lighted security breaches (Bagchi and Kapilavai 2018). The invalidation of the initial EU–US 'Safe harbour' agreement in 2015 further under-scored the divergent approaches between these states, as did the 2018 US CLOUD Act, which gave the US government wide extra-territorial ability to obtain personal data on non-US citizens (Thieulin 2019).

For the EU, these divergent approaches between the leading providers of cloud storage and its own 'values' has driven its digital sovereignty strategy. For the EU, this is not data nationalism as a means of economic protectionism but a system of ensuring EU values are encapsulated within the European portion of the internet (Kuner 2015, EC 2020d). These themes are also shaped by the nexus between sovereignty and security, based on the perception that a global digital system is a vulner-able system (Burwell and Propp 2020). EU action is keen to ensure that any response to such issues should not lead to renewed fragmentation within the EIS insofar that it further inhibits a core objective of the scaling up of the European information industry. Thus digital sovereignty seeks self-determination through the creation of European competence in the information industry, and security can be a driver of this process (Taylor and Hoffman 2019). By 2020 states were at different stages of development with regard to awareness of the need to adapt legal frame-works to the shifting digital economy (EC 2020d). Bauer et al. (2016) found over 20 cases where states limited data flows between EU states across a number of areas. States are increasingly restricting what data can and cannot be moved outside state borders – typically accounting, banking and government data. These cases were compounded by another 35 where there was an indirect impact upon data flows between states.

The EU has begun a push-back by moving away from cloud services offered by non-EU companies and towards an EU capability in this area to counter the accumulation of power by large (mainly US) technology businesses (Besley and Persson 2009). Typical of this is the Gaia-X initiative, which seeks to develop cloud services based on European standards by linking EU cloud service suppliers into an integrated system. This creation of a European cloud service is pushing towards data localisation (Taylor 2020). This is also compounded by the General Data Protection Regulation (GDPR). This reflects that regulation is at the heart of digital sovereignty, with the EU seeking to ensure its core principles are enshrined within digital systems. The EU is underscoring that any party that wishes to move, access or store data within the region has to conform to agreed common standards. The GDPR is underpinned by a narrative that any push towards data localisation within Europe should not (again) come at the expense of the scaling up of the EU information system. If states are going to engage in these policies then it is best to do it via co-ordination so that other objectives are not compromised. Despite this intent, the regulation does allow considerable state discretion to sustain flows to a third state if GDPR compliance is not assured. They are also allowed to diverge for clear territorial aims – notably cohesion, control (public safety) and security. In short, national security can override the GDPR (Brehmer 2018).

The GDPR offers a perspective that free movement of data is allowed so long as certain guarantees are made with regard to usage, with data protected through a credible governance framework. On that basis, where adequate protection is offered, then data flows are sanctioned. The GPDR is also supported by measures to promote the free flow of non-personal data within the EU by seeking to remove national barriers as to where firms can store data across the EU. This reflects that across the EU, despite pressure to promote the single digital market, states retain restrictions on data mobility. These restrictions are still allowed where there are security concerns. Whilst the EU is keen to scale up the EU-wide cloud market, it has to address business concerns over the commercial use of data, with many not wanting to undertake activity in states that do not adhere to the GDPR. Of course, data localisation comes at a cost for cloud businesses as they need to build local data centres to meet the requirements of the legislation. The accusation of such policies is that they are essentially an exercise in digital mercantilism promoting the local information industry at the expense of the efficiency of the global information system (Cory 2017). Such policies towards the localisation of content also inhibit the ability of firms to deploy ICTs in their most efficient manner (OECD 2019). Bauer et al. (2014) argue that the process is harmful, hindering flows of data and imposing costs on cloud infrastructure owners and resulting in net welfare losses created by impacts on trade flows.

Interwoven with these themes of digital sovereignty is how the EIS adapts to pressure within the global system towards fragmentation (O'Hara and Hall 2018). It has been widely accepted that the notion of a global information system as an homogenous, borderless system is outdated and there is pressure from commercial, technical and governmental forces that are fragmenting the system (Drake et al. 2016). At the state level, this is driven by the aforementioned challenges of states seeking to assert territoriality over this system. These macro trends are also suggestive of a meta trend where the internet is starting to splinter at the international level (Internet and Jurisdiction Policy Network 2019). This is based on the emergent technological rivalry between the US and China which the EU finds itself caught in. On the whole, European businesses are not large operators within the global information system. The major tech giants are US- and, increasingly, Chinese-based businesses. The presumption is that competition between these two states could create two rival digital ecosystems – one of which Europe would have to choose to adhere to (Lippert and Perthes 2020).

As technological prowess has become seen as a proxy for a state's hard power, so its ability to export this capability can shape a state's sphere of influence. Whilst the US is still the leader with regard to technological superiority, it is evident that China feels that its security is best protected by independence from this US-based information ecosystem (Hoffman et al. 2020). Thus it is seeking to develop and export its own information infrastructure hardware. The result is the development of two competing information system spheres which overlap in Europe. The main issue with regard to the EIS (as mentioned above) is the lead that China has established in 5G technology, where EU-based businesses have invested heavily in Chinese equipment from firms such as Huawei and ZTE (ENISA 2019). This has placed Europe in a quandary as limiting access to 5G within the EIS would delay the roll-out of the technology across the continent.

How these systems evolve is as yet unknown; but they do offer the potential for these respective systems to not facilitate interworking resulting in trade and other barriers between these potentially competing systems being hindered. Clearly the potential for this division ebbs and flows with the state of international relations between these states. Evidently the more these systems fragment the more the technological leader can impose its values on its sphere of influence, notably over issues like standards, legal frameworks and so on (Farrell and Newman 2019). There are also potential security risks where the powers can monitor data traffic from all states within their respective sphere (Slaughter 2017).

The EU, whilst having no comparable digital champions to insert themselves between these spheres, does nonetheless have the ability to assert power through its regulatory competences such as the GPDR. This reflects that the EU's market power could act as some degree of counter-balance to these trends. The intensity of the dispute between China and the US has the potential to erode this power. In some ways, the digital sovereignty strategy is part of the mechanism to cope with this. Evidently if the EU takes one side or the other it risks incurring sanctions from the offended party. The overlap with the US position is tending to be stronger even if there are differences between them (Taylor and Hoffman 2019). However it is also suggested that the EU acts pragmatically in seeking to utilise technologies from both emergent information ecosystems. Europe is not without a bargaining position in terms of skills and markets (ECFR 2020, Lippert and Perthes 2020). This will be enhanced – so it is believed – with the creation of the European Digital Market, which should further enhance the market. O'Hara and Hall (2018) argue that in seeking to push its attitudes of prudence, civility and virtuousness online the EIS is creating a 'bourgeois internet' stressing dignity over liberty, with safety being the main focal point of usage strategies. This is based on a mistrust of free markets and stands in contrast to the US model that more readily accepts such notions of development, and also to the Chinese model, which is more authoritarian in its approach (Hoffman et al. 2020).

CONCLUSION

There has, arguably, been no other infrastructure system subject to as much change over the past two decades as information infrastructure. This infrastructure has evolved from being a simple, analogue-driven voice system to an all-encompassing infrastructure ecosystem. Whilst many parts of Europe had relatively mature NIIs at the onset of this process, these states have gradually lost ground to existing (US and Japan) and new rivals (China) in the development and use of these technologies. For the European Commission, this decline in relative position has been driven by the continued fragmentation of national infrastructure markets. Whilst the national focus in the EII remains pre-eminent, there has been longstanding inter-governmental action to remove inconsistencies and discontinuities between NII. This has been compounded by supranational action which has sought to promote further integration through the progressive liberalisation but also through the stimulation of cross-border projects or those trial projects that can be rolled out throughout the rest of the EU. The long-term intention is for such action to promote the scaling up of an information industry rather than seeking to integrate NIIs into a single system. However against this process are renewed forces of fragmentation within the global information system which is highlighting divergent approaches between states with regard to the development and deployment of new components of NIIs.

NOTES

1. Broadband infrastructure comprises those systems with the capability to simultaneously support multiple streams of information at speeds generally above 2 megabits per second (Mbps), though the EU also identifies further levels: 30 and 100 Mbps.
2. These are defined as those businesses with at least ten employees.
3. This includes access to at least one of the following technologies: DSL, cable, FTTP or WiMAX. The EC identifies three distinct broadband types: basic (at least 2 Mbps), fast (at least 30 Mbps) and ultrafast (at least 100 Mbps).
4. This includes access to one of the following NGA technologies: VDSL, FTTP or Cable DOCSIS 3.0.
5. This is based on access to two technologies – Long-Term Evolution (LTE) and High Speed Packet Access (HSPA), both of which are common across Europe.
6. eGoverment is a catch-all term to denote the provision of public services through electronic channels.
7. It is estimated that the EU needs to spend €500 billion on infrastructure to meet the needs of the Digital Single Market (DSM) (EC 2017b).
8. In Eastern Europe, competition tends to be based on competing infrastructures, which eschews the dependence upon incumbent networks by new entrants.
9. Phishing is the receipt of fraudulent messages; pharming is the redirection to fake websites asking for personal information.

REFERENCES

5G Industry Association (5G-IA) (2020). 5G Pan-European trials roadmap version 4.0. Available at www.5g-ia.eu; date accessed 19/11/2020.

5G Industry Association (5G-IA) (2020a). 5G strategic deployment agenda for connected and automated mobility in Europe. Available at www.5g-ia.eu; date accessed 19/11/2020.

Bagchi, K., and Kapilavai, S (2018). Political economy of data nationalism. 22nd biennial conference of the International Telecommunications Society (ITS): 'Beyond the Boundaries: Challenges for Business, Policy and Society', Seoul, Korea, 24–27 June 2018.

Bauer, M., Ferracane, M. F., Lee-Makiyama, H., and Van der Marel, E. (2016). Unleashing internal data flows in the EU: An economic assessment of data localisation measures in the EU member states. ECIPE Policy Brief No. 3/2016.

Bauer, M., Lee-Makiyama, H., Van der Marel, E., and Verschelde, B. (2014). The costs of data localisation: Friendly fire on economic recovery. ECIPE Occasional Paper No. 3/2014.

Besley, T., and Persson, T. (2009). The origins of state capacity: Property rights, taxation, and politics. *American Economic Review*, Vol. 99, No. 4, pp. 1218–1244.

Bourreau, M., Feasey, R., and Nicolle, A. (2020). Assessing fifteen years of state aid for broadband in the European Union: A quantitative analysis. *Telecommunications Policy*, Vol. 44, No. 7, p. 101974.

Brehmer, H (2018). Data localization: The unintended consequences of privacy litigation. American University Law Review, Vol. 67, No. 3, Article 6. Available at: http://digitalcommons.wcl.american.edu/aulr/vol67/iss3/6; date accessed 11/10/2020.

Briglauer, W., and Gugler, K. (2019). Go for gigabit? First evidence on economic benefits of high-speed broadband technologies in Europe. *JCMS: Journal of Common Market Studies*, Vol. 57, No.5, pp. 1071–1090.

Briglauer, W., Cambini, C., Cave, M., Shortall, T., Parcu, P., Rossi, M.-A., Silvestri, V., and Valletti, T. (2016). The future of broadband policy: Public targets and private investment. A report by the Florence School of Regulation Communications and Media for the Public Consultation on the Needs for Internet Speed and Quality Beyond 2020. Available at https://cadmus.eui.eu/handle/1814/38884; date accessed 11/09/2020.

Briglauer, W., Cambini, C., Fetzer, T., and Hüschelrath, K. (2017). The European Electronic Communications Code: A critical appraisal with a focus on incentivizing investment in next generation broadband networks. *Telecommunications Policy*, Vol. 41, No. 10, pp. 948–961.

Broadband Commission (2013). Planning for progress: Why national broadband plans matter. Available at www.broadbandcommission.org; date accessed 09/09/2020.

Broadband Commission (2019). The state of broadband 2019. Available at www.broadbandcommission.org; date accessed 09/09/2020.

Burwell, F. G., and Propp, K. (2020). The European Union and the search for digital sovereignty: Building 'Fortress Europe' or preparing for a new world? Atlantic Council Issue Brief. Available at www.atlanticcouncil.org; date accessed 13/10/2020.

Cave, M. (2006). Encouraging infrastructure competition via the ladder of investment. *Telecommunications Policy*, Vol. 30, No. 3, pp. 223–237.

Cave, M. (2014). The ladder of investment in Europe, in retrospect and prospect. Telecommunications Policy, Vol. 38, No. 8, pp. 674–683.

Cave, M., and Prosperetti, L. (2001). European telecommunications infrastructures. *Oxford Review of Economic Policy*, Vol. 17, No. 3, pp. 416–431.

Cave, M., Genakos, C., and Valletti, T. (2019). The European framework for regulating telecommunications: A 25-year appraisal. *Review of Industrial Organization*, Vol. 55, No. 1, pp. 47–62.

Clifton, J., Díaz-Fuentes, D., and Revuelta, J. (2010). The political economy of telecoms and electricity internationalization in the single market. *Journal of European Public Policy*, Vol. 17, No. 7, pp. 988–1006.

Cory N. (2017). Cross-border data flows: Where are the barriers, and what do they cost? Information Technology and Innovation Foundation. Available at itif.org; date accessed 11/10/2020.

Digital Summit (2018). Digitale Souveränität und Künstliche Intelligenz: Voraussetzungen, Verantwortlichkeiten und Handlungsempfehlungen. Downloaded from https://www.de.digital/DIGITAL/Redaktion/DE/Digital-Gipfel/Download/2018/p2-digitale-souveraenitaet-und-kuenstliche -intelligenz.pdf; date accessed 11/10/2020.

Drake, W. J., Vinton, C. G., and Kleinwächter, W. (2016, January). Internet fragmentation: An overview. World Economic Forum Future of the Internet Initiative White Paper. Available at www.wef.org; date accessed 12/11/2020.

Dutta, S., and Lanvin, B. (eds) (2019). *Network Readiness Index 2019*. Washington DC: Portulans Institute.

European Commission (EC) (2004). Intermediate evaluation of the eTEN (formerly TEN-Telecom programme). Available at www.europa.eu.int; date accessed 28/09/2020.

European Commission (EC) (2010). Communication on a Digital Agenda for Europe. Available at www.europa.eu.int; date accessed 01/09/2020.

European Commission (EC) (2013). Commission staff working document impact assessment accompanying the document Proposal for a regulation of the European Parliament and of the Council laying down measures concerning the European single market for electronic communications and to achieve a connected continent. Available at www.europa.eu.int; date accessed 01/09/2020.

European Commission (EC) (2014). Digital Agenda for Europe. Available at www.europa.eu.int; date accessed 01/09/2020.

European Commission (EC) (2016). Connectivity for a competitive digital single market: Towards a European gigabit society. Available at www.europa.eu.int; date accessed 23/09/2020.

European Commission (EC) (2016a). 5G for Europe: An action plan. Available at www.europa.eu.int; date accessed 24/09/2020.

European Commission (EC) (2017). Study on national broadband plans in the EU-28. Available at www.europa.eu.int; date accessed 14/09/2020.

European Commission (EC) (2017a). Identification and quantification of key socio-economic data to support strategic planning for the introduction of 5G in Europe. Available at www.europa.eu.int; date accessed 20/09/2020.

European Commission (EC) (2017b). Mid-term review on the implementation of the digital single market strategy: A connected digital single market for all. Available at www.europa.eu.int; date accessed 22/09/2020.

European Commission (EC) (2017c). Commission staff working document accompanying the document Communication from the Commission to the European Parliament, the Council, the European Economic and Social Committee and the Committee of the Regions on the Mid-Term Review on the implementation of the digital single market strategy: A connected digital single market for all. Available atwww.europa.eu.int; date accessed 22/09/2020.

European Commission (EC) (2018). Guidelines on market analysis and the assessment of significant market power under the EU regulatory framework for electronic communications networks and services (Text with EEA relevance) (2018/C 159/01). Available at www.europa.eu.int; date accessed 22/09/2020.

European Commission (EC) (2019). Broadband coverage in Europe 2018: Mapping progress towards the coverage objectives of the Digital Agenda. Available at www.europa.eu.int; date accessed 01/09/2020.

European Commission (EC) (2019a). EU coordinated risk assessment of the cybersecurity of 5G networks. Available at www.europa.eu.int; date accessed 01/09/2020.

European Commission (EC) (2019b). Investing in European networks. The Connecting Europe Facility: Five years supporting European infrastructure. Available at https://ec.europa.eu/inea/en/connecting-europe-facility; date accessed 17/11/20.

European Commission (EC) (2020). Digital Economy and Society Index (DESI) 2020: Connectivity. Available at www.europa.eu.int; date accessed 03/09/2020.

European Commission (EC) (2020a). European 5G Observatory 8th report, June 2020. Available at www.5gobservatory.eu; date accessed 16/09/2020.

European Commission (EC) (2020b). EU Security Union strategy. Available at www.europa.eu.int; date accessed 03/10/2020.

European Commission EC (2020c). Secure 5G deployment in the EU: Implementing the EU toolbox. Available at www.europa.eu.int; date accessed 07/10/2020.

European Commission (EC) (2020d). A European strategy for data. Available at www.europa.eu.int; date accessed 10/10/2020.

European Council for Foreign Relations (ECFR) (2020). Europe's digital sovereignty: From rule maker to superpower in the age of US–China rivalry. Available at ecfr.eu date; accessed 13/11/2020.

European Court of Auditors (ECA) (2019). Challenges to effective EU cybersecurity policy. Available at www.eca.europa.eu.int; date accessed 11/10/2020.

European Investment Bank (EIB) (2020). The growing digital divide in Europe and the United States. EIB Working Paper 2020/07. Available at www.eib.org/economics; date accessed 05/10/2020.

European Parliament (EP) (2018). The European digital single market. Available at www.ep.europa.eu; date accessed 23/09/2020.

European Parliament (EP) (2020). Digital sovereignty for Europe. Available at www.ep.europa.eu; date accessed 11/10/2020.

European Policy Centre (EPC) (2010). The economic impact of a European digital single market. Available at www.epc.eu; date accessed 23/09/2020.

European Round Table for Industry (ERT) (2020). ERT position on regulatory framework for 5G. Available at www.ert.eu; date accessed 24/09/2020.

European Telecommunications Network Operators (ETNO) (2019). 5G and us: A European story. Available at www.etno.eu; date accessed 15/09/2020.

European Union Agency for Cybersecurity (ENISA) (2019). Threat landscape for 5G networks. Available at https://www.enisa.europa.eu; date accessed 07/10/2020.

European Union Agency for Cybersecurity (ENISA) (2020). Telecom services security incidents 2019. Available at https://www.enisa.europa.eu; date accessed 07/10/2020.

European Union Agency for Cybersecurity (ENISA) (2020a). Trust services security incidents 2019. Available at https://www.enisa.europa.eu; date accessed 07/10/2020.

Eurostat (2020). Digital economy and society indicators. Available at www.europa.eu.int/Eurostat; date accessed 31/03/2020.

Falch, M., and Henten, A. (2018). Dimensions of broadband policies and developments. *Telecommunications Policy*, Vol. 42, No. 9, pp. 715–725.

Farrell H and Newman A. L. (2019). Weaponized interdependence: How global economic networks shape state coercion. *International Security*, Vol. 44, No. 1, pp. 42–79.

Feasey, M., Bourreau, M., and Nicolle, A. (2018). State aid for broadband infrastructure in Europe: Assessment and policy recommendations. Centre on Regulation in Europe (CERRE) report, November. Available at www.cerre.eu date accessed 28/09/2020..

Garcia Calvo, A. (2012). *Universal service policies in the context of national broadband plans*. Paris: OECD.

Grajek, M., and Roller, L.-H. (2012). Regulation and investment in network industries: Evidence from European telecoms. *Journal of Law and Economics*, Vol. 55, No. 1, pp. 189–216.

Gruber, H., Hätönen, J., and Koutroumpis, P. (2014). Broadband access in the EU: An assessment of future economic benefits. *Telecommunications Policy*, Vol. 38, No. 11, pp. 1046–1058.

Henry, C. (1993). Public service and competition in the European community approach to communications networks. *Oxford Review of Economic Policy*, Vol. 9, No. 1, pp. 45–66.

Hoffmann, S., Lazanski, D., and Taylor, E. (2020). Standardising the splinternet: How China's technical standards could fragment the internet. *Journal of Cyber Policy*, Vol. 5, No. 2, pp. 239–264.

inCITES Consultancy (2020). Europe 5G Readiness Index. Available at www.incites.eu; date accessed 16/09/2020.

Institut Montaigne (2019). 5G in Europe: Time to change gear! Available at https://www.institutmontaigne.org; date accessed 15/09/2020.

Institut Montaigne (2019a). Europe and 5G: The Huawei case. Available at https://www.institutmontaigne.org; date accessed 15/09/2020.

Internet and Jurisdiction Policy Network (2019). Internet and Jurisdiction global status report 2019. Available at https://www.internetjurisdiction.net; date accessed 13/11/2020.

Irion, K. (2013). Government cloud computing and national data sovereignty. *Policy and Internet*, Vol. 4, No. 3–4, pp. 40–71.

Johnson, D., and Turner, C. (1997). *Trans-European networks: The political economy of integrating Europe's infrastructure*. Basingstoke: Macmillan.

Johnson, D., and Turner, C. (2007). *Strategy and policy for trans-European networks*. Basingstoke: Palgrave Macmillan.

Kuner, C. (2015). Data nationalism and its discontents. *Emory Law Journal*, Vol. 64, pp. 2089–2098.

Kyriakidou, V., Michalakelis, C., and Sphicopoulos, T. (2011). Digital divide gap convergence in Europe. *Technology in Society*, Vol. 33, No. 3–4, pp. 265–270.

Lacey, S. (2011). Implementation of national broadband plans: Agreed regulatory principles and their evolution. Available at SSRN 2072855; date accessed 10/09/2020.

Lemstra, W., and Melody, W. H. (eds) (2014). *The dynamics of broadband markets in Europe*. Cambridge: Cambridge University Press.

Liaropoulos, A. (2011). Power and security in cyberspace: Implications for the Westphalian state system. In *Panorama of global security environment*. Bratislava: Centre for European and North American Affairs.

Lippert, B., and Perthes, V. (2020). Strategic rivalry between United States and China: Causes, trajectories, and implications for Europe. SWP Research Paper, 4. Berlin. Available at www.swp-berlin.org; date accessed 12/11/2020.

Mann, M. (2012). *The sources of social power, Vol. 4: Globalizations, 1945–2011*. Cambridge: Cambridge University Press.

Markopoulou, D., Papakonstantinou, V., and de Hert, P. (2019). The new EU cybersecurity framework: The NIS directive, ENISA's role and the General Data Protection Regulation. *Computer Law and Security Review*, Vol. 35, No. 6, pp. 1–11.

McKinsey Global Institute (MGI) (2016). Digital globalization: The new era of global flows. Available at https://www.mckinsey.com; date accessed 21/08/2020.

Melody, W. H. (2013). Moving beyond liberalization: Stumbling toward a new European ICT policy framework. *Info*, Vol. 15, No. 2, pp. 25–38.

O'Hara, K., and Hall, W. (2018). Four internets: The geopolitics of digital governance. CIGI Papers No. 206, December 2018. Available at www.cigionline.org; date accessed 13/11/2020.

Organisation for Economic Co-operation and Development (OECD) (2011). *National broadband plans*. OECD Digital Economy Papers No. 181. Paris: OECD.

Organisation for Economic Co-operation and Development (OECD) (2017). *OECD digital economy outlook 2017*. Available at www.oecd.org; date accessed 20/3/2020.

Organisation for Economic Co-operation and Development (OECD) (2017a). *OECD territorial reviews: Northern sparsely populated areas*. Paris: OECD.

Organisation for Economic Co-operation and Development (OECD) (2018). *Bridging the rural digital divide.* Available at www.oecd.org; date accessed 05/10/2020.

Organisation for Economic Co-operation and Development (OECD) (2018a). *Policies for the protection of critical information infrastructure: Ten years later.* Available at www.oecd.org; date accessed 05/10/2020.

Organisation for Economic Co-operation and Development (OECD) (2019). *Telecommunications database: OECD telecommunications and internet statistics.* Available at www.oecd.org, date accessed 20/3/2020.

Organisation for Economic Co-operation and Development (OECD) (2019a). *The road to 5G networks: Experience to date and future developments.* Available at www.oecd.org; date accessed 20/09/2020.

Rand Europe (2008). Final evaluation of the eTEN programme. Available at www.europa.org; date accessed 28/09/2020.

Rinaldi, S. M., Peerenboom, J. P., and Kelly, T. K. (2001). Identifying, understanding, and analyzing critical infrastructure interdependencies. *IEEE Control Systems*, Vol. 21, No.6, pp. 11–25.

Shahin, J. (2011). The European Union's performance in the International Telecommunication Union. *Journal of European Integration*, Vol. 33, No. 6, pp. 683–698.

Slaughter, A.-M. (2017). *The chessboard and the web: Strategies of connection in a networked world.* New Haven, CT: Yale University Press.

Taylor, E., and Hoffman, S. (2019). EU–US relations on internet governance. Research Paper, 14 November. Available at www.chathamhouse.org; date accessed 12/10/2020.

Taylor, R. D. (2020). 'Data localization': The internet in the balance. *Telecommunications Policy*, Vol. 44, No. 8, p. 102003.

Thieulin, B. (2019). Towards a European digital sovereignty, Policy report to Economic, Social and Environmental Council. *Official Journal of the French Republic.* Available at https://www.lecese.fr/en/publications; date accessed 11/10/2020.

Turner, C. (1997). *Trans-European telecommunication networks: The challenges for industrial policy.* London: Routledge.

Turner, C. (2001). Accelerating the development of the European information economy: The European Commission's eEurope initiative. *European Business Review*, Vol. 13, No. 1, pp. 1–21.

Turner, C. (2018). The governance of polycentric national infrastructure systems: Evidence from the UK National Infrastructure Plan. *Environment and Planning C: Politics and Space*, Vol. 36, No. 3, pp. 513–529.

Turner, C. (2020). *The infrastructured state: Territoriality and the national infrastructure system.* Cheltenham, UK and Northampton, MA, USA: Edward Elgar Publishing.

World Economic Forum (WEF) (2019). Global competitiveness report 2019. Available at www.wef.org; date accessed 14/09/2020.

World Population Review (2020). Internet speeds by country 2020. Available at https://worldpopulationreview.com/country-rankings/internet-speeds-by -country; date accessed 14/09/2020.

5. European infrastructuring as co-operative territoriality

INTRODUCTION

The European Infrastructure System (EIS) operates as an interactive network of national networks. The national infrastructure systems (NIS) have evolved to underpin the territorial needs of European states as they seek to secure and enhance their territoriality (Taylor 1994). As a component of territorial strategy, NIS underpin actions by the state to control, secure, develop and integrate the territory under their jurisdiction (see Mann 2008). However territorial strategies are subject to the adaptive tensions created by external pressures acting on the state (Agnew 1994). This generates an overlap between territorial strategy and geostrategy. Regionalism operates as one such tension which – either through formal or informal channels of interaction – has the capability to reshape the form and structure of territorial strategy (see for example Söderbaum 2003). The research within this work has sought to investigate the legacy of this through the concept of co-operative territoriality. This explores the notion that states adapt to regionalism by co-operating with each other to solve common problems or co-ordinate activity for mutual benefit. This work investigated this through longstanding and evolving interactions between NIS in the transportation, energy and information sectors.

EUROPEAN INFRASTRUCTURAL INTEGRATION AND STATE TERRITORIALITY

States as territorialising agents develop strategies not only to preserve and enhance their territoriality but also to ensure that the state can safeguard its territorial interests within the international system (Taylor 1995). For the territory under its jurisdiction, infrastructuring is a core component of territorial strategy (Turner 2020). These infrastructures can comprise a diverse set of physical assets; but the focus of the state remains on economic infrastructures (transport, energy and information) which remain the primary infrastructural means through which the state can assert its territoriality (Murphy 1996). These economic infrastructures are central to the notion of territoriality insofar as they are a means of enabling flows of tangibles and intangibles to reach all parts of the space over which the state is the main territorialising agent. These flows are important in enabling the state to assert control over this space and in seeking to bind this space together. Turner (2018) refers to the idea of the infrastructure mandate (IM). This reflects that the state and infrastructure systems are intimately linked as the NIS needs to be territorially extensive with the capacity to intensively support flows that enable territorial control, security, growth/development, cohesion and sustainability. Whilst the literature on infrastructural violence (Rodgers and O'Neill 2012) suggests that under-provision can proffer some territorial advantage, the overwhelming consensus is that the development of an NIS that is universally accessible is central to state legitimacy and operation (Edwards 2003).

The central paradox is of managing territorially fixed systems to cope with – and adapt to – territorially fluid flows that operate across them. Whilst these flows have always existed and national systems have adapted to varying degrees to them, the challenge of regionalism is that these flows rise in volume, intensity and extensity. The consequence of such processes is that a state's territorial interests overlap with geostrategic concerns as it faces rising regional interdependence. This means the NIS has to be adapted to enable these flows driven by regionalism as part of the state's territorially defined infrastructural mandate. There is also a trade-off within the infrastructural mandate as refocusing hard and soft infrastructure systems to secure external flows can compromise security and – possibly – control. These tensions shape adaptation within the IM. Ultimately most of the flows within systems are national both in terms of source and destination, thereby reinforcing the national mindset within NIS.

The EIS is more than simply a collection of national assets. In this context, the conceptualisation of the EIS and the emergence of influence over these systems by international forces can act as catalysts for NIS evolution where such systems may be resistant to change, though it has to be stressed the impact upon NIS of regionalism is unlikely to be total. Regionalism will by its very nature have its greatest impact where the component parts of the national systems interact. In physical terms, this is in border infrastructure. However regionalism's impact can extend beyond such physical infrastructures into 'softer' components of the system, notably ensuring mutually acceptable standards and terms of use so that traffic can flow seamlessly between national systems (Star 1999). Ideally the basis of a regional system is the invisibility of the divide between such systems, though this rarely happens in practice.

The pressures of regionalism and the tensions placed upon NIS and their respective mandates incentivise states to co-operate and co-ordinate aspects of their infrastructure systems. This strategy of co-operative territoriality is based on an amalgam of factors. These include:

- the management of cross-border spillovers to sustain control;
- the enablement of the benefits of scale for small states in a global system;
- the offering of collective geostrategy vis-à-vis third states;
- the mutualisation of security;
- the management of those tensions on states that are, by their nature, de-territorial;
- managing and supporting a high intensity of flow de- and re-territorialisation; and
- formalising the informal integration and reflecting longstanding coalescence of political interests.

In short, the benefits of regionalising NIS do not merely reflect narrow concerns embedded within the logic of the competition state (Cerny 1997); they also reflect a broader range of territorial and geostrategic factors – though, in the case of the EIS, the competition state narrative shaped by the logic of the single market remains a powerful driver behind the process (Johnson and Turner 1997, 2007). However – at the state level (and as the main driver behind NIS and by default EIS evolution) – there exist strong incentives for states to seek to interconnect and even integrate their respective systems for a multitude of territorial and geostrategic reasons.

Of course, the territoriality supported by the evolving EIS is that of states and not of the European Union as a supranational entity. The EU has no real notion of territoriality beyond that of the component states (Mamadouh 2001). As Wissel (2014) notes, the EU has no infrastructural power, so lacks capability to assert control on or through civil society. This remains a state-based capability. Moreover, despite the EU's stated intent, it has little direct ability to promote security, and cohesion remains at best a shared competence. As such, arguably the EU's most effective impact of the IM is through 'soft' infrastructure capabilities of shaping the growth/competitiveness agenda of states (Johnson and Turner 2007). The EU largely acts as a supranational forum for inter-governmental co-operation and co-ordination across a limited range of activities, and these are largely based around economic integration and the creation of a single economic space. Its efficacy is to create common positions between states to secure the benefits noted above, but also to formalise the ongoing informal processes of integration within the EU. Such action does not remove the potential for fragmentation, competition and conflict between states, with each still having its own set of often divergent national territorial and geostrategic interests.

Looking globally at EU policy strategies on infrastructure, it is evident that these actions build upon pre-existing, longstanding actions at inter-state level to interconnect systems where it is in their interests to do so (Van der Vleuten and Kaijser 2005). EU direct action on infrastructure can at best be seen as a support to state territorial strategies rather than a parallel system of action (Johnson and Turner 2007). Indeed EU action in terms of infrastructure is limited to economic infrastructure; it has no capability as regards the direct development of social infrastructure. The funding offered across each of the respective sectors (see below) further indicates the limited power the EU has over the development of economic infrastructure, with available finance being a fraction of what is desired (EP 2014, 2020). In this sense, despite the grand ambitions for the programme, the Trans-European Networks (TENs) initiative has been underwhelming, with much of the work done by other actors – notably the member states and/or commercial operators. Across the infrastructures targeted by the EU within the TENs programme, informal integration (that is, formally outside the EU's treaties) remains a powerful driver of infrastructural integration, with bilateral/multilateral action between states seeming to have more impact on the EIS. There can be little doubt that the most effective means through which the EU has the capability to influence the development of the EIS is through soft infrastructure systems. In a market-driven process of infrastructure development, the co-ordinated liberalisation of network services to drive increase in traffic acts as a stimulant to infrastructure investment. These trends in soft infrastructure underscore the role of the EU in promoting co-operation and co-ordination over integration in the EIS (Florio 2017). In so doing, it underlines the position that the EU is more effective in promoting market integration (that is, the integration of network services markets) than it is in promoting systemic infrastructural integration. This has been evident across each of the economic infrastructure sectors identified by the EU (Johnson and Turner 2007).

TRANSPORT

The integration of the transport sector pre-dates the formation of the EU by as much as a century. This long-term trend towards integration of road and rail systems between states reflected the operators' desire for integrated services across borders (see for example Schot 2010). These were – and continue to be – reflected within longstanding co-operation in the development of standards through international bodies. However these international links became fragmented due to a combination of intra-European conflict, the borders created by the cold war, and the ebb and flow of infrastructure nationalism (Schipper and Van der Vleuten 2008). This indicates that the desire for infrastructural integration between European states tended to vary with both the prevailing geostrategic context and the priorities inherent within states' territorial strategy. The trend towards integration began to flow again with the expectation that the advent of rising cross-border interactions stimulated by the single market programme would require a new investment in infrastructures with a clear 'European dimension' (Johnson and Turner 1997).

However the states – and their respective national transport systems (NTS) – remain the primary focus of the European Transportation System (ETS). Freight and passenger flows within the EU have an overwhelmingly national focus (Eurostat 2019). As such, the ETS develops on a national basis to meet needs of the state and not those of the broader regional grouping. Such a national focus exposed the weaknesses of supranational policy as embedded within the Trans-European Transportation Network strategy (TEN-T) (Sichelschmidt 1999). TEN-T has been through a series of transformations since its conception, but the focus on national schemes within a transnational programme has been a core consistency. Arguably this reflects that – for many states – enabling the international dimensions of NTS is not as important for states as it is for supranational bodies. This has had its most evident expression in the limited funding offered for EU priority projects by the respective public sectors. However simply viewing the ETS as the sum of NTS risks understating the complexity of transport flows where the international dimension can be hidden.

The latest version of TEN-T seeks to rationalise the national focus within the more systemic approach offered by the prioritisation of corridors (EC 2018). This follows a two-tier approach. The first is to complete a 'core' network of nine transport corridors by 2030; the second was a more broadly based comprehensive networks to be completed by 2050. The logic of these corridors was not merely to contextualise national projects within a broader European system, but also to offer more forums for intense co-operation between states in transportation systems (Öberg et al. 2018). This refocus was designed to ensure alignment between national priorities and those of the broader European system and add impetus to their development. However this process seems to have added little to the TEN-T development process. Indeed it can very feasibly be argued that the EU's greater contribution is in soft (as opposed to hard) infrastructure, where the progressive liberalisation of the transport sector has stimulated investment in response to increased flows. This again underscores that national market integration has been a major theme underpinning infrastructure development (EP 2014).

The ETS has also been subject not merely to the adaptive tension between the national and supranational but also to tension between states in the broader transport European systems. Europe has had longstanding co-operation between states to develop interconnected national road and rail systems through the UN's trans-European motorway and rail initiatives (UNECE 2011). Whilst these operate little beyond inter-state co-operation and depend on state finance, they do reflect a longstanding desire by states to promote pan-European mobility. These strategies have been long on ideals but short on practical action as finance and inter-state disputes limit their efficacy. The salience of such broader pan-European programmes have been added to not just by the evident external dimension of TEN-T (such as in the Motorways of the Sea initiative) but also by China's proactivism in the development of the ETS (EP 2016). China has tended to act in a non-systemic fashion as it seeks entry points for its exports to the European market, largely through investment in port facilities (Zeng 2017); though it is also targeting high-speed rail facilities in Central and Eastern European states. In combination these infrastructure investments (especially the port facilities) are designed as a bridgehead between Eurasia and EU-based transport systems. This engagement by states with China's Belt and Road Initiative further underlines how state discretionary actions can further challenge a coherent EU-wide approach to the ETS (Vergeron 2018).

Peters (2003) argues that there innate conflicts within TEN-T as it seeks to balance desires for security, cohesion, competitiveness and sustainability. The market-led strategy of the process and the extent to which it relies on states to implement the process reflects the source of conflict as it will focus on the wealthier areas. Thus states seeking to use TEN-T to support or enhance their own infrastructural mandates will steer the system towards their objectives, and will only consider non-domestic issues where there is clear overlap and mutual dependence between states. Thus TEN-T happens where there is alignment between the respective NTS to the extent that interconnection between them is justified to the degree that such flows can be rendered seamless where alignment in soft infrastructure is matched by investment in physical capacity.

ENERGY

Like transport, Europe has longstanding patterns of infrastructural integration within the energy sector (Kanellakis et al. 2013). These have been shaped by shifting patterns within states' energy mix as they moved away from dependence solely on domestic sources of energy towards those sourced from more distant locations. This was especially evident in the increased reliance on more distant sources of oil and gas (Kandiyoti 2015). The dislocation between European demand for energy and its dependence on external sources has exposed core energy security issues where disruptions to supply and/or rapid oscillations in price have (at times) left the European economy vulnerable (see for example Högselius 2012) . Consequently one of the major trends within the European Energy System (EES) over the past few decades has been the shift towards turning what was often considered a hidden aspect of European integration into a more explicit process. This has generated the more complete integration of the respective national energy systems to mutualise energy security to render it a common problem (Clavin 2005, Benson and Russel 2015).

Energy remains an overwhelmingly national competence. Despite an increased presence by supranational bodies within the energy sector, it is states that have the ultimate power over the system. It is states that decide the energy mix and the form and nature of the interconnection between the respective systems. That is, it is the states that decide the form and direction of EES integration (Aalto and Korkmaz Temel 2014). These systems have undergone a transition initially from coal towards oil and gas; but more latterly a second transition from hydrocarbons towards renewables is underway. These transitions are reflected in the interconnections between the national systems where extensive links between national and international gas and oil systems have been a longstanding feature of EES. These regional systems scale up the process of energy transmission between national systems where not all systems have large national markets to support such investments or allow the energy source to be transmitted from third states into the EU (ENTSO-G 2019). These communal links also allow landlocked states access to energy sources distributed through maritime channels from third countries. These interconnections have also extended to electricity systems where all EU states exchange electricity via a series of interconnectors which allow states to balance out supply and demand (ENTSO-E 2018). However such links can be a mixed blessing if they undermine territorial strategy (Aurora 2016).

The widening and deepening of these interconnections lies at the heart of the Trans-European Energy Networks (TEN-E) programme (Johnson and Turner 2007). The main thrust of TEN-E was to establish a series of projects of common interest within the sector (especially in gas and electricity) which would offer the greatest contribution to the themes engendered within the EU's wide-ranging Energy Union Strategy, which seeks to promote energy security whilst promoting a market-driven energy transition (Andersen et al. 2016). Within a broader context, the Energy Union Strategy and TEN-E can also be seen as geostrategic tools by states seeking to integrate systems to – at least partially – remove dependence on non-EU sources of energy (Szulecki et al. 2016). However state territorial themes remain the pre-eminent focus within the EES as states tend to use interconnections as 'valves' for national energy systems rather than as a tool for the strategic mutualisation of energy risk. As a result, a truly co-ordinated and co-operative approach is still absent, with each state seeking to look after its own interests rather than focusing on the health of the system as a whole (Helm 2014). As a result, TEN-E has had limited success, especially in developing the required physical links, with many states not really seeing the need for such a programme. Arguably the greater impact of TEN-E is in seeking to militate the transaction costs involved in developing cross-border energy systems by creating an enabling soft infrastructure system to allow commercial and other state-based operators to develop these links by simplifying permission and other regulatory processes (Hawker et al. 2017).

Reinforcing the salience of EU soft infrastructural action has been narrative surrounding the development of the Internal Energy Market (IEM). With the EU lacking any meaningful sense of power within the energy infrastructure field, the IEM is arguably one area where it can have a tangible impact on promoting interconnection as an enabler of security through competition (Siddi 2016). This reflects a desire for the development of the IEM to scale up the European energy system to enable it to cope with any supply disruptions by the simple operation of market forces based on an integrated supply base. In practice, the IEM has been a mixed bag in its ability to meet these market-driven security objectives (Pollitt 2019). The interconnectivity across the EU still falls short of that required to make an IEM truly realisable (ACER 2017). As with TEN-E, EU action regarding the IEM has met with ongoing resistance from states that see the underpinning geostrategic logic of the market-based approach as being at odds with the main territorial themes inherent within national energy security.

The longstanding links that inform EU energy security have also stimulated the development of links between EU and non-EU systems, including those to Western and Eastern Europe (notably Russia) as well as Eurasia (Amirova-Mammadova 2017). These international systems (especially the gas links with Russia) have come under increasing scrutiny as fears grow that Russia could use these facilities as a geopolitical weapon (Bozhilova and Hashimoto 2010). The EU has tried to rein in this potential risk (largely through the application of the rules of the internal energy market). However this met with limited success, in part because individual states have been prepared to pursue their own interests in dealing with Russia (Johnson and Derrick 2012). This undermines the ability to use collective action as a means of mutualising energy security.

In examining the infrastructural impact of the energy transition, there are two apparently contradictory forces at work – namely integration and fragmentation. The former reflects that renewable generating capabilities are spread unevenly throughout the EU; thus there needs to be a further enhancement of systemic interconnection if all states are to integrate renewables into their energy mix as envisaged within the EU-wide agreed targets (see Chapter 3). The latter reflects that the integration of renewables into the energy mix offers the opportunity for the descaling/decentralisation of energy generation, opening up the possibility of systemic fragmentation. Alongside these processes are those that exist as a hybrid of these trends: namely that, across the EU, there is the likelihood that the transition will be a very uneven process. It also underlines that progress towards these objectives will be informed by state actions and how they each plan to shift their respective energy mixes to adapt to the energy transition (Szulecki et al. 2016).

INFORMATION

As with the other systems, there are longstanding interconnections between Europe's National Information Infrastructure (NII) systems. These were through organisations such as the International Telecommunications Union (ITU) or Europe-wide bodies such as the European Conference of Postal and Telecommunications Administrations (CEPT), which historically covered simple, basic telecommunication flows between states (Johnson and Turner 1997). These arrangements underscored the intergovernmental nature of the European Information Infrastructure (EII) system for much of its evolution (Turner 1997). The past two decades have seen a rapid change within NII, with the spread of the internet driving a desire for upgrades of these systems to cope with greater volumes and a change in the form of traffic which is increasingly bandwidth hungry. The spread of broadband across the EU+4 has been uneven, with evident gaps between the relative maturity of national infrastructure systems (EC 2020). This unevenness of development, the consequent threat to territorial cohesion and the belief that the European states were falling behind their major rivals have been catalysts for regional action (Turner 2007).

Such supranational activity is secondary to the prevalence of national broadband strategies that are ubiquitous across European states (OECD 2019). Though there is overlap with EU-driven targets (these are effectively meaningless), these strategies underscore the national emphasis in information infrastructure development within the EII. Whilst states are open to co-operation in areas like R&D and standards, it is states that drive the EII via their respective territorial actions. The EU can merely seek to steer their development in a manner that is complicit with the development of an interconnected EII (see Briglauer et al. 2017). This has largely been driven by the EU's impact on soft infrastructure and its re-regulation of the sector that has fostered pan-European connectivity without formally integrating national markets. This interconnectivity has been driven by the objective of creating a common information area. This has been the cornerstone of supranational initiatives, many of which seek to apply the principles of the single market to information infrastructures.

In the absence of any clear territorial mandate for the EU by member states, supranational actions have been largely facilitatory (Johnson and Turner 2007). Early ambitions of proactivity in plotting the migration of EU-wide telecommunications infrastructure have been overtaken by a mix of state action, but more importantly of the maturing of information markets that have rendered such activism meaningless (EC 2004). Consequently TEN-based actions have been gradually downscaled from being infrastructure-based towards the deployment of public service applications/services where the programme is a mere flanking policy of the larger, strategic ongoing digital agenda promoted by the EU. This is where co-operation and co-ordination between states have had a greater impact on the EII, not in the sense of integrating NII but in seeking to create a common operating environment across these markets (Lemstra and Melody 2014). This has led not simply to a broad re-regulation of the sector but also to support in areas such as R&D and inter- and intra-state cohesion. As the NIIs have become embedded within other infrastructure sectors – and as international data exchange has risen as a commercial flow – so this co-operation between states has evolved beyond market-creating and market-facilitating measures towards issues of security and mutually assured data sovereignty (see for example Kuner 2015).

This benign role of the supranational institutions within the NII is perhaps best illustrated within the current strategies towards roll-out of 5G mobile technology. These are areas where the state is driving change, with all national strategies setting (market-driven) targets for the deployment of this technology. The states themselves decide on what technology to deploy and who to source it from – thus eschewing a common security approach based on concerns about Chinese suppliers (see for example Institut Montaigne 2019). Whilst the EU is keen to promote the deployment of this technology and is aligned with states over the need to prevent European states falling further behind in the widespread utilisation of 5G, in those areas where the EU should be leading (i.e. promoting cross-border projects) the states appear to be driving the process. This has been evidenced by state-driven cross-border 5G interconnection projects.

CONCLUSION

The prevailing narrative of national infrastructure systems functioning as an apparent paradox of territorial fixity in a world of de-territorialisation misinterprets the political economy in which such systems are formed and develop. In a global system based on state territoriality, these are systems designed not just to support and enable the territoriality of the state but also to reflect the nature of flows within them – namely that domestic flows (by any measure) heavily outweigh cross-border flows even in cases of intensifying regionalisation. However there remains links between European NIS; and these links (within a contemporary context) are shaped by a range of concerns across the infrastructural mandate in seeking to support states to sustain, secure and enable the transmission of energy, goods and data between these states to enable and support state territoriality. Consequently co-operative territoriality is indicative of this process where interconnection and interaction between NIS is driven by pragmatism and expedience rather than some broader overarching supranational strategy.

REFERENCES

Aalto, P., and Korkmaz Temel, D. (2014). European energy security: Natural gas and the integration process. *JCMS: Journal of Common Market Studies*, Vol. 52, No. 4, pp. 758–774.

Agnew, J. (1994). The territorial trap: The geographical assumptions of international relations theory. *Review of International Political Economy*, Vol. 1, No. 1, pp. 53–80.

Amirova-Mammadova, S. (2017). *Pipeline politics and natural gas supply from Azerbaijan to Europe*. Wiesbaden: Springer.

Andersen, S. S., Goldthau, A., and Sitter, N. (eds) (2016). *Energy Union: Europe's new liberal mercantilism?* London: Palgrave Macmillan.

Association for the Co-operation of Energy Regulators (ACER) (2017). Annual report on the results of monitoring the internal electricity and gas markets in 2016. Available at www.acer.europa.eu; date accessed 22/06/2020.

Benson, D., and Russel, D. (2015). Patterns of EU energy policy outputs: Incrementalism or punctuated equilibrium? *West European Politics*, Vol. 38, pp. 185–205.

Bozhilova, D., and Hashimoto, T. (2010). EU–Russia energy negotiations: A choice between rational self-interest and collective action. *European Security*, Vol. 19, No. 4, pp. 627–642.

Briglauer, W., Cambini, C., Fetzer, T., and Hüschelrath, K. (2017). The European Electronic Communications Code: A critical appraisal with a focus on incentivizing investment in next generation broadband networks. *Telecommunications Policy*, Vol. 41, No. 10, pp. 948–961.

Cerny, P. G. (1997). Paradoxes of the competition state: The dynamics of political globalization. *Government and Opposition*, Vol. 32, No. 2, pp. 251–274.

Clavin, P. (2005). Defining transnationalism. *Contemporary European History*, Vol. 14, No. 4, pp. 421–439.

Edwards, P. N. (2003). Infrastructure and modernity: Force, time, and social organization in the history of sociotechnical systems. *Modernity and Technology*, Vol. 1, pp. 185–226.

European Commission (EC) (2004). Intermediate evaluation of the eTEN (formerly TEN-Telecom) programme. Available at www.europa.eu.int; date accessed 28/09/2020.

European Commission (EC) (2018). Indicative TEN-T investment action plan. Available at www.europa.eu.int; date accessed 28/10/2020.

European Commission (EC) (2020). Digital Economy and Society Index (DESI) 2020: Connectivity. Available at www.europa.eu.int; date accessed 03/09/2020.

European Network of Transmission System Operators for Electricity (ENTSO-E) (2018). Electricity in Europe 2017. Available at www.entsoe.org; date accessed 20/05/2020.

European Network of Transmission System Operators for Gas (ENTSO-G) (2019). The European gas network. Available at www.entsog.org; date accessed 15/05/2020.

European Parliament (EP) (2014). *The cost of non-Europe in the single market in transport and tourism, I: Road transport and railways.* Brussels: European Union.

European Parliament (EP) (2016). One Belt, One Road (OBOR): China's regional integration initiative. Available at http://www.europarl.europa.eu/ date accessed 24/04/2020.

European Parliament (EP) (2020). Financing the Trans-European Networks. Available at https://www.europarl.europa.eu/factsheets/en/sheet/136/financing-the-trans-european-networks; date accessed 22/10/2020.

Eurostat (2019). EU transport in figures. Available at http://epp.eurostat.ec.europa.eu; date accessed 25/10/2020.

Florio, M. (ed.) (2017). *The reform of network industries: Evaluating privatisation, regulation and liberalisation in the EU.* Cheltenham, UK and Northampton, MA, USA: Edward Elgar Publishing.

Hawker, G., Bell, K., and Gill, S. (2017). Electricity security in the European Union: The conflict between national capacity mechanisms and the single market. *Energy Research and Social Science*, Vol. 24, pp. 51–58.

Helm, D., (2014). The European framework for energy and climate policies. *Energy Policy*, Vol. 64, pp. 29–35.

Högselius, P. (2012). *Red gas: Russia and the origins of European energy dependence.* London: Palgrave Macmillan.

Institut Montaigne (2019). Europe and 5G: The Huawei case. Available at https://www.institutmontaigne.org; date accessed 15/09/2020.

Johnson, C., and Derrick, M. (2012). A splintered heartland: Russia, Europe, and the geopolitics of networked energy infrastructure. *Geopolitics*, Vol. 17, No. 3, pp. 482–501.

Johnson, D., and Turner, C. (1997). *Trans-European networks: The political economy of integrating Europe's infrastructure.* Basingstoke: Macmillan.

Johnson, D., and Turner, C. (2007). *Strategy and policy for trans-European networks.* Basingstoke: Palgrave Macmillan.

Kandiyoti, R. (2015). *Powering Europe: Russia, Ukraine, and the energy squeeze.* Basingstoke: Palgrave Macmillan.

Kanellakis, M., Martinopoulos, G., and Zachariadis, T. (2013). European energy policy: A review. *Energy Policy*, Vol. 62, pp. 1020–1030.

Kuner, C. (2015). Data nationalism and its discontents. *Emory Law Journal*, Vol. 64, pp. 2089–2098.

Lemstra, W., and Melody, W. H. (eds) (2014). *The dynamics of broadband markets in Europe*. Cambridge: Cambridge University Press.

Mamadouh, V. (2001). The territoriality of European integration and the territorial features of the European Union: The first 50 years. *Tijdschrift voor economische en sociale geografie*, Vol. 92, No. 4, pp. 420–436.

Mann, M. (2008). Infrastructural power revisited. *Studies in Comparative International Development*, Vol. 43, No. 3–4, pp. 355–365.

Murphy, A. B. (1996). The sovereign state system as political territorial ideal: Historical and contemporary considerations. In Biersteker, T. J. and C. Weber, C. (eds), *State sovereignty as social construct*. Cambridge: Cambridge University Press, pp. 81–120.

Öberg, M., Nilsson, K. L., and Johansson, C. M. (2018). Complementary governance for sustainable development in transport: The European TEN-T core network corridors. *Case Studies on Transport Policy*, Vol. 6, No. 4, pp. 674–682.

Organisation for Economic Co-operation and Development (OECD) (2019). Telecommunications database: OECD telecommunications and internet statistics. Available at www.oecd.org; date accessed 20/3/2020.

Peters, D. (2003). Cohesion, polycentricity, missing links and bottlenecks: Conflicting spatial storylines for pan-European transport investments. *European Planning Studies*, Vol. 11, No. 3, pp. 317–339.

Pollitt M.G (2019). The European single market in electricity: An economic assessment. *Review of Industrial Organization*, Vol. 55, pp. 63–87.

Rodgers, D., and O'Neill, B. (2012). Infrastructural violence: Introduction to the special issue. *Ethnography*, Vol. 13, No. 4, pp. 401–412.

Schipper, F., and Van der Vleuten, E. (2008). Trans-European network development and governance in historical perspective. *Network Industries Quarterly*, Vol. 10, No. 3, pp. 5–7.

Schot, J. (2010). Transnational infrastructures and the origins of European integration. In Badenoch, A. and Fickers, A. (eds), *Materializing Europe: Transnational infrastructures and the project of Europe*. London: Palgrave Macmillan, pp. 82–109.

Sichelschmidt, H. (1999). The EU programme 'trans-European networks': A critical assessment. *Transport Policy*, Vol. 6, No. 3, pp. 169–181.

Siddi, M. (2016). The EU's Energy Union: A sustainable path to energy security? *International Spectator*, Vol. 51, No. 1, pp. 131–144.

Söderbaum, F. (2003). Introduction: Theories of new regionalism. In Söderbaum, F., and Shaw, T. M. (eds), *Theories of new regionalism: A Palgrave reader*. New York: Palgrave Macmillan, pp. 1–21.

Star, S. L. (1999). The ethnography of infrastructure. *American Behavioral Scientist*, Vol. 43, No. 3, pp. 377–391.

Szulecki, K., Fischer, S., Gullberg, A. T., and Sartor, O. (2016). Shaping the 'Energy Union': Between national positions and governance innovation in EU energy and climate policy. *Climate Policy*, Vol. 16, No. 5, pp. 548–567.

Taylor, P. J. (1994). The state as container: Territoriality in the modern world-system. *Progress in Human Geography*, Vol. 18, No. 2, pp. 151–162.

Taylor, P. J. (1995). Beyond containers: Internationality, interstateness, interterritoriality. *Progress in Human Geography*, Vol. 19, No. 1, pp. 1–15.

Turner, C. (1997). *Trans-European telecommunication networks: The challenges for industrial policy.* London: Routledge.

Turner, C. (2018). *Regional infrastructure systems: The political economy of regional infrastructure.* Cheltenham, UK and Northampton, MA, USA: Edward Elgar Publishing.

Turner C. (2020). *The infrastructured state.* Cheltenham, UK and Northampton, MA, USA: Edward Elgar Publishing.

United Nations Economic Commission for Europe (UNECE) (2011). Master plan of the Trans-European Motorway (TEM) and Trans-European Railway (TER) Part 1: Main report, Available at www.unece.org; date accessed 16/10/2020.

Van der Vleuten, E. and Kaijser, A. (2005). Networking Europe. *History and Technology*, Vol. 21, No. 1, pp. 21–48.

Vergeron, K. L. D. (2018). The new silk roads: European perceptions and perspectives. *International Studies*, Vol. 55, No. 4, pp. 339–349.

Wissel, J. (2014). The structure of the 'EU'ropean ensemble of state apparatuses and its geopolitical ambitions. *Geopolitics*, Vol. 19, No. 3, pp. 490–513.

Zeng, J. (2017). Does Europe matter? The role of Europe in Chinese narratives of 'One Belt One Road' and 'new type of great power relations'. *JCMS: Journal of Common Market Studies*, Vol. 55, No.5, pp. 1162–1176.

Index